WOMEN IN THE CHURCH

A BIBLICAL THEOLOGY OF WOMEN IN MINISTRY

STANLEY J. GRENZ

WITH DENISE MUIR KJESBO

InterVarsity Press
Downers Grove, Illinois

© 1995 by Stanley J. Grenz and Denise Muir Kjesbo

All rights reserved. No part of this book may be reproduced in any form without written permission from InterVarsity Press, P.O. Box 1400, Downers Grove, Illinois 60515.

InterVarsity Press® is the book-publishing division of InterVarsity Christian Fellowship®, a student movement active on campus at hundreds of universities, colleges and schools of nursing in the United States of America, and a member movement of the International Fellowship of Evangelical Students. For information about local and regional activities, write Public Relations Dept., InterVarsity Christian Fellowship, 6400 Schroeder Rd., P.O. Box 7895, Madison, WI 53707-7895.

All Scripture quotations, unless otherwise indicated, are taken from the HOLY BIBLE, NEW REVISED STANDARD VERSION®. Copyright © 1989, Division of Christian Education of the National Council of the Churches of Christ in the United States of America. Used by permission. All rights reserved.

Cover illustration: June M. Burrows

ISBN 0-8308-1862-6
Printed in the United States of America ∞

Library of Congress Cataloging-in-Publication Data

Grenz, Stanley, 1950-
    Women in the church: a biblical theology of women in ministry/
Stanley J. Grenz, with Denise Muir Kjesbo.
        p.   cm.
    Includes bibliographical references.
    ISBN 0-8308-1862-6 (pbk.: alk. paper)
    1. Ordination of women—Christianity.   2. Women clergy.   3. Women
in Christianity.   4. Evangelicalism.   I. Kjesbo, Denise Muir.
II. Title.
BV676.G74   1995   95-38605
262'.14—dc20   CIP

17	16	15	14	13	12	11	10	9	8	7	6	5	4	3
09	08	07	06	05	04	03	02	01	00	99	98			

To
Edna Grenz
and
Allen Kjesbo

PREFACE

◆

"How long did it take you to write that sermon, Pastor?" queried a congregant after hearing an unusually inspiring message. The minister responded, "All my life." Both Denise and I would be tempted to say the same thing about this book. In a sense, *Women in the Church* has been in the making all of our lives.

Because I was raised a "preacher's kid" among pietist Baptists of immigrant stock, it is not surprising to find a strong egalitarian strand in my own background. My mother readily spoke of my father as the "head of the house," and the churches my father served as pastor all boasted strong male leadership. Yet evident within what may have appeared to be the male-dominated contexts of home and church was an obvious, unquestioned partnership of male and female that assumed the value and equality of all persons in Christ.

Hence, no one in the churches I knew as a child ever questioned the propriety of inviting veteran missionary leader Laura Reddig to address the congregation (that is, to preach) at a Sunday-morning worship service. Nor can I recall that my father ever made a crucial family decision alone; rather, what some might have seen as "his" decisions—

such as whether to accept the call to another church—were always *our* decisions. My sense, whether in our home or in our church, was that we were all in this together and that each person was to be honored and welcomed into the corporate life without regard to gender distinctions.

The basic openness to the ministry of women I gained from my upbringing was deepened after my marriage to Edna. I had always assumed that my life's partner would also be a partner in ministry. But when I became the youth director at the Northwest Baptist Church in Denver (1972), Edna quickly transformed "my" ministry into *our* ministry. For this reason it was quite natural for our three-year sojourn at the church during my seminary days to climax in June 1976 with Edna kneeling beside me as the deacons and area pastors laid hands on the two of us while our pastor spoke the ordination prayer. Edna has repeatedly remarked that she looks back on this event as in a sense her ordination as well as mine.

Yet God had additional plans for her. Soon after I moved from the pastorate to the seminary (1981), our Lord opened the door for Edna to embark on a church music ministry. First as choir director and eventually as a member of the pastoral staff in the capacity of minister of music, she has truly been "pastor" to the people in her care. I have been able not only to support her in this role but also to sit under her leadership and benefit from her prayerful, diligent work, as she faithfully exercises the gifts the sovereign Spirit has given her.

My desire to write a book exploring the question of women in the church was sparked nearly a decade ago. Like many other evangelical groups, the denomination of my upbringing was in the throes of a hotly contested, emotional debate over women's ordination. As the theology professor at the denomination's seminary, I witnessed the negative effect much of the rhetoric was having in the lives of many students. For some, the joy and anticipation of church ministry was being clouded by uncertainty, doubt and even fear. Others were being caught up in the dogmatism generated by the debate, and many fell prey to a creeping suspicion of those whose position differed from their own.

The heat of this controversy led me into a sustained study of the issue. Both my personal interaction with the biblical texts and my understanding of the implications of the foundational tenets of our evangelical theology confirmed the basic outlook I had gained from my upbringing. The time had come to speak out, I concluded—not in a belligerent manner, but irenically yet firmly, believing that no side in a controversy among concerned Christians could be either devoid of truth or totally free from error.

Early in 1991 I began discussing with Rodney Clapp and others at InterVarsity Press the idea for a book that would move beyond the debate over the proper exegesis of specific biblical texts and would draw from Christian theology to shed light on the role of women in the church today.

The project was still in its infancy in summer 1992 when Denise came to Regent College to teach a course in this exact subject. I had come to appreciate Denise's giftedness for ministry when we were both at the North American Baptist Seminary in Sioux Falls, South Dakota. She had served ably as my teaching assistant the academic year 1982-1983 and had later returned to the school as a much-appreciated faculty colleague. As we discussed my proposed book, it became evident that Denise's involvement would add a needed dimension to the project. Consequently, she served as the primary author of the first two chapters (I came in later as editor of these). In addition, her careful eye and keen mind surveyed the rest of the book at each stage in its production. As a result, the entire volume reflects Denise's thinking on the topics covered and therefore is in a real sense her book as well as mine.

* * *

I was the youngest of three girls born to a farming family on the plains of southern Minnesota. Throughout my childhood and adolescence my parents laid the foundation for my ministry pilgrimage. My mother continually told her children that we were the most important persons in her world and that she loved us no matter what. And my father, who believed in our potential, instilled in us the conviction that we could do anything we set ourselves to do—with God's help.

During my high-school days I was involved in my home church as well as Youth for Christ. Because I had no role models of women in vocational ministry (apart from foreign missionary work), I did not know how to process what I sensed to be the urging of God toward vocational ministry. As I moved on to college, I decided to act on my calling by pursuing Christian counseling, which seemed an appropriate avenue for a conservative Christian woman to fulfill her ministry yearnings. The college experience exposed me to a variety of approaches to biblical interpretation, which led me to question the veracity of the restrictions on women in ministry which I had been taught. A course in "Women in Ministry" at Bethel Seminary, taught by a female seminary professor and an ordained Southern Baptist woman minister, proved to be a turning point. With these women as role models, I was finally able to begin to process my personal sense of God's call to vocational Christian ministry.

I met Allen, my husband and best friend, during college. Allen had sensed God's calling to youth ministry, and he strongly encouraged me to pursue ministry in partnership with him. As life partners, and with the support of family and friends, we ventured into the realm of seminary. Some students questioned my presence in the M.Div. program, of course, but their attitude generally changed once they came to know us and sensed our heart for ministry. Because clergy couples were nonexistent in our denominational setting, many people cautioned us that no church would call both of us to the pastoral staff. Nevertheless, we knew we needed to follow God's leading. And God was faithful, graciously providing a church context in Edmonton, Alberta, where Allen and I enjoyed several years of joyous ministry as a clergy couple.

Allen put his plans for ordination on hold for the sake of another dream—that we be ordained as a couple. After a five-year wait during which our dream collided with "reality," Allen proceeded alone. The experience was bittersweet for us as he moved through a credentialing process denied me solely because of my gender. I resigned myself to the fact that this was not the time to fight a battle that might ultimately cost me valued ministry opportunities.

Then came our return to Sioux Falls, South Dakota. Allen moved into a youth ministry position at First Baptist Church (where I had served for six months as interim director of Christian education), while I turned to teaching at our alma mater. After seeing us function for a year as a team in ministry, the leadership of First Baptist approached us with the idea of reviving our dream of joint ordination. Allen's credentials needed to be transferred to the American Baptists, and this would be the occasion for a service involving us together. We were overwhelmed at the goodness of God and the openness of the people of the congregation. After seeking counsel, we proceeded and saw our dream fulfilled on May 11, 1991.

That event has by no means marked the end of my involvement in the discussion regarding the ordination of women. As a seminary professor I am in dialogue with students continually—sometimes verbally as questions are voiced in the classroom or over lunch, and always nonverbally as I daily live out my calling as a woman in ministry. Through all of this, I am continuing to learn and grow, and I want to remain open to other people's points of view, whether or not I agree with them.

I met Stan Grenz during my years as a seminary student. He was my theology professor and offered me the opportunity to serve as his teaching assistant. At that time I appreciated his scholarship, as well as his love for Christ and the church. When I later returned to North American Baptist Seminary as a faculty member, he welcomed me and encouraged my ongoing professional development. Stan has been a wonderful mentor and a treasured friend over the past fifteen years. His offering me the opportunity to collaborate on this project is one more example of his continuing support for my professional goals and his willingness to invest in my life. I am thankful for him and the model he offers of a respected scholar who invites a younger colleague into partnership.

* * *

Together we offer our gratitude to those persons who have contributed to this volume: to our respective institutions, which not only provide a context in which to learn from colleagues and students but also granted each of us sabbatical time for working on this project; to the support staff at these institutions—Beverley Norgren, administrator, and teaching assistants Bob Tees and George Capaque at Carey Theological College, as well as Pat Asche, faculty secretary at the North American Baptist Seminary; to the many people at InterVarsity Press, especially Rodney Clapp; and to Professor Craig Keener, who willingly read the manuscript in an earlier form and offered many helpful comments. In addition, I (Stan) gratefully acknowledge the Association of Theological Schools, whose Theological Scholarship and Research Award program (fall 1993) provided additional funding for research that fed into my work on this project.

Above all, we acknowledge our respective spouses—Edna Grenz, minister of music at the First Baptist Church, Vancouver, and Allen Kjesbo, associate pastor of youth at the First Baptist Church, Sioux Falls. Edna serves a model of a woman in church ministry. And Allen stands as an example of a man who supports the ministry of women in the church. In gratitude for their ministry in our lives and in the lives of many others, we gladly dedicate this book.

INTRODUCTION

◆

In high school Sally was a well-liked member of her church youth group. She led various youth activities ranging from planning Sunday-evening worship services to organizing car washes to raise money for summer mission trips. Sally always sensed that God was calling her to a lifetime of Christian ministry, but she thought this meant being a pastor's wife.

After high school Sally naturally chose to attend a Christian liberal arts college. In her third year she was required to declare a major, so she chose Christian education. She consistently earned excellent grades in her coursework, and through working in a local Sunday school, she discovered an ability to teach. Sally began to dream about the possibility of one day becoming a Christian education director. But to pursue this goal she needed further training. So she enrolled in the master's level Christian education program offered by her denomination's seminary.

As Sally proceeded through seminary, she sensed that her gifts and calling could be more adequately expressed if she explored pastoral ministry and the master of divinity track. This move, however, placed Sally into traditionally "male-only" courses such as Church Administration and Homiletics. In her homiletics class, Sally discovered a genuine love for preaching and demonstrated keen skills in constructing sermons. And although some of her male classmates were offended at the presence of a woman in a homiletics course, most sat spellbound when she delivered her first sermon. Her exposition was well conceived, intellectually stimulating and captivating. Once again Sally was left to reconsider her call. It seemed evident that God wanted her to enter pastoral ministry.

Sally completed the M.Div. degree with highest honors. Her name went out to various churches searching for pastors with her qualifications. But when she was repeatedly passed over for placement by less gifted men in her graduating class, Sally questioned her sense of call. Had God played a cruel joke on her? Had he led her step by step through several years of diligent study only to abandon her when the preparation was complete and the ministry was ready to begin?

Sally's story highlights the experience of many evangelical women who have sensed a call to ministry. Although most mainline Protestant bodies officially favor the inclusion of women in all areas of pastoral work, many evangelical groups are sharply divided on the issue. Denominations as diverse as the Mennonite Brethren[1] and the Christian Reformed Church[2] now find themselves embroiled in what is perhaps the most divisive debate they have faced in decades. And denominational periodicals have often served as forums for both proponents and opponents of women in ministry.[3]

Not only are specific denominations caught up in the debate over women's ordination, the issue of women's roles in the church has engulfed evangelicalism in general. Since 1975, *Christianity Today*, the flagship periodical of the evangelical family, has repeatedly provided a platform for contending positions.[4] Evangelical scholars have frequently joined the foray, publishing a battery of articles and books on the various aspects of the question. Nevertheless, strong divisions remain at every level of the evangelical community, including denominations, seminaries, and local congregations.

After the 1986 meeting of the Evangelical Theological Society, which focused on the theme "Male and Female in Biblical and Theological Perspective," polarization of the issue took organizational form through the founding of two competing coalitions, Christians for Biblical Equality and the Council on Biblical Manhood and Womanhood. As the existence of these two organizations suggests, the debate has coalesced around two broad positions, although there may be shades of differences within each.[5] Christians following the lead of the Council on Biblical Manhood and Womanhood believe that the Bible places restrictions on the public ministry of women. Those who voice agreement with Christians for Biblical Equality are convinced that God calls gifted persons into all aspects of public ministry regardless of gender. Hence, at the center of the controversy is the question of "male leadership" versus "shared leadership."

Some proponents of the ordination of women find a deeper issue at stake: the equality of women and men. They see their struggle as a battle for justice, as a matter of human rights. Stephen C. Barton articulates this connection: "I think also that there is a strong argument from natural justice in favor of the ordination of women. Today, there would be a public outcry if, because of gender, a woman was barred entry into, say, the caring professions. Such appointments are (meant to be) made, not on the basis of a person's gender, but on the basis of his/her qualifications and experience gained in courses of training."[6]

Gretchen Gaebelein Hull voices the same argument in more theological terms: "Just as discrimination in the area of natural rights is contrary to God's will, so also is discrimination in the area of spiritual rights. All persons should have the right to spiritual freedom. Certainly the Bible teaches that both women and men have the right to know God, the right to act on that knowledge, the right to learn about God, and—once regenerate—the right to serve God as He calls. Discrimination is any act that restricts those spiritual rights and thus harms or diminishes a person's spiritual standing or limits a person's opportunities to serve God."[7]

Others, however, want to ensure that society not be allowed to set the church's agenda. Mark E. Chapman, for example, challenges us to keep our focus on the issue of ordination itself and not be sidetracked by the contemporary emphasis on justice and human rights: "The ordination of women, then, precisely by virtue of its being an issue related to *ordination*, cannot be an issue of sexual equality or of women's rights."[8] Chapman then pinpoints the fundamental consideration: "The only reason why the church should ordain women is that it legitimately can be expected that God would call women to be his ministers. If the possibility exists that God, without violating his own gospel, can call women as well as men to be ministers of that gospel, then the church has the obligation of providing for and investigating the circumstances in which women as well as men may actually be called to that ministry. And if the church discerns that there are such women called to the ministry, the church should then ordain them."[9]

Chapman's statement raises the central question, Whom does the Holy Spirit call to leadership ministries in the church? Some Christians, based on their reading of the Bible, conclude that the Spirit does not call women into such leadership roles or bestow on them the necessary gifts for such a call simply because of their gender. Other Christians, by contrast, believe Scripture teaches that the Spirit may call both men and women to any responsibility in the church.

In this volume we take up the challenge posed by this fundamental disagreement within evangelicalism, conscious that sincere believers stand on both sides of the divide. In an attempt to gain clarity on the issue, we address the question of women in ministry from three vantage points: church history, Scripture and Christian theology. If there is no historical, biblical or theological basis to conclude that the Spirit calls women into leadership roles in the church, then the contemporary cry for women's justice is ill-founded. The church, in such a case, would need to stand firm against the contemporary egalitarian mindset.

Our thesis, however, is that historical, biblical and theological considerations converge not only to allow but indeed to insist that women serve as full partners with men in all dimensions of the church's life and ministry. We believe that the sovereign Spirit calls women, together with men, to positions of leadership in the church and that God's Spirit bestows on women and men the gifts necessary to fulfill such responsibilities. Consequently, to categorically deny women the opportunity to obey the Spirit places us in the position not only of acting unjustly toward women but, more important, of standing in opposition to the work of the sovereign Holy Spirit.

In advocating the full participation of women in ministry, we are not arguing that women should *displace* men. On the contrary, our contention is that the ministry of the church is best facilitated through a mutuality of leadership. The mandate to the church is advanced as men and women serve together in all aspects of ministry.

We have purposely focused our reflections in this book on the issue of women in the ordained ministry. This narrow focus arises out of the current situation in the church, namely, that only the propriety of *women* in church leadership is in question. Our goal is to address this specific issue. Consequently, we do not attempt to develop a theology of pastoral ministry and church leadership in general. Nor do we set forth an apologetic for ordination in general. Rather, we seek only to articulate what we believe is the case for the inclusion of women in all aspects of church life, including pastoral ministry and church leadership, and hence the case for the ordination of women. Yet we realize that the inclusion of women does carry implications for how we view the pastoral office.

Further, we approach this question from a decisively evangelical stance. As participants in the evangelical wing of the Christian church, we readily affirm the central authority of Scripture for belief and practice—that is, our convictions must be biblically based and theologically grounded. We affirm the God-intended distinctiveness of male and female. And we do not advocate rescinding the biblical language for God as the triune One who is Father, Son and Spirit.[10]

Not only is this book by evangelicals, but it is also primarily for evangelicals. Specifically, we desire to speak to three groups within the evangelical family. We hope those who are now opposed to women in ministry will give the book a fair reading and perhaps be persuaded by its argument. We also want to offer a clear, biblically grounded statement for women's ordination to those who sense in their hearts that women and men should serve together in all areas of church life but have been led by the forceful pronouncements of others to conclude that such a position cannot be biblical. Above all, we seek to provide an apologia for women who have sensed God's call to ministry but have been shaken by well-intentioned believers who question their call solely because they are women.

Finally, a word about labels. Most writers refer to the two major positions concerning male-female relationships as the "hierarchicalist" (or "traditionalist") view and the "egalitarian" view. In their apologetic for the former position, however, John Piper and Wayne Grudem express discomfort with the term *traditionalist* and reject the label *hierar-*

chicalist.[11] They suggest that the position they advocate is based on the concept of "complementarity," because it suggests both equality and beneficial differences between the sexes. According to their understanding, God created male and female equal but also designed the woman to complement the man by subordinating herself to his leadership. Although critics of the Piper-Grudem position question whether complementarity lies at the center of their argument,[12] out of deference to those who hold this view we will designate their position the "complementarian" view.

Because *egalitarian* has raised no corresponding reaction from proponents of the full inclusion of women in ministry, we readily retain the use of this term. Egalitarians seek to replace the hierarchical ordering of male over female with a focus on reciprocal relations and mutuality in relationships. In contrast to the claim set forth by complementarians that God created the second gender specifically to complement the first, egalitarians argue that God intends that men and women mutually support each other in all dimensions of life, including within the church and the church's ministry.

We are committed to this egalitarian position. And we have written this book to show that the vision of male-female mutuality is grounded in the Bible, is the logical outcome of evangelical theological commitments and best serves the practical needs of God's people.

ONE

WOMEN IN THE CHURCHES

◆

IN NOVEMBER 1992, THE CONFERENCE of Mennonites in Manitoba gave its blessing to the ordination of a woman serving as a staff member in a local church. The Christian Reformed Church voted in June 1993 to open the door for councils and churches to ordain women, but one year later reversed their decision. One month after the initial CRC decision, the Mennonite Brethren voted to continue barring women from senior pastor positions in all MB churches. In November 1993, the General Synod of the Church of England voted overwhelmingly to allow women to be ordained as priests.

As these four events—occurring over the course of a single year—suggest, the word that best characterizes the current situation of women in church leadership is *polarization*. Evangelicals today are divided into two clearly defined groups: those who believe that all facets of ministry ought to be open to women (egalitarians) and those who are convinced that women can properly serve only in supportive roles (complementarians). Despite a protracted discussion on the issue, the chasm between the two viewpoints seems to be widening. And proponents from both sides of the controversy are often guilty of using the question of women in ministry as a "litmus test" of Christian orthodoxy.

The widening gulf over women's roles is likewise evident in recent decisions by several churches to rescind their previous openness to women serving in lay leadership roles and in professional ministry staff positions. Some groups have enacted stricter limitations on women than at any previous time in their history. New directives prohibit women from chairing committees, teaching mixed gender adult classes, serving on the governing bodies of local congregations or being considered for any positions on the pastoral staff.

This chapter will set forth the context of the current dialogue between complementarians and egalitarians. We begin by exploring the formation in the late 1980s of two national organizations, each of which provides a network for those who hold to its stated positions. From there we assess the ongoing phenomenon of women entering seminaries to prepare themselves for vocational ministry. We conclude by tracing the recent struggles of several denominations to set policy regarding the ordination of women and the difficulties encountered in discussing and studying the issue.

The Council for Biblical Manhood and Womanhood

As the decade of the 1980s drew to a close, evangelicals were instrumental in the formation of two organizations that grew out of the ongoing debate over women's roles. Each group has one overarching purpose, namely, to facilitate networking among Christians holding similar beliefs regarding women in Christian leadership.

A meeting of evangelical scholars in Danvers, Massachusetts, in December 1987 marked a new beginning for transdenominational cooperation among church leaders and scholars. Calling themselves the Council for Biblical Manhood and Womanhood, this group set out to formulate a manifesto on the relationship between the sexes, especially in the church and the home. The product of their labors was the "Danvers Statement," named after their original meeting place, even though the statement was not finalized and published until November 1988.

The organization publicly set forth its agenda through a full-page "ad" in the January 13, 1989, issue of *Christianity Today*. Through this innovative format the council members informed the wider evangelical family of the intent of their work: "We now offer this statement to the evangelical world, knowing that it will stimulate healthy discussion among Christians, and hoping that it will gain widespread assent."

Those who signed the statement claim that confusion in the Christian community over male and female roles motivated them to form the council. They assert that God created men and women "equal in personhood and in value, but different in roles." Consequently, they uphold male leadership in the church and the home, while encouraging women's participation.

To propagate its position, the council carved out an ambitious agenda. It promised to "publish books, articles and pamphlets, hold seminars for scholars as well as large conferences for laypersons." One major work arising out of its efforts is a lengthy collection of essays published in 1991, *Recovering Biblical Manhood and Womanhood*, edited by John Piper and Wayne Grudem.[1] In addition, the council regularly produces pamphlets on related topics, which it distributes to those on its mailing list.

Christians for Biblical Equality

As complementarians were launching the Council for Biblical Manhood and Womanhood, egalitarians were giving birth to a parallel organization for transdenominational cooperation that represented a quite different approach to the questions of men and women in the church and the home. The fledgling organization called itself Christians for Biblical Equality.

Susan McCoubrie dates the founding of the group to August 28, 1987: "Catherine Clark Kroeger called together a group of people to pray and examine the need for evangelicals to be informed about the basic biblical teaching regarding equality of men and women of all races, ages, and economic classes." McCoubrie suggests that this was the climax of several earlier developments: "Prior to this gathering, in the winter of 1987 Catherine and Richard Kroeger had begun publishing a journal, *Priscilla Papers*, as an extension of a study center based in their home in St. Paul, Minnesota. In addition, egalitarian-minded persons in the Twin Cities area were already meeting under the name Christians for Biblical Equality."[2]

Christians for Biblical Equality incorporated as a nonprofit organization on January 2, 1988. In the summer of 1989, at its first biennial conference, the group unveiled its own position document, a "Statement on Men, Women, and Biblical Equality." This declaration, which was distributed to several national magazines in 1990, generated keen interest both nationally and internationally. On the basis of Galatians 3:28 and other biblical texts, CBE asserts that the Bible affirms the equality of men and women. Its mission strategy includes publishing newsletters and journals, sponsoring conferences, workshops and seminars, and facilitating the formation of local chapters. They operate a distribution service for books, article reprints, as well as audio and video cassettes dealing with biblical equality. In addition CBE has established a resource center and speaker's bureau to commission specific research projects to further develop a biblical theology of women and men and to provide prayer support for Christians in discriminatory situations.[3] As of February 1994, CBE had thirty-four chapters in the United States and six international chapters.

Women in Theological Education

Both the Council for Biblical Manhood and Womanhood and Christians for Biblical Equality seek to bring together women and men—both lay and clergy—who share similar viewpoints. The existence of these two organizations clearly illustrates the persistent divisions within evangelicalism concerning the role of women in ministry.

While the debate goes on, women continue to sense God's call to ministry, and many of them pursue that call by preparing themselves through seminary training. But their presence in theological education and church leadership is not always greeted with celebration.

Some historians view the current stream of women seminarians as the "second wave," flowing from the post-World War II historical milieu. This present wave follows on the heels of the "first wave," those pioneer women who entered seminaries in the late 1800s and early 1900s. Certain observers question the "wave" analogy because it implies that women entered in large numbers. Others, however, respond by noting that the movement of women into this previously all-male institution has indeed had a ripple effect on faculty, students, curriculum and ultimately the church itself.

The second wave of women in theological education dates back to 1956. That year Harvard and Yale divinity schools opened their doors to women in all degree programs. In addition, the United Methodist and United Presbyterian denominations opened the way for the ordination of women.

Despite these significant steps, women tended to limit their sights to master's programs in religious education rather than divinity programs.[4] By 1948 two-thirds of the directors of religious education in American churches were women. This apparent openness to women is countered by the fact that two-thirds of the ministers with whom they worked would have preferred a man in that position. In addition, the status, security and pay for these women were low, and their average length of stay in a congregation was only two years.[5]

The presence of women in theological education, however, has made a significant and lasting impact on the learning community. We can trace these developments within almost any denominational seminary by following Nancy Hardesty's four stages of progression in the relationship of women to seminary.[6] In addition to noting how seminaries have responded to the presence of women, Hardesty's outline also uncovers some of the dynamics women experience in seminary life.

Stage 1: A few women are granted the opportunity to pursue seminary studies. They are grateful and hope to find an avenue of ministry on the fringes of the church. Male students are not threatened by the presence of women; they respond in a friendly yet patronizing fashion to "coeds." Meanwhile, male faculty assume a paternal role in training women students.

Stage 2: Small groups of women gather to deal with their anger over what they perceive to be sexism in the church and seminary. They form women's caucuses, which sparks hostility from their male peers and resistance from the faculty.

Stage 3: More women students arrive, and the passion of the second stage subsides. The seminary inaugurates changes such as adding women to the faculty, devising courses relevant to the specific concerns of women in ministry and urging faculty and students to use inclusive language. Harmony seems to govern this stage.

Stage 4: Women seminarians come to terms with past gains and struggles, and they voice a realistic appraisal of the remaining barriers to ministry. At the same time, the changes at the seminary and in the church become solidified. Women are an integral part of the faculty. Seminary courses are generally informed by women authors and women's perspectives. Women take their places in ministry on the basis of giftedness rather than gender. Clergy couples find support as they seek flexible solutions to issues of career and family.

Most mainline seminaries have moved through this pattern and find themselves comfortable at "stage four." Thus, the percentage of women enrolled in M.Div. degrees at seminaries related to the Association of Theological Schools more than tripled from 1972 to 1979, rising from 4.7 percent to 15 percent.[7] Today 25-30 percent of the students enrolled in seminary degree programs in the United States are women.[8] Many mainline schools now have at least as many women as men in their M.Div. programs. Churches that ordain women have witnessed the emergence of a group of well-prepared, well-trained female candidates for ministry in their congregations.

In contrast to most mainline schools, seminaries affiliated with denominations that do not ordain women find themselves in a difficult situation. The large number of women in the current pool of potential students exercises a great influence on seminary admissions policies. But if these schools admit women into all of their degree programs, they face an ethical dilemma. Can they accept women into programs that lead to ordination, knowing that their gender will prohibit—or at least inhibit—them from being ordained after graduation? And is it ethically responsible to accept tuition dollars from women when the seminary leadership recognizes that their gender will hamper these women as they travel the pathway to ministry?

Evangelical seminaries find themselves caught in this dilemma. A *Christianity Today* survey of thirty-four schools conducted in the mid-1980s determined that women made up 20 percent of the student population at evangelical seminaries, double their 10 percent representation in 1965.[9] Even many traditionally conservative seminaries are admitting women to all programs of study. Nevertheless, the casual observer of seminary life will note that most evangelical schools fall somewhere between stage 1 and stage 3 of Hardesty's progression. Only a few institutions have moved along with the mainline seminaries to stage 4.

The situation at Dallas Theological Seminary is typical of many evangelical schools. Dallas admitted its first woman to the Th.M. program in 1986. However, the school carefully states that it retains its long-standing belief that women should not seek ordination or serve as senior pastors. Similarly, in 1981 the faculty of Western Conservative Baptist Seminary (Portland, Oregon) reaffirmed that "the M.Div. degree was open to women with the understanding that they were not being trained to be senior pastors."[10] Despite these disclaimers, the number of women students at these schools matches the 20 percent average for evangelical seminaries in general.

These enrollment statistics, which show increasing numbers of female students, do not reflect several crucial opposite trends within evangelical theological education. One trend compares the number of women preparing for congregational or parish ministry with those aiming for counseling and chaplaincy ministries. Many schools report that the number of women applying to program tracks designed for church ministry (M.Div. and C.E.) is dwindling, whereas a growing number are entering the fields of pastoral care and counseling.

Another trend concerns the denominations in which women graduates choose to serve. Various schools note that the seminary experience offers students of denominations that do not ordain women the opportunity to explore other options. It is not unusual for women students and graduates to leave the denomination in which they were raised in order to affiliate with one that endorses an egalitarian vision of ministry and therefore offers them better opportunities for service. This phenomenon suggests that conservative denominations are losing capable female leaders to more open groups.

While women students and faculty continue to influence the current milieu of theological education, women clergy are beginning to make significant advances in church ministry. As women move into ministerial positions, they bring a renewed understanding of ministry. They tend to challenge the older hierarchical understanding of church leadership, and in its place promote a cooperative approach. Women leaders often emphasize a collaborative, mutually facilitating and participative style of leadership.

The more consensual style of female leadership finds its parallel in a more egalitarian understanding of the church. This stands in stark contrast to hierarchical models that focus on the distinctions between clergy and laity. Female ministers tend to view the primary task of clergy as empowering the laity for ministry. In addition they tend to see the church as a caring community of faith, which encourages character traits typically associated with the feminine, such as compassion, mercy and the giving of nurture. As a result the presence of women in ministry leads the church to confront social injustice and oppression more aggressively.[11]

In many ways women upset the older assumptions about the Christian life and its institutional expression. Egalitarians celebrate the presence of women, together with men, within the ranks of the clergy. They believe that this development sets the church on the brink of a genuine renewal in ministry. They see the new partnership of women and men in church leadership as a potential catalyst for positive change. Complementarians, in contrast, fear that this will only lead to "feminization" of the church. They wonder if the inclusion of women will discourage men not only from entering the ministry but from participating in church life in general.

Denominational Discussions
Within evangelical denominations one can observe what is perhaps the most intense struggle and protracted conflict over women in ministry. Today many denominations wrestle with questions related to women's role in the church. And decisions made today often face challenges and reevaluation tomorrow.

In the last two or three decades, American denominations that presently are or at one time considered themselves to be evangelical have been ordaining women. Examples include the Evangelical Lutheran Church in America, the United Church of Christ, the American Baptist Churches, the Presbyterian Church USA, the Christian Church (Disciples) and the United Methodist Church. Other denominations, in contrast, have staunchly rejected the idea of ordaining women. And still others have been unable to come to agreement on the question.

In this section, we will look at select denominations that have studied the issue in recent years. These are, of course, only a sampling of the many bodies that are finding the question divisive. But they demonstrate the variety of responses denominations offer today.

Baptists and Ordination

Baptist emphasis on congregational autonomy places them in an interesting position. Theoretically, ordination is largely a concern of the local church, and each congregation may ordain its own leaders. Associations and national conferences, in turn, cannot make binding rules governing local affairs. At the same time, local churches may ordain only with the blessing of regional and national bodies. And these larger organizations can dismiss an errant congregation from their membership. Let us look at how three Baptist denominations, all of which share to some extent this basic polity, have dealt with the question of women's ordination.

The Southern Baptist Convention. Of the major Protestant denominations that have debated the question of women's ordination, none has been more embattled than the Southern Baptist Convention (SBC). Initially, small pockets of openness to women in ministry emerged among Southern Baptists. Although their numbers were never large, ordained women served in various capacities in convention life. Yet the denomination never officially sanctioned the inclusion of women in pastoral positions.

After the inerrancy controversy of the 1970s died down and the new conservative leadership solidified its hold within the denomination, the issue of women's ordination flared up with great intensity. The first volley fired in the new battle came during the 1984 Southern Baptist convention, where the membership passed a resolution designed to discourage women from seeking pastoral leadership positions. Then in 1987 the Home Mission Board voted to cut off financial support to any church that had a female pastor on its staff.

As the previously open policies toward women began to tighten, egalitarians organized the Southern Baptist Women in Ministry and published *Folio* to provide a forum among men and women who hold to a more egalitarian stance. In 1987, the newly formed Southern Baptist Alliance, which was designed to operate within the SBC, accepted as one of its first projects financial assistance for churches that had female pastors.

At first, the battle within the convention did not completely close the door to women in ordained ministry. As late as 1993 Mark Wingfield could report: "Currently about 900 women are ordained for professional ministry roles by Southern Baptist churches. That figure does not include unordained women serving on church staffs or women ordained as deacons . . . the number of ordained women ministers is rising faster among Southern Baptists than any other American religious body."[12] During the tumultuous years between 1986 and 1992, the number of ordained women in the denomination increased by 291 percent. At the same time women still only comprised 1 percent of the ninety thousand ordained Southern Baptist ministers. And the majority of ordained women were serving in capacities other than senior pastor, working instead as chaplains or church staff members in youth, Christian education and music.[13]

Whether the current ferment will slam the door shut to women's ordination remains to be seen. The current SBC leadership, however, maintains a closed-door policy when it comes to giving women greater opportunities for service in the church.

The North American Baptist Conference. Several denominations currently struggling with the issue of women in ministry have appointed task forces, study groups and resolution committees to deal with the issue. The North American Baptist Conference (NAB) gives us an example of this approach. According to NAB polity, the local congregation, acting with the advice and consent of the regional association, is responsible for ordination. Nevertheless, North American Baptists engaged in an important general discussion on the role of women in the church at their 1985 triennial convention in Anaheim, California. Debate at the convention focused on a task force document that the denominational General Council had affirmed and now sought to present to the general session. The document placed its treatment of the role of women within the context of guidelines for ordination in general. After summarizing the arguments of biblical scholars on both sides of the question, the document offered a compromise: "The Task Force considers it biblical and appropriate for women to be ordained by North American Baptist Conference churches, provided that they meet the prerequisites and general principles for ordination as outlined in our Conference's guidelines for ordination. However, it is deemed inadvisable for women to serve in the office of a senior pastor in our Conference churches."[14]

The task force's conclusion met stiff resistance from the floor of the conference. The conference decided to send the document to the various associations for further study and discussion. However, few associations looked at the document in any organized, systematic fashion, thereby effectively postponing the decision indefinitely.

During the years immediately following the drafting of the initial task force document no women were ordained within the NAB conference. However, soon after the ordination of two women seven years later, the conference leadership commissioned another task force. The second committee reaffirmed the ordination of women according to the guidelines of the earlier study. Like its predecessor, this second document triggered another heated debate at a triennial convention. The official discussion within the NAB conference has now spanned more than a decade.

The Conservative Baptist Association. The North American Baptists are not alone in their attempt to resolve this issue by appointing task forces and publishing study documents. Their colleagues in the Conservative Baptist Association (CBA) have taken the same approach. The official discussion in the CBA was launched by a church seeking advice from the National Coordinating Council (NCC) concerning the possibility of ordaining a woman on its pastoral staff. The NCC turned to Earl D. Radmacher and Western Conservative Baptist Seminary (Portland, Oregon) to study the matter. In January 1989 the study committee presented its findings to the NCC, which then suggested that the committee be broadened to include representatives of all three seminaries related to the CBA.

The expanded committee produced a revised document that outlined three positions. These included the egalitarian (all ministry positions should be open to qualified women and men), the moderate (the office of elder [senior pastor] should not be open to women, but women should participate fully in all other areas of ministry) and the hierarchical (women should be restricted from participating in ministries that involve exercising authority over, or teaching, men).

In June 1989 the final draft, "Women's Ministry Roles and Ordination: Study Packet," appeared in a report to the NCC. The document concludes with a call for clarification regarding the meaning of ordination in the light of two possible alternatives. The first limits ordination to elders, with other persons (such as church staff members, missionaries, chaplains, and those in parachurch organizations) being licensed rather than ordained. This option, the task force noted, requires a significant change in the understanding of licensure. Licensure "would give ecclesiastical endorsement for ministerial service including qualification for tax benefits and the professional stature associated with ministerial positions."[15]

According to the committee a second alternative would be to "ordain all official vocational ministers of the Word," including anyone who "derives their livelihood from their ministry." The committee noted that this option requires a change in the understanding of ordination: "Ordination would cease to be understood as requiring or certifying fitness for the pastorate of a local church or installation in an ordered ministry of the church."[16] While agreeing that either alternative would be an improvement over current practice, the committee was equally divided between those preferring the first option and adherents of the second.

At the July 1992 annual meeting in Orlando, the CBA decided to deny any church with a female senior pastor admission into the association. To date, the Conservative Baptists have ordained only one woman. And no other churches are coming forward with female candidates for ordination.

Christian Reformed and Evangelical Free

The Baptists, of course, have not been the only ones to struggle over the role of women in the church. Therefore, we now round out this discussion by briefly looking at current debates within two additional evangelical denominations, the Christian Reformed Church and the Evangelical Free Church.[17]

The Christian Reformed Church. Unlike Baptist churches, the Christian Reformed Church (CRC) does not claim to follow strict congregational polity. Consequently it offers an illuminating case study of a denomination in the broader Reformed tradition.

The CRC has been studying the question of women's ordination for over two decades. Synod 1990 finally broke with long-standing church tradition and voted to allow congregations to ordain women to all church offices, but left individual congregations with the decision as to whether or not to do so.

The decision to open the offices of minister, evangelist and elder to women sparked much unrest within the church. Consequently Synod 1992 refused to ratify the change in church order proposed by Synod 1990, claiming that the scriptural support for the earlier directive was insufficiently persuasive and that the innovation would escalate the divisiveness within the church. Despite this reversal, the synod encouraged the CRC membership "to use the gifts of women members to the fullest extent possible in their local churches, including allowing women to teach, expound the Word of God, and provide pastoral care under the supervision of the elders."[18] The architects of the statement carefully chose the word *expound* in lieu of terms such as *exhort, proclaim* or *preach*. Their precision demonstrates the potentially incendiary nature and polarizing effect of word selection in the current climate.

But the story does not end in 1992. Synod 1993 reversed the decision of its predecessor, electing to open the door once again to women's ordination. However, changes in church order such as those proposed by the body in 1993 require ratification by the next annual synod. By a vote of 95 to 89 the all-male delegates to Synod 1994 failed to endorse the proposal passed the previous year.[19] Once again, the denomination "flip-flopped" on the role of women in CRC ministry, indicating how difficult and polarizing the question had become.[20]

The decision by Synod 1994 failed to bring the twenty-year debate to a close. At Synod 1995, proponents of women's ordination gained passage of a "local option" solution that places the decision in the hands of each district governing body (called a "classis"). The resolution would allow a classis to declare inoperative the requirement that ordained officers be male, thereby opening the door for the ordination of women within its jurisdiction. The proposal adopted in June 1995 exhibited an irenic spirit. It recognizes "two different perspectives and convictions, both of which honor the Scriptures as the infallible Word of God."[21]

Despite the attempt of the CRC to give attention to all sides, the debate has led to internal wounds within the denomination. Several churches opposed to the ordination of women have already left the CRC. Others may follow.

The Evangelical Free Church. The Evangelical Free Church provides us with an example of a theologically conservative denomination with a pietistic heritage. It too has grappled with the question of women in ministry. Current Evangelical Free Church policy is based on the results of a study on ordination and a denominational vote in 1988. Women cannot be ordained, but they can obtain a Christian ministry license. This license is designed for people in a variety of positions, including workers who focus on children, youth, music or women's ministries, pastoral care and counseling, pastoral administration, evangelism or missionary service.

A Christian ministry license remains valid only for the particular position in which the licensee is serving at the time of application. In the event of a move or change of position, a person must reapply. Although licensure does not require seminary training, candidates must be able to articulate their theological position both in writing and orally before an examining board. The license confers no title upon the recipient. Nevertheless, licensees receive the tax benefits enjoyed by ordained clergy.

The current Evangelical Free Church policy attempts to address the uncertainty over women in church ministry noted by the Conservative Baptist study committee. By focusing the question of ordination on the senior pastorate and providing licensure for other professional ministers, it exemplifies the second option that the CBA committee outlined. This policy effectively closes the door to the ordination of women. At the same time it affirms the calling of women to positions other than that of senior pastor and the preaching-teaching role in the church.

The Evangelical Free Church stands as a clear example of a denomination that has opened selected doors of ministry for women while retaining the position of senior pastor for men only. As in the case of the other denominations in this survey, it is too early to speculate whether this compromise will function as a long-term solution to the question.

Implications of the Debate

This rather brief perusal of representative denominations suggests that despite their seeming dissimilarities the discussions share certain significant features. First, the question of women's ordination repeatedly triggers a rethinking of the meaning of ordination and the authority of the ordained office. Sometimes this rethinking leads to new structures, such as stratified ordination, while in other cases ordination is confined to a particular office and an expanded licensure covers all other positions in the church. Of course any changes in the meaning of ordination and the place of licensure has legal and/or governmental implications, as well as ramifications for professional certification.

Second, several evangelical denominations are moving toward a compromise or moderate position. This position allows churches to ordain women, but only to a limited number of ministry roles. Typically, evangelical moderates deny women access to the position of "authority" in the congregation (the role of senior pastor), which on the basis of "headship theology" they reserve for men. Many moderates forget that women have been serving in most of these denominations for many years as vocational staff members, as denominational leaders and teachers, and in a variety of authoritative positions on the mission field. Their service has made a significant contribution to their denominations and ultimately to the kingdom of God. Only in recent years, in the wake of the feminist movement, has the question of their gender become an issue.

Finally, various denominations find a wide chasm between what they proclaim in official documents and what local churches practice. In the process of change, procedural statements often precede implementation. Denominational task forces may form a position on the role of women in the church after a relatively short period of study, but endorsement and implementation of this position in local churches will take much longer. Change occurs very slowly, particularly when opening ministry options to women involves moving against long-standing denominational practice.

What, then, can be said about contemporary evangelical divisions over the issue of women in ministry? Many complementarians conclude that the time is simply not ripe for women in ministry. They caution the church to wait for a more opportune season. Some offer an even more pointed rejection of the push toward women's ordination, claiming that it reflects the dangerous inroads of contemporary secular culture into the church. J. I. Packer, for example, declares that

the present-day pressure to make women presbyters owes more to secular, pragmatic, and social factors than to any regard for biblical authority. The active groups who push out the walls of biblical authority to make room for the practice fail to read out of Scripture any principle that directly requires such action. Future generations are likely to see their agitation as yet another attempt to baptize secular culture into Christ, as the liberal church has ever sought to do, and will, I guess, rate it as one more sign of the undiscerning worldliness of late twentieth-century Western Christianity.[22]

Egalitarians, in contrast, are convinced that the time is ripe for changes in the church. They believe that rather than being the result of unwholesome secular ideas invading the church, the push for women's ordination represents the work of the Spirit. And empowering women for ministry could possibly revitalize the contemporary church.

Some voices suggest that the full inclusion of women may offer an occasion for a wholesale rethinking of how the church carries out its mandate. Patricia Gundry, for example, writes, "We have all too easily beaten ourselves bloody knocking at the closed doors of the institutional church asking to be allowed into the established avenues of ministry, thinking all the while that this is the way to do it. . . . Actually, if we think about it, many of us will admit that we always thought some of those avenues were too stylized and rigid and outdated anyway. We really would like to improve things, to innovate some, and refurbish the place a bit. Why keep knocking to get in? Why not circumvent the obstacles entirely and re-invent the church along more vital, even more biblical lines?"[23]

While Gundry's statement may seem too radical for some, most egalitarians agree that there is truth in what she says. Attitudes and structures that restrict women also frustrate many men in ministry. Consequently, egalitarians hope to enlist men and women in the work of bringing about a new face for the contemporary church. They are convinced that God desires to bring new life into the church, and they see the growing partnership between women and men in Christian leadership as a means of God's work in reawakening a truly biblical vision and purpose.

Patricia Gundry's comments shed light on how the move to include women may fit into this renewal:

When people with ability are shut out of an established way of doing things, they tend to generate new ways of doing things. And those ways frequently turn out to be better—not because the people generating them are necessarily superior in ability, but because, over time, institutional structures decay. . . . When a new idea is put into practice, a new idea for ministry, or a way of thinking about ministry, . . . a change that may have been small begins to generate other changes.[24]

In the following chapters we will evaluate the debate between complementarians and egalitarians. Specifically, we aim to demonstrate that the cautionary stance voiced by complementarians is simply wide of the mark historically, biblically and theologically. Now is the time for change! With other egalitarians we are convinced that even though some Christians attempt to discourage them, women "will continue to answer God's call, and God will continue to choose whomever God wills."[25]

TWO

WOMEN
IN CHURCH
HISTORY

◆

EVANGELICALS SUPPORT THEIR DIVERGENT POSITIONS on the issue of women in ministry by appealing to the Bible, theological conviction and practical considerations. Yet a careful reading of history also gives important perspective to the contemporary discussion.

Complementarians and egalitarians agree that throughout most of history women have played a secondary role in church life. But the two groups disagree on the extent to which women have been marginalized and the historical significance of male dominance. Complementarians tend to emphasize that men have traditionally exercised authority in the church, and they relegate examples of women in leadership to the fringes of Christian church life. They suggest that history supports their opposition to women in ministry and that to open the door to women in leadership roles would move against a nearly two-thousand-year ecclesiastical tradition.

Egalitarians, in contrast, tend to highlight historical examples of women engaged in church leadership, claiming these persons as precedence for their position. In contrast to complementarians who celebrate the relative absence of female church leadership, egalitarians such as Robert P. Meye respond to the history of women in the church with "a certain amount of tears, a certain amount of rejoicing, and a lot of patience (How long, O Lord, how long?)."[1]

In the past, discussion surrounding the place of women in the church largely focused on the extent to which male dominance precluded female leadership. Recently, however, certain historians have been raising a more difficult question. They not only want to learn why men have traditionally dominated church life, but why women leaders reemerge. Their research yields an interesting historical pattern. The ebb and flow of women's participation in leadership does not merely fluctuate according to changes in biblical exegesis or the reigning interpretation of particular passages of Scripture. Rather, the pattern can also be traced to institutionalization of the church (the development of organizational structures), influences from the surrounding culture and the theology of leadership at work in the church. Thus renewal movements initially open the door to greater female involvement, only to shut the door as they subsequently become institutionalized and seek respectability in the broader culture.

Maria L. Boccia describes this pattern, which she claims repeats itself over and over in the history of the church:

When leadership involved the charismatic choice by God of leaders through the gifting of the Holy Spirit, women are included. As time passes, leadership is institutionalized, the secular patriarchal culture filters into the Church, and women are excluded.[2]

Indeed, revival and renewal do not only break through gender distinctions, they also call into question the barriers of socioeconomic class and professionalization. The dichotomies of rich versus poor, old versus young, educated versus uneducated, ordained versus lay are put aside when the Spirit of God visits the church with revival. As walls that divide people crumble, the church experiences a new oneness in Christ, in keeping with Paul's vision: "There is no longer Jew or Greek, there is no longer slave or free, there is no longer male and female; for all of you are one in Christ Jesus" (Gal 3:28).

In her 1993 address to the North American Professors of Christian Education, Roberta Hestenes articulated a similar historical thesis. She pointed out that women played crucial roles in the initial pioneering stages of religious movements, only to be replaced by men as the movements became more "respectable."[3] According to Hestenes this phenomenon typically occurs through a three-stage process.

During the charismatic phase, the early days of revival movements, women serve as evangelists, church planters and teachers. The ministry spawned by Dwight L. Moody stands as a clear example. Records of the Moody Bible Institute speak about women evangelists, Bible conference speakers and Bible teachers, who even lectured to mixed audiences through the school's extension department. Janette Hassey offers this appraisal: "Moody Bible Institute provides the clearest documentation of a turn-of-the-century Evangelical institution outside the Wesleyan holiness camp that actively promoted public church ministry for women."[4] This support for women's public ministry stood alongside the school's solid commitment to Scripture as inspired and inerrant.

In contrast to the ad hoc leadership style of the first-generation revivalists, the second and third generations of leaders desire the respectability afforded by credentials. As this occurs, the initial, charismatic phase gives way to the second, credentialing phase. This bid for respectable credentials takes many forms, but in the past it was often characterized by a push for higher education (Bible college or seminary training) and ordination. Consequently, the process discriminated against women, insofar as various factors made it difficult, if not impossible, for women to achieve the prerequisites necessary to gain credentials.

The third phase—the bid for full institutional respectability—completes the marginalization of women. As participants in the movement desire acceptance by other, respectable denominations, most of which do not sanction female leadership, women are increasingly excluded from positions of responsibility.

In this chapter we will examine this pattern within the broad sweep of church history and within the history of evangelicalism itself. The presence of this pattern carries significant weight in the contemporary debate over women in ministry. Men have indeed dominated church structures through much of Christian history. Yet if male dominance is linked historically to institutionalization and the bid for cultural respectability, then the traditional practice of the church is not necessarily an indication of God's will but may well be the result of sociological and cultural forces. And if female involvement emerges among renewal movements, only to be replaced by male leadership as revival gives way to institutionalization, then the contemporary call for a mutuality of men and women in ministry may be a manifestation of the Spirit's renewing work in the church today.

Women in the Early Church

A cursory look at the history of the church reveals the presence of the pattern that Boccia and Hestenes explicate. Women served together with men in the early years until the institutionalization of the church transformed leadership into the sole prerogative of men.

From the fulfillment of Joel's prophecy at Pentecost ("Your sons and your daughters shall prophesy") through the early years of the church, women and men contended for the faith side by side. According to Catherine Clark Kroeger's research, women acted in various leadership roles, including bishop (or elder) and deacon.[5] The early church may have even recognized the ministry of the widows as a "clergy" function.[6] In any case, in the second and third centuries the church ordained women deaconesses along with male deacons. These women ministered to other women in a variety of ways, including instructing catechumens, assisting with women's baptisms and welcoming women into the church services.[7] In addition to these particular ministries to women, they mediated between members of the church, and they cared for the physical, emotional and spiritual needs of the imprisoned and the persecuted.

Christian art from the first and second centuries depicts women performing various ministerial activities—administering the Lord's Supper, teaching, baptizing, caring for the physical needs of the congregation and leading in public prayers. Later revisionists, however, apparently attempted to cover traces of women's involvement in what had subsequently become male prerogatives. One example is the fresco in the Catacombs of Priscilla, which may originally have depicted a celebration of the Eucharist in which the leader and all of the participants are women. But the fresco has been altered so that the leader appears to be male rather than female.

Another such example of tampering lies outside the chapel of St.

Zeno in the Church of St. Praxida in Rome. An inscription denoting a woman in the mosaic as "Episcopa Theodora" was changed by dropping the -ra ending, thereby transforming a feminine into a masculine name. Because *episcopa* is the feminine form of the Greek word for bishop or overseer, the inscription suggests that Theodora was a woman bishop. Church council records and tombstone epitaphs substantiate the presence of women bishops in the early church.[8]

Many of the church fathers also acknowledge the presence of women in leadership.[9] Jerome offers an especially lucid example. Although the fourth-century leader is not noted for his advocacy of women, he bore witness to the importance of Paula, whom he greatly respected. Together, Jerome and Paula established monasteries for men and women. Paula functioned as abbess of the women's monasteries and was later succeeded by her daughter. Jerome also expressed high praise for Paula's learning, admitting that her mastery of Hebrew was better than his own and that she could recite the Psalms in that original language without an accent.[10] Even though some historians describe him as a misogynist, Jerome could not overlook the leadership, gifts and abilities of this woman whom God had called.

The Institutionalization of the Church

The wave of spiritual vitality that characterized the early church eventually receded, leaving an established religion in its wake. Establishment elevated men to leadership and reduced women to subservient roles. According to Boccia, "Women were systematically excluded by decrees of the Church Councils, actions of bishops and popes, and sociocultural pressures." She points to the 300s and 400s as a critical time in this development:

> As the church institutionalized and absorbed the surrounding culture, it adopted a negative view of women generally and in leadership in particular, something it did not have prior to this time. Consequently, several Church Councils produced statements restricting and prohibiting women from holding the offices they had held in earlier centuries.[11]

Yet women found ways to exercise their leadership gifts, especially in monasteries. In fact, ascetic communities of female virgins predated the male monastic movement. Women flocked to monasteries for various reasons, including the privilege of studying, writing and traveling. By avoiding the dangers associated with pregnancy and childbirth, they were able to pursue holiness without the expectations of marriage and family. In addition, women in female monasteries freely governed themselves with minimal male influence. Consequently, women within these communities functioned as leaders and teachers from the beginning. But their influence extended beyond the walls of the abbey. In fact, the church recognized the significance of two of these women leaders—Teresa of Ávila and Catherine of Siena—by bestowing on them the title "Doctor of the Church." Consequently, they stand alongside such notable men as Jerome, Chrysostom, Augustine, Anselm and Aquinas.

Abbesses held great power within the monastic movement. They supervised large tracts of land and managed the funds brought to the abbey by the women who entered the order. Many of the abbeys, being ruled directly by the pope, functioned independent of the local bishop. Because these abbeys were not required to pay tithes to the bishop nor to follow his rulings, tensions often arose between bishops and abbesses.

In addition to governing their own lands, abbesses appointed local parish priests, heard confessions and cared for the material and spiritual needs of their people. Nuns and monks, as well as male and female laity, submitted to the abbesses' authority. Boccia summarizes their important spiritual role:

These women leaders attended and participated in church councils, nominated priests, appointed and licensed priors, and received vows of obedience from those who were under them. . . . The popes sanctioned, supported, and acknowledged the right of these women to exercise this authority and receive the obedience of those under her care.[12]

Apparently abbesses were originally ordained. They received the symbols of the office of a bishop—the miter, ring, crosier, gloves and cross. However, later translations obscure much of the earlier written evidence surrounding the ordination of abbesses by rendering the Latin term "blessed" rather than "ordained."

The abbesses' authority and power gradually declined from the twelfth to the sixteenth centuries. Boccia reports that the final stroke came at the Council of Trent in the middle of the sixteenth century, when the council ruled that all of the women's and double monasteries ruled by abbesses had to either join with a male monastery and submit to the rule of a male abbot, or come under the direct control of the male bishop. This was the final stroke eliminating women from leadership in the church up to that time.[13]

The erosion of papal authority resulting from growing nationalism and the years of "captivity" in Avignon (1309-1377) meant that succeeding pontiffs could do little to support the abbesses in their struggles with local bishops over land and money. In addition, the rising middle class, populated by guilds of merchants and artisans, as well as the emerging university system, contributed to the decline of monasteries. At the same time, renewed interest in Greco-Roman culture revived a negative view of women. These factors combined to reduce female leadership in the church.

This short survey suggests that the growing exclusion of women from authoritative leadership did not come from advances in biblical exegesis. Rather, as Boccia argues, the institutionalization of the church, accompanied by ever-present conflicts over power and control, found that "monks and priests who had once pointed to the examples of Deborah, Huldah and others in the Bible to support their submission to the abbesses were now proclaiming that it was contrary to the laws of God and nature for a man to submit to a woman."[14]

Indeed, throughout history people have twisted the meaning of Scripture to support their own questionable positions on particular issues. The question of women in leadership is no exception to this tendency.

Women in the Wesleyan Revival

Neither church decrees nor the struggles between local bishops and abbesses could completely squelch women's involvement in ministry. Subsequent renewal movements revived female leadership. Revivals among Protestants in Britain and North America represent the most important of these developments for evangelicals. As Ruth Tucker and Walter Liefeld note, these revivals fostered shared leadership among men and women: "Revivalistic religion has always provided both men and women—but especially women—with greater outlets for self-expression and innovation than have the established churches."[15]

John Wesley's preaching and the rise of Methodism arrived at a crucial moment in English history. As aristocratic, hierarchical patterns of British society were crumbling, the lower classes were gaining power in the workplace. Within this historical setting, uneducated, fiery, Spirit-gifted Methodist preachers began to supplant the educated clergy of the established church. As a result, Methodism became known as "a religion of the heart rather than tradition or training."[16] From the beginning, women played a key role in the Wesleyan revival, organizing and teaching the class meetings.

Some historians suggest that women owed their participation to Susannah Wesley's powerful influence. John Wesley acknowledged his mother's formative influence on him personally. He called her "a preacher of righteousness."[17] Her habit of spending time with her children in spiritual instruction planted egalitarian seeds within her famous son, which later bore fruit in his leadership of the Methodist revival. But Susannah Wesley's influence extended beyond her family. She held meetings within her home, which grew in popularity until over two hundred attended and more were turned away because they were unable to find a place to sit or stand where they could hear. Susannah was never a campaigner for "women's right to preach," however. She simply shared her understanding of the gospel and invited others to journey with her. God used her simple faith to ignite the hearts of many—both men and women.

If Susannah Wesley struck the flint of revival, John Wesley caught the spark and fanned it into a blazing fire. His characteristic practicality played an important role in the revivals, including the modification of his views on women's involvement. Wesley had always allowed women to participate fully in the class meetings, including serving as leaders. But he gave women leaders permission to "exhort" rather than to "preach," a demarcation that has recurred throughout church history. He advised women to be mindful of the higher pitch of their voices and to keep their "exhortations" short, so as not to be misconstrued as sermons. He also advised them to call their gatherings "prayer meetings," lest anyone think that they were forming a congregation with a female preacher.

In spite of the warnings of their leader, Methodist women moved beyond "exhorting" to "preaching." The success of their efforts eventually led Wesley to conclude that a woman's call was the key factor in determining her ministry. If a woman sensed that God was urging her to serve in the church, Wesley believed she was justified in obeying that call, even if it fell outside the normal practices of church leadership. In his later years Wesley publicly affirmed and privately encouraged women to preach, regardless of the prevailing public opinion. Women engaged in itinerant preaching and moved into leadership roles in local bands and class meetings. Thus Wesley's initial reservations about women preaching could not continue in view of the evident fruit of their preaching ministries.

The Wesleyan revival offered women new opportunities to experience freedom in ministry. Janette Hassey summarizes some of the features that contributed to these new opportunities:

> First, revivalism carried an implicit egalitarianism which tended to undermine traditional structures of authority. Second, the revival turned to Christian experience as central along with doctrine. Third, the revivalist leaders generally possessed pragmatic qualities. These factors helped open the doors for women to serve as Methodist class leaders.[18]

Unfortunately, the typical pattern of male dominance reemerged in the Wesleyan revival. When Methodism abandoned its fluid revival structure to become more institutional, women's roles diminished. As Tucker and Liefeld note,

> the success of . . . women preachers was closely related to the support and backing of Wesley. Although Wesley believed in his later years that opposition to women in ministry had decreased, such was not the case. Indeed, the opportunities for women to publicly minister quickly declined following his death.[19]

Wesley's public affirmation demonstrates the crucial role of male support for women in ministry at denominational, institutional and congregational levels.

Women in the North American Revivals
The second installment in the evangelical revivals occurred on American soil in the 1700s and 1800s. Frontier women flocked to revival meetings as a welcome respite from the drudgery of everyday pioneer

life and as an outlet for social interaction with other women. At these gatherings the Holy Spirit touched the lives of women as well as men, and they both responded in typical revivalist fashion—with heartfelt prayers of repentance. During the revival meetings emotions flowed freely as people experienced God's power afresh.

Women responded to their revived spirituality in various ways. Most notably, they reached out to their communities by caring for the imprisoned, the poor and the sick. As a result, women were instrumental in founding "voluntary societies" both within their own churches and across denominational lines. Through these societies, women ministered to other women, to children as well as to men. Christian volunteers, who principally carried out the work of these societies, felt responsible to act on their faith—to "put hands and feet on the gospel."

The Sunday-School Movement. Sunday school served as an important outlet for women's creative energies. Originally, the Sunday-school movement in the United States grew out of a concern for impoverished children. Because these children worked long hours during the week, they could not take advantage of public education, and so had little opportunity to learn even the basic skills of reading and writing.

At first, church leaders were cool to the idea of teaching literacy skills on Sunday. Martin Marty notes the underlying reason: "Ministers at first opposed the early Sunday school movement not simply because it was new or was a threat to established ways of doing things but because it was often in the hands of women."[20] Tucker and Liefeld offer a poignant characterization of the situation: "Fearing that 'these women will be in the pulpit next,' some pastors and church boards denied the use of their facilities for Sunday-school work."[21]

Despite this initial opposition, the Sunday-school movement grew, largely through the untiring efforts of women. Then, however, the typical historical pattern emerged once again. Not wanting to be "outdone by the women," the male leadership co-opted the movement, forming the American Sunday School Union. The men set policy and governed the organization, while women, who composed the majority of its teachers, did the grassroots work. As the movement gained respectability and became established, women effectively handed over the reins of leadership to the men. Once again institutionalization virtually eliminated women from leadership positions within an important area of the church's ministry.

The Revivals of Charles Finney. One revivalist, Charles Finney, stood out from the others in giving women a more visible place in his ministry. He created quite a stir among the "more respectable" revivalists by encouraging women to pray aloud and to exercise their gifts of preaching by testifying within his revival meetings. In fact, Finney strongly encouraged women not merely to minister in the background but if they were so gifted and called, to move their ministries into public gatherings of both women and men.

Historians differ, however, as to what motivated Finney to advocate public roles for women in ministry. Donald Dayton, Lucille Dayton, Nancy Hardesty and others assert that feminism found its roots among evangelical revivals.[22] They cite Charles Finney as a key figure in laying the foundation for modern-day biblical feminism in general and the full ordination of women in particular. Tucker and Liefeld disagree, however. They claim that Finney was simply "reacting against the conservative Calvinists in the East who were seeking to tighten up controls on women." Consequently, although he was open to the public ministry of women, Finney was by no means a vocal advocate of women's ordination. Rather, it may have been his dependence on the support of women for his revival meetings that led him to conclude that "the church that silences the women is shorn of half its power."[23]

Regardless of his own motivation, Finney served as the first professor of theology at Oberlin College, a school open to women students. At Oberlin he taught Antoinette Brown, the first woman ordained in America. Luther Lee, a Wesleyan Methodist preacher, spoke at her ordination service, which was held in a Congregational church in 1853.[24] This one example reveals some of the varied denominational threads that weave through the history of the modern openness to female leadership in the church.

Women and the Western Frontier. On the North American frontier women fulfilled various roles at home and in society. Frontier life required women and men to work together as partners in order to survive. In her book *Petticoats in the Pulpit*, Elizabeth Gillan Muir examines the history of women on the Canadian frontier. Women had been "programmed to be delicate and passive, to cling like sea anemones to their conjugal rocks." On the Western frontier, however, "if they wished to survive, they had to be brave, aggressive, resourceful. Fragile silk was gradually replaced by strong canvas."[25]

Frontier patterns of men and women working side by side contributed to egalitarian developments in the church. Yet the connection was not uniformly evident on the Western frontier. Muir illustrates this by comparing the plight of Methodist women preachers in the United States and Canada. According to Muir, the number of Canadian women preachers declined in the middle and late 1800s, while their American counterparts steadily increased. Why the difference?

Canadian and American cultures both experienced urbanization and industrialization during this period, and their respective churches underwent the same kinds of institutionalization and professionalization. However, Canada's political climate increasingly assumed a conservative air, which led Canadian Methodists to dissociate from American Methodism and to align themselves with the more conservative British Wesleyan Methodists. Consequently, as Methodist women in the United States rapidly moved toward ordination in the late 1800s, Canadian women preachers gradually disappeared.

The Conservative Reaction

While revivalism and frontier egalitarianism renewed opportunities for women in leadership, the late 1800s prompted a conservative response. What made the inclusion of women in church leadership so difficult for many Christians in the waning years of the nineteenth century? One crucial factor was the prevailing ideals of marriage and family. The closing years of the 1800s witnessed a shift from the farm to the cities, which led to a reexamination of family life.

In the rural environment, gender roles remained distinct. Women functioned primarily as wives, mothers and homemakers. Nevertheless, men and women sensed their partnership with each other, and their worlds intersected frequently throughout the day. Industrialization eroded these traditional connections.

Sociologist Betty A. DeBerg has explored the effects of industrialization on the male psyche.[26] DeBerg theorizes that men in preindustrial society obtained their vocational identity through the type of work they did—as warriors/hunters and patriarchs in the family structure. Preindustrial society considered work "manly" if it required great physical strength or faced the dangers of injury. Thus the warrior/hunter role elevated competitiveness and aggression to primary status within the male identity. And patriarchal family structure gave husbands/fathers great power over other family members. Industrialization and urbanization, however, called this version of the male psyche into question. Although many factory jobs continued to require physical strength and some posed real threats of physical injury, many men worked in positions where physical strength was irrelevant and the risk of bodily harm was minimal.

In addition to robbing men of their previous vocational identity, industrialization and urbanization kept men away from the home for many hours each day. As a result, women gained more influence over the daily functioning of the home and child rearing. At the same time, the change in men's work transformed the metaphors used to describe it; work became "the battleground" or "the jungle." This effectively sanctioned the public sphere as the new male domain. DeBerg summarizes the result:

> The stability of the economic warrior (or breadwinner) symbol depended on keeping women out of the male sphere of business, labor, politics and government. Women were assigned to the home, where they could not jeopardize, symbolically or practically, the deep and unambiguous sense of manhood fostered in and dependent on an exclusively male workplace and public domain.[27]

As a counterpart to the battleground of the workplace, home became a refuge, a place of virtue that revolved around the woman. Christopher Lasch argues that the American situation was both unique and extreme: "In no other country in the world was the distinction between the two genders, in the popular mind, so uncompromisingly rigid."[28]

Home also replaced the church as the primary religious institution of society. The home attained this new status when "the woman of the house" became a "religious agent and moral guardian,"[29] influencing society through raising godly children rather than by entering the public sphere. A "feminization" of the church accompanied the "divinization" of the home. If home was the primary religious institution, and women were the guardians of home and hearth, then religion was largely a female matter.

In this new milieu, male church leaders found it increasingly difficult to construct any semblance of the traditional masculine identity. This difficulty led many fundamentalist clergymen into a campaign to reclaim the church for men. Convinced that men would respond to Christ only in a context of male leadership, they sought to limit the presence of women in positions of authority. In addition, military metaphors dominated the church, and aggressive, militant language abounded in the writing and music of the day. Based on an analysis of popular fundamentalist literature between 1880 and 1930, DeBerg concludes, "Regarding matters of gender, perhaps especially so, late twentieth-century evangelicalism is truly the heir of its own past."[30]

The Deaconess Movement. The conservative reaction to women's involvement assumed various forms. One example was the opposition in America to the deaconess movement. This movement, which began in Germany, offered women opportunities to minister in contexts as diverse as hospitals, teacher training centers, programs for the rehabilitation of female criminals, homes for the mentally ill, orphans' homes, facilities for homeless women and high schools for young women. Deaconesses in England were even considered a type of women's religious order.

From Europe the deaconess movement spread to the United States. Tucker and Liefeld report that by the late 1800s "more than one hundred homes, representing many different Protestant denominations" had joined the movement. However, on this side of the Atlantic the deaconess movement met with stiff opposition. Its emphasis on a celibate life in service to God and the church ran counter to the overriding ethos of American Protestantism and to the established ideals of women devoted to home and family. Tucker and Liefeld explain:

> These celibate Protestant sisterhoods smacked of Roman Catholicism, and some of the strongest sentiment against the Catholic concept of female religiosity came from the pen of evangelical women. The evangelical emphasis on female piety that was centered on the home and family was diametrically opposed to the Catholic ideal of celibacy and complete oneness with God.[31]

Women Social Activists. Social activism characterized much of the nineteenth century. It is not surprising, therefore, to find women involved in various activist movements, ranging from suffrage and abolition to temperance. Women's leadership within these movements gave them platforms from which to speak. In fact, the first women to address mixed audiences in America spoke on the subject of abolition. However, their role was not always clear, nor was their leadership welcomed.

The temperance movement offers a lucid example. From its beginnings, women constituted the backbone of the temperance movement. However, men headed most of the early organizations. Women were not allowed to serve in leadership positions or to speak in public gatherings.

A case in point occurred at the World's Temperance Convention in New York City in 1853. When Antoinette Brown, the duly elected delegate of her local society, tried to speak, she met with strong opposition:

> There was a great furor, and I stood on the platform for three hours except when someone brought me a chair, and I did not have a chance to open my mouth. So much stamping and pounding with canes that the air was full of dust.[32]

In response to this type of treatment, women formed their own temperance organizations. In so doing, women who had been kept in the shadows now took the spotlight in the fight against the "demon liquor." The Women's Christian Temperance Union (WCTU) became the most well known of these organizations, and it demonstrated the Christian underpinnings of this social movement.

The temperance movement provided one of the few widely acknowledged opportunities for nineteenth-century women to fulfill a call to ministry. The close link between temperance and home life "allowed" women to serve in leadership positions. The evils of liquor ravaged families and destroyed sons who had been carefully reared by godly women. Hence, it was entirely appropriate for women to engage in saving husbands and sons from the downward spiral of alcohol. As a part of their temperance work, women taught Bible studies in prisons, police stations and railroad terminals. They also evangelized among sailors, lumbermen and soldiers.

Frances Willard, founder and director of the WCTU, combined social concern with a personal call to Christian ministry. Although she lacked formal biblical training, she was invited to conduct afternoon Bible studies and speak at women's meetings associated with Dwight L. Moody's revivals. Willard treasured Moody's endorsement of her ministry.

By the twilight of the nineteenth century, Willard publicly endorsed the equality of women with men and became an active proponent of women in church leadership. She maintained that "a vast army of women functioned outside the church, not because they wish to be so, but because the church is afraid of her own gentle, earnest-hearted daughters." Her commitment to the church led her to encourage younger women to listen to the voice of God and answer the call to ministry. She dreamed of the church living out Paul's call for equality in Galatians 3:28-29:

> It is therefore my dearest wish to help break down the barriers of prejudice that keep women silent. I cannot but think that meetings in which "the brethren" only are called upon, are one half as effective as those where all are freely invited. . . . As in the day of Pentecost, so now, let men and women in perfectly impartial fashion participate in all services conducted in His name in whom there is neither bond nor free, male nor female, but all are one.[33]

Women Preachers. The nineteenth-century conservative reaction perhaps most deeply affected the cadre of women who sensed God's call to preaching ministries. Although women social activists of the 1800s enjoy greater recognition, important Christian women preached during this time. These women served without the official church recognition of ordination. They typically did not have a parish or congregational home, but instead traveled among several churches of varied denominational affiliation. Some conducted revival meetings and served as itinerant evangelists. Many regularly visited new churches or churches unable to obtain the services of a credentialed, ordained clergyman.

Although the congregations these women served generally welcomed their ministry, women preachers also met with opposition. Sometimes the objections were mild. In 1851, for example, James Porter commented that women must not be kept from speaking, but they must take care not to speak too loud or too long. As long as women were not "contending with a man in public . . . finding fault with men . . . usurping authority over them . . . dictating to men . . . or being disloyal to men in public," they could speak.[34]

On other occasions, however, the objections were severe. Muir states that "over the centuries, there has been something particularly offensive or threatening about a woman preaching." She notes that some men see such preaching by its very nature as obtrusive and tiresome:

> As one male churchgoer in the United States commented after hearing a woman preach, "Oh, the sermon was all right, but you see I hear a woman preach six days a week, and on Sunday I like to get a rest." It is this pejorative understanding of preaching . . . which has traditionally been ascribed to women.[35]

The cult of domesticity fueled this pejorative attitude toward women preaching, for it looked to "home and hearth" as the defining factor of true womanhood.

The nineteenth-century church also followed the typical historical pattern of male leadership usurping female leadership. Many churches readily allowed women to lead if they were struggling to survive. But if a woman preacher managed to build the church into a thriving congregation, she worked herself out of a job and was generally replaced by a permanent male pastor. Churches often viewed their ability to "afford" a male preacher, rather than "settling" for a woman, as a testimony to their viability.

Women preachers and evangelists tended to be involved in the more sectarian groups. Women pastors in mainline parish ministries remained relatively rare throughout the nineteenth century, numbering as few as twenty by the late 1800s. The mere fact they existed at all testifies to their courage and to the work of the Holy Spirit. In contrast, women who desired to follow what they viewed as God's call flocked to groups more on the fringe of American religious life—Quakers, Free Methodists, Freewill Baptists and deeper life movements. Hence, by the end of the century there were some 500 women evangelists, 350 Quaker women preachers and many female Salvation Army officers.

Ordination for women proved to be an uphill battle. Women faced not only arguments from biblical texts but also sociological arguments, especially the prevailing belief that a woman could not be ordained to pastoral ministry and maintain a healthy family life. If called to choose between them, the godly woman would opt for the family. Nevertheless, ordained women could be found among the Methodists, Congregationalists and Baptists.[36]

Some women moved beyond the boundaries of perceived orthodoxy into heterodox groups that practiced a consistent egalitarianism. Ellen

Harmon White founded the Seventh-day Adventists, who have always accepted women as preachers. The Oneida Community of the 1850s exercised complete equality and freedom for women. Mother Ann Lee, founder of the Shakers, believed that women and men had equal responsibility to pray, testify, preach and teach in public, although the Shakers did not formally ordain men or women. Tucker and Liefeld offer one important rationale for the stance of these groups. The partnership between men and women was "a smart strategy for any developing sect that needed all the willing laborers that could be recruited to propagate the new creeds or doctrinal emphases."[37]

Some complementarians, of course, explain this historical phenomenon by asserting that women by their very nature are prone to be led astray from orthodoxy. Egalitarians rightly counter by pointing out that women simply found more open doors for ministry among marginalized religious bodies. In contrast to the conservative mainline denominations, groups that welcomed women focused on a direct experience of God's calling, which took precedence over church bylaws and ordination guidelines. They believed that the Holy Spirit endowed God's children with spiritual gifts irrespective of gender; both women and men could serve as leaders, administrators and preachers. The sectarian movements reasoned that if God so gifted men and women, who were we mere mortals to stand in the way of the Spirit's work?

Women in Evangelical Denominations

The evangelical movements of the 1700s and 1800s provide lucid examples of the typical cycle of women's roles. What was true of the revivals in general also proved true in many evangelical denominations. Women frequently led during the early, formative years of a new church body, only to be replaced by men as the denomination "came of age." The founding of several evangelical groups illustrates this tendency.

The Salvation Army. Many denominations owe their existence to the pioneering work of male and female leaders. The Salvation Army is an obvious example. Catherine Booth founded the Salvation Army with her husband, William. She was a noted speaker. Some hearers even preferred her preaching over her husband's, and she typically drew much larger crowds than he. The Booths practiced a "team" approach to ministry and parenting, each one taking a turn at home with the children while the other preached.

In keeping with the Booths' legacy, the Salvation Army has kept its long history of men and women sharing leadership roles. Denominational policy provides for men and women to serve side by side and be offered similar opportunities for "advancement."

Despite its official egalitarian policy, however, the Salvation Army has not consistently provided a healthy context for women in ministry. Nor has the organization been free of internal struggles over the role of women. The ebb and flow of women's roles within the organization can be seen in the changes to its official stationery, which for a time only acknowledged William Booth as founder, thereby omitting reference to Catherine's contribution.

Holiness Churches. Ferment within late nineteenth-century Methodism gave birth to what church historians refer to as the holiness movement. Like the Wesleyan revival that preceded it, the holiness renewal welcomed the participation of women.

Lay evangelist Phoebe Palmer, an important leader in the holiness movement, strongly advocated for women's right to preach. Another highly gifted leader, Aimee Semple McPherson, founded the Foursquare Gospel Church. Seth Cook Rees, one of the founders of the Pilgrim Holiness Church, reflects the characteristic holiness attitude toward women:

Nothing but jealousy, prejudice, bigotry, and a stingy love of bossing, in men have prevented woman's public recognition by the church. No church acquainted with the Holy Ghost will object to the public ministry of women. We know scores of women who can preach the Gospel with a clearness, a power, and an efficacy seldom equalled by men. Sister, let the Holy Ghost fill, call and anoint you to preach the glorious Gospel of the Lord.[38]

Several denominations that grew out of the holiness movement testify to the abiding influence of women such as Palmer and McPherson. These holiness groups officially recognize a shared leadership of men and women in the church. Yet as they became more institutionalized and sought inclusion in the mainstream of evangelicalism, many compromised their earlier enthusiasm for women leaders.

The Church of the Nazarene serves as a prime example. The original constitution of the denomination specifically recognized the right of women to preach. However, the official stance no longer reflects the actual situation. According to Harold E. Raser, professor of the history of Christianity at Nazarene Theological Seminary, the percentage of women among Nazarene clergy has dropped from 30 percent to less than 5 percent, and fewer than 1 percent of Nazarene churches in the United States now have women pastors. The reason is simple: "Holiness churches have tried so hard to blend in with the evangelical 'mainstream,' which has tended to oppose women in ministry."[39]

Baptists. In the early days of the Baptist work in England and North America, women preached and served as ordained deacons. Historian Leon McBeth, for example, reports that in the mid 1600s Dorothy Hazzard was known as "a teacher, preacher, Bible study leader, soulwinner, and founder of one of the most famous Baptist churches in England" (the Broadmead Baptist Church).[40] These early Baptist women endured the same persecution as their male colleagues—being frequently beaten, fined and jailed.

As the British Baptists moved from despised sect to established denomination, however, the role of women leaders declined. By the mid-1800s Baptists questioned the right of women to vote in church conferences, as well as their right to speak in mixed assemblies. At the same time, some congregations also abolished the office of female deacon (or deaconess).

Baptists in North America always held divergent views on women in church leadership. In New England and the middle colonies, Baptists generally traced their heritage to England's Particular Baptists, who were strongly institutional. Consequently, they tended to develop qualifications for leadership that excluded the laity in general and women in particular. Many Baptists in the Southern colonies, by contrast, followed the English Separate Baptists, where women played a larger role, serving as deaconesses and even elders and preachers.

Institutionalization in America led to the same male-dominated leadership as it did in Britain. However, the Separate Baptist tradition never completely died out. Even when the prevailing mood of the denomination restricted women's roles, women continued to serve in leadership positions in various places.

Tucker and Liefeld give a brief appraisal of where women stood within the church at the turn of the century:

Women had made great gains in organizational work, particularly in regard to home and foreign missions and humanitarian endeavors. Equally significant was the prominent role played in sectarian movements that flourished in the nineteenth century. But by the end of the century, women had made very little official headway in the established churches. The vast majority of institutionalized churches barred them from ordination and from equal status on the lay level as well.[41]

Women in Education (1830-1900)

In the past, the transition within renewal movements from the charismatic to the credentialing phase generally led to the loss of leadership roles for women. We have already noted one factor that contributed to this phenomenon in the 1800s, namely, the cultural perception that a woman's place was in the home. But the lack of concern to educate women played an equally significant and related role in the marginalization of women. Credentialing generally included educational qualifications that women simply could not fulfill. Consequently, we will conclude this historical survey by sketching the challenges that women faced in gaining access to ministerial education.

Andrew Peiser cautions against a superficial reading of women's struggle for education:

The history of women in education has long been ignored. It is rare for more than one paragraph to be devoted to the entire development of education for women. . . . The facts that women literally fought their way into colleges and universities, that their admission followed agitation by determined would-be students, and that they were treated as subservient to male students at even such pioneering institutions as Oberlin, are always absent. The simple statement that they were admitted suffices.[42]

Women's struggle for access to education stems, at least in part, from the unprecedented political significance given to the family in the early 1800s. The family was responsible for the moral instruction of the next generation, and mothers served as the primary educators in the home. With the concept of women as citizens not yet on the horizon, women only received political significance as the educators of the republic's future male citizens.

Women were permitted to attend elementary schools in order to gain the necessary skills for managing a household. Admission to secondary schools, however, occurred much later, colleges later still, and graduate training followed much later. The girls' schools of the mid-1800s, or "seminaries" as they were frequently called, saw their primary purpose as training young women to become wives and mothers.

Troy Seminary, founded by Emma Willard in 1821, was the first permanent institution to offer women a curriculum similar to that of men. Willard sought to "educate women for responsible motherhood and train some of them to be teachers." Troy offered an interesting blend of well-defined ideals for "true womanhood" and attentiveness to women's intellectual capabilities. Willard's ability to integrate an ideology of women's domestic roles with feminist concerns probably contributed to her success. When asked to justify higher education for women, she offered the following four-point argument: (1) Government has a duty to secure the present and future prosperity of the nation. (2) This prosperity depends on the character of its citizens. (3) Character is formed by mothers. (4) Only thoroughly educated mothers are equipped to form the quality of character necessary to ensure the future of the republic.[43]

Willard was a remarkable woman. In addition to being a wife and mother, she founded the best-known women's school in the nation, wrote a series of widely distributed textbooks, served as a political adviser and formulated respected scientific theories. In so doing, she became a model of the newly educated woman.

Students who graduated from Troy Seminary became "agents of cultural diffusion,"[44] spreading Willard's approach to women's education throughout the country. Willard intentionally created a network of graduates held together by a common conception of womanhood, which included the pursuit of intellectual development without fear or shame and the ability to think for oneself.

Historians debate the extent to which seminaries (girls' schools) moved women's education forward. Some conclude that they only trained women for the domestic roles of wife and mother. Others claim that these schools provided high-quality education, where women were encouraged to learn for the sake of learning. Whatever impact sem-

inaries generally made, Troy's effects extended well beyond the generation it served. The ideal Willard espoused led to increased educational
expectations in the daughters and granddaughters of those first graduates.

In the mid-1800s women began to enter as "coeds" in previously all-
male institutions. The situation at Oberlin College provides insight into
those early days. Oberlin was linked to a farm where male students
would work to pay for their education. Soon after opening the school,
administrators realized they needed a domestic staff to clean resi-
dences, prepare meals and wash dishes, and launder and mend the male
students' clothes. To this end, they concluded, women students were
essential.

Jill Conway characterizes the significance of the duties assigned to
women: No classes were held on Mondays so that women could take
care of the male students' clothes. However, no time was allocated for
the laundering and repair of women's clothing. The daily routine for
women students included cooking the meals, serving the tables of male
students and cleaning up afterward. Women students were valued for
their contribution to the emotional and mental well-being of the male
students, thereby allowing them to maximize the male students' time.[45]
Although women entered Oberlin as early as 1837, their domestic role
did not encourage women to think for themselves.

Scholars continue to debate the significance for women's intellectual
development of these early coeducational institutions. In any case,
coeducational schools ensured that men and women would follow a
similar curriculum. Yet by the end of the nineteenth century, when a
college education for women was generally acceptable, very few wom-
en actually attended college.

Even fewer women entered doctoral studies. The first woman to
receive a doctorate was Helen Magill, who graduated from Boston University in 1877. Although only 25 doctorates were granted to women
prior to 1890, by the dawn of the new century 204 women had been
awarded doctoral degrees.[46] Despite tremendous barriers, women were
beginning to make their presence known.

The door for women in education did not swing open without significant opposition. One long-standing argument against women in
higher education stated that such learning would make them unattrac-

tive to men and thus reduce marriage and birth rates.[47] As women entered higher education, they were indeed less likely to marry, and if they did marry, their families were significantly smaller than average.[48] Higher education also served to distance the nineteenth-century woman from her family of origin. Marriage had been the acceptable mode of female upward mobility. Consequently, women who climbed the social ladder through education often found themselves ostracized not only by their family of origin but also by their "class of origin."[49]

The path to women's higher education stood like a winding mountain trail with limited access and a well-defined speed limit. As Joyce Antler notes, women continually "struggle[d] for access to institutions."[50] When some of the educational barriers came tumbling down, more rigid and prejudicial barriers against women in the public sphere arose. Indeed, the very institutions that educated women refused to hire them to faculty positions.[51] In 1906 Stanford University president David Staff Jordan pronounced a significant benediction on women's education in the nineteenth century, stating, "If the college woman is a mistake, nature will eliminate her."[52]

Women in Theological Education

The restricted pace for women entering higher education in general paralleled their pursuit of theological studies. The first woman to gain access to theological training was Antoinette Brown.[53] Brown studied at Oberlin College, which from its founding was open to women. But an Oberlin professor actively discouraged Brown from entering the seminary. He stated his case in the school journal, claiming that women were emotional, illogical, physically delicate, weak-voiced, vain, dependent and ordained by God to be mothers and homemakers.[54] Brown persisted and was finally admitted, albeit to a hostile environment where she was prevented from speaking in the classroom or pulpit. Pamela Salazar notes that at Brown's graduation in 1850 "it was deemed improper for her to sit before an audience, receive a degree, or be recommended for ordination."[55] The pioneer woman sat in the audience watching all her male colleagues receive their degrees but was not even given the privilege of having her name listed on the graduation record.

Despite her unfortunate seminary experience, Brown was ordained in 1853 and served a Congregational church. Twenty-eight years after her graduation, she received an honorary master's degree from her alma mater. In 1908 she was given the doctor of divinity degree. She wrote nine books in her lifetime and preached until she was ninety years old.

Olympia Brown, another early woman seminarian, graduated from St. Lawrence University in 1863 and was ordained shortly thereafter. Although she did not face the degree of opposition Antoinette Brown had suffered, her classmates ridiculed her, gathering outside her bedroom window at night to mimic her "funny preaching voice."[56]

From its inception, the University of Chicago (Baptist) admitted women to all degree programs. Nevertheless, the school catalog stated that "women are to receive no encouragement to enter upon the work of public preaching, but on the contrary are distinctly taught that the New Testament nowhere recognizes the ordination of women to the Christian pastorate."[57] The dean of the school once declared that women in the divinity school were preparing for pagan pastorates. That is, women could prepare for foreign service among "pagans" but could not prepare for similar work in North America.

Anna Oliver's story illustrates another difficulty women students often faced. After initially enrolling at Oberlin, in 1873 she transferred to Boston University, where she found greater receptivity. She was even asked to give an oration at Boston's commencement. Overt opposition to Oliver did not come from male faculty or students, but from her own family. Her educational endeavors so embarrassed family members that they essentially disowned her. The severity of the ostracism even caused her to change her name on admission.

Anna Howard Shaw, another Methodist woman enrolled at Boston University's School of Theology, almost starved to death while pursuing her educational dreams. The seminary did not offer room and board or scholarships to women students, so Shaw tried to support herself by speaking at temperance meetings, preaching and working with a missionary society. The Methodist Women's Home Missionary Society finally agreed to assist Shaw financially after a society member found her collapsed from hunger and exhaustion in a school stairway.

In 1889 Hartford Theological Seminary became the first school to recruit women actively. Although men and women studied alongside one another in all subject areas, the administration directed women away from congregational or parish ministry into religious education, social work, women's education and missionary service.[58] In addition, Hartford's female students did not receive financial assistance. Only "special funds" could be allocated to educate them, because no woman should be allowed to "subtract from the funds built up over the years to help men get through school."[59] The irony is that many of the funds earmarked for financial aid were raised through the efforts of women.

In addition, female students soon discovered that graduation from seminary did not guarantee access to ordination. In 1880 Anna Howard Shaw and Anna Oliver petitioned the New England Annual Conference of the Methodist Episcopal Church for ordination. Although the General Conference had removed all gender barriers, the presiding bishop refused to ordain them. In fact, he encouraged them to leave the church if they planned to continue their quest for ordination. Soon Anna Oliver's church experienced financial strain, and in 1883 she left the pastorate tired and disillusioned. Anna Howard Shaw requested ordination from the Methodist Protestant Church and was ordained in 1880. However, the battle she encountered during her schooling and her rocky pathway to ordination left her discouraged; she soon left the ministry as well. As Pamela Salazar states,

Through the 1890's, the academic credentials which women painstakingly earned—that were not considered essential for most male ministerial candidates of the day—were insufficient to assure either ordination or a parish position to women who completed seminary programs, accounting to a large extent for the very small numbers of women in these programs.[60]

The early pioneers paved the way for later nineteenth-century women seminarians. However, the path to theological education remained treacherous. A woman who gained admission to seminary would likely be the only female in a class of males. She also found no female faculty members who could serve as role models. Women students were also isolated from community life, which focused on male dormitories and dining halls. Many professors resented having women in their classes and continually harped on their responsibilities as mothers and homemakers.

Despite these difficulties, women repeatedly rose to the challenge.

The first woman graduate from Garrett Biblical Institute (1887) was valedictorian of her class. In many seminaries, women students earned top academic honors. Indeed, women persistent enough to gain admission proved to be academically keen and handled their studies in admirable fashion.[61]

At the dawn of the twentieth century, 181 women were enrolled in seminary. The first wave of women in theological education had begun. And women were finally receiving their rightful educational credentials. These pioneers set a clear historical precedent for women serving in the gospel ministry. Therefore those who would bar them from preaching and teaching must turn from history to the Bible and theology in an attempt to make their case.

THREE

WOMEN
IN THE FAITH
COMMUNITY

◆

T HE PREVIOUS CHAPTER FOLLOWED the ebb and flow of women's roles in the church from the patristic era to the present. This chapter focuses on the biblical era. Using Scripture as our guide, we consider the following questions: What was the status of women in the early faith communities? In what ways did women serve? What roles did they fulfill?

These questions will help us see the wider context of God at work among his people in the Old and New Testaments. Did the biblical era set the stage for a movement of the Spirit expanding the role of women? And does the way in which women served in the early faith communities suggest anything about God's larger purposes?

In the first century the gospel message made such a powerful impact on women and attracted so many that critics satirically declared Christianity "a religion of widows and wives."[1] In part, women found the message of Jesus appealing because it gave them equal status with men and new avenues of religious service. They sensed that the gospel granted women, as well as men, the opportunity to participate fully in the community of God's new people.

The freedom women found in the gospel was not mere wishful thinking. Throughout the biblical era God was moving the community of faith toward an understanding of his egalitarian purposes. God set out to create a new family where all barriers to equality could be overcome to the praise of his name. Every member of this new community would be encouraged to use their gifts to build up the community of faith.

This biblical survey naturally begins with the Old Testament. What was the place of women within the ancient community? The Old Testament, in turn, provides the context for an inquiry into the new community of faith that Jesus formed. What attitude did our Lord demonstrate toward women during his earthly sojourn? And what status did women enjoy within his band of disciples? Finally, how did the early Christian communities seek to imitate what they had seen in the Master? Is there evidence of women sharing equally with men in the gospel ministry, even fulfilling leadership capacities?

Women in the Hebrew Community

The Old Testament narrates God's covenant relationship with Israel. God entered into covenant with this nation in order to create a holy people who would worship and obey him alone. God established this people as the means by which he would bless all nations (e.g., Gen 12:2-3). What was the status of women in the ancient community of faith? More specifically, Does the Old Testament teach by precept and example that women should not be leaders among God's people because of their gender? Or did God call both men and women to fulfill various roles in the faith community?

To answer these questions, we must first consider the status of women in Israelite society at large.[2] Taken as a whole, the Old Testament bears witness to a strong patriarchal social order, where males dominated public and private life. Closer inspection, however, reveals that this patriarchal structure was not so rigid as to exclude women completely from positions of leadership.

Ancient Hebrew society centered on family life. The extended family formed the primary social unit, which generally included a male leader (patriarch), his wife or wives, their offspring and the family servants. Patriarchalism established tribal identity, for members of a tribe traced their roots through their male ancestors.

The centrality of the family life in the Old Testament world led to a strong emphasis on women's bearing children, especially sons. A woman's chief function was to become a "fruitful" wife, whereas "barrenness" was a grave reproach (for example, Ex 23:25-26; 1 Sam 1:1—2:10; Job 24:21; Ps 113:9). A man's name lived on through his sons, but when a daughter married, she left her family of origin and became part of her husband's family.

This emphasis on the male as progenitor and the woman as childbearer led to a subordinate, restricted position for women. Pamela J. Scalise offers a succinct summary:

> The place of women in Israelite society was narrowly circumscribed by law and custom. An adult woman was a minor in the eyes of the law and lived under the authority of her nearest male relative. Even her vows to God could be cancelled by her father or husband (Num 30:3-16). Her husband could divorce her (Deut 24:1-4) or take another wife (Ex 21:10; Deut 21:15-17), but she could not divorce him. She was subject to a terrible ordeal if her husband even suspected her of unfaithfulness (Num 5:11-31). She could inherit the family lands only if there were no male heirs, but she could only marry within her own clan because the land would then pass to her husband (Num 27:1-11; 36:1-13).[3]

The patriarchal family structure guaranteed male dominance of public life in Israel. While the ideal wife "watches over the affairs of her household" (Prov 31:27 NIV), the Israelite man joins his peers at the city gates, taking "his seat among the elders of the land" (v. 23). As this passage suggests, the politics of public life also remained an almost exclusively male domain. From the beginning Israel's leaders were male, although an occasional woman assumed authority. During the monarchy, kings usually governed Israel, although in one instance a queen functioned as head of state (2 Kings 11:3).

Men also took the lead in religious matters. As the representatives of their households, they brought most of the prescribed sacrifices to the tabernacle or temple. In addition, the Torah stipulated that only men could serve as priests. However, the Old Testament gives no theoretical or theological explanation as to why women were barred from the priesthood.[4] Some scholars suggest that on practical grounds, women would have found it very difficult to serve as priests while also fulfilling their primary social role of bearing children and managing the household. Or perhaps they could not do the various types of work involved in the sacrificial system, such as killing and lifting heavy animals. Others offer a more theological explanation, seeing the prohibition as prompted by the struggle against Canaanite fertility cults, which had female priests serving as sacred prostitutes. In any case, only males descended from Aaron could hope to become priests.

Despite the dominance of men in Israel's public life, women were not limited to household management. Women occasionally took the lead in family affairs outside the home. Examples include the "clever and beautiful" Abigail, who intervened on behalf of her foolish and mean husband (1 Sam 25:2-35), and the Shunammite woman who suggested to her husband that they build a lodging for Elisha (2 Kings 4:8-10). Under certain circumstances daughters could inherit family property (Num 27:1-11; 36:1-9; Josh 15:13-19; Job 42:15), and women frequently engaged in commerce (Prov 31:13-18, 24). The ideal wife used these resources to assist the needy (Prov 31:20).

Women sometimes exercised great influence in local public life. For example, when David's army besieged the town of Abel Beth-maacah, a "wise woman" persuaded the townspeople to meet the demands of Joab, the commander (2 Sam 20:14-22). Consequently, this unnamed woman stands as an example of what Edmund Jacob describes as "a special class, distinct from prophets and priests . . . who by their counsel have an active influence on the course of events."[5]

Although the priesthood was restricted to men, women participated in Israelite worship, for God had entered into covenant with both men and women (Deut 29:1-11). Women were to be present for the public reading of the Torah (Deut 31:9-13; Neh 8:1-3). They served at the tent of meeting (Ex 38:8; 1 Sam 2:22) and offered sacrifices (Lev 12:1-8; 1 Sam 2:19). Women sometimes played a more significant role than their husbands in God's redemptive acts (Judg 13:1-23). And without the mediation of their husbands, women could inquire of God through prophets or in prayer (1 Sam 1:1-28).

During the intertestamental period, women's role in worship dimin-

ished. Their access to the temple was greatly restricted, being limited
to the outer courts of the building. Despite such severe constraints,
women continued to serve God at the temple. This is exemplified by
Anna, who "never left the temple but worshiped there with fasting and
prayer night and day" (Lk 2:37).

According to Mary Evans's concise summary, Israelite women were
"subordinate to their husbands and generally of lower status than men.
They were seen for the most part as child-bearers, or at best homemakers, but in some cases they were acknowledged as companions and
partners, and it was not impossible for them to have wider spheres of
interest and work. How they were treated and the sort of life a woman
lived depended largely on the attitude of her husband and on his position in society."[6]

The Old Testament narrates the stories of some great women chosen
by God to lead Israel. But we should not assume that the few women
specifically named constitute the total number of women acting in such
authoritative roles. The Old Testament gives every indication that unnamed women and men served in authoritative capacities throughout
Israel's history. Scripture offers no evidence that the Israelites ever
rejected a woman's leadership simply on the basis of gender. On the
contrary, we get the impression that Israel acknowledged the authority
of God-ordained women leaders to the same extent as their male
counterparts. In what authoritative roles did women serve?

Women as Leaders. Early in Israel's history, various women assumed
leadership roles. Prominent among them were Miriam, the sister of
Moses, and Deborah, one of Israel's judges. Miriam was one of the
three siblings whom God chose to lead Israel out of Egypt. The Bible
refers to her as a prophet, a role she performed soon after Israel's
escape from the pursuing Egyptian army. In celebration of God's great
victory, Miriam led the Israelite women in a song and dance of praise
(Ex 15:20-21).

The fact that this song was performed by a women's chorus does not
mitigate against the public nature of her leadership role.[7] On the contrary, the psalmist later spoke of these women as public heralds of the
word of God. In reciting God's glorious victory over his enemies in the
conquest of Canaan, the biblical poet declares, "The Lord announced
the word, and great was the company of those who proclaimed it" (Ps

68:11 NIV). However, the feminine form of the Hebrew text is better translated, "great was the company of the women that heralded it."[8]

At Hazeroth, Miriam exercised her leadership capabilities in a sinful manner (Num 12:1-15). Together with Aaron, she spoke against Moses because he had married a Cushite woman. They justified their criticism by claiming an authority to speak in God's name equal to that of Moses. In response, God confirmed Moses' superiority over his siblings. Nevertheless, God's rebuke of Miriam and Aaron assumed their role as prophets who received divine communication through visions and dreams. God then singled out Miriam for punishment. This act and the listing of Miriam's name before Aaron's suggests that she may have been the primary instigator of the challenge. However, nowhere does the text suggest that Miriam sinned by circumventing male headship. Rather, she and Aaron went astray by questioning Moses' status.

Despite her sin, Miriam gained a positive place in Israelite history. The biblical authors considered her of sufficient importance to record her death (Num 20:1) and to include her in the lengthy genealogies of the Israelite clans (Num 26:59; 1 Chron 6:3). Miriam's position as a leader in Israel is unquestionable. In fact, she was so prominent that a later prophet, Micah, could invoke her name. As Micah records the case against Israel, God himself confirms Miriam's place among Israel's leaders at the exodus: "I brought you up from the land of Egypt, and redeemed you from the house of slavery; and I sent before you Moses, Aaron, and Miriam" (Mic 6:4).

Perhaps the most prominent early female leader in Israel was Deborah (Judg 4—5). Whereas Miriam functioned as part of a leadership team of which Moses was clearly the more important, Deborah served as the highest leader of her people. Although she was married, her leadership role included the exercise of authority over men.

Deborah's position combined the work of prophet and judge (Judg 4:4). As a member of the prophetic community, she acted as the mouthpiece for the word of God (4:6-7). Deborah announced God's command to Barak, telling him to assemble the Israelite army against the Canaanites. Probably due to Deborah's prophetic function, the commander insisted that she accompany the expedition (4:8).

God used the judges to lead Israel from the time of Moses until the monarchy (Acts 13:20-21). Judges functioned as Israel's highest legal tribunal (Deut 17:8-13). In keeping with this function, Deborah "held court . . . and the Israelites came to her to have their disputes decided" (Judg 4:5 NIV). In so doing, Deborah assumed the role of national judge in much the same way as Moses had done earlier (see Ex 18:13).

Israel's judges also performed a political function. God repeatedly raised up judges in order to deliver Israel from foreign oppressors (Judg 2:18). Deborah also fulfilled her political role when she commanded Barak to assemble Israel's army to repel the foreign oppressors (4:6). In the same way, Samuel later commissioned Saul to be Israel's political ruler even before he became king (1 Sam 10:1). Deborah also directed the plans for the military expedition against the Canaanites, including the day of the attack (Judg 4:14).

In addition to their political importance, judges served as spiritual leaders. God intended judges to foster true worship and morality in Israel (Judg 2:19). Deborah fulfilled this aspect as well. After defeating Sisera's army, she—like Miriam generations earlier—praised God in song for the victory (Judg 5). The text indicates that Barak joined her in this praise. The narrator does not include Barak's name to demonstrate Deborah's submission to the male headship principle, as some complementarians claim.[9] Rather, this detail climaxes a narrative in which Deborah and Barak together are the chief figures. This military victory resulted in forty years of peace (5:31).

Judges obviously carried out their responsibilities in public view. The biblical text notes that Deborah exercised her office in the hill country near Bethel (Judg 4:5). Throughout Israel's history this strategic location was connected with religious practices and the prophetic community (see 1 Sam 7:16; 2 Kings 2:3; 17:28; Amos 7:10-13). Further, the language used in the Judges 4:5 passage—"and the Israelites came up to her for judgment"—is reminiscent of Moses' earlier ministry (Ex 18:13-16). Nothing in the text suggests that Deborah acted in a purely private manner.[10] As the mediator of public disputes, she, like Moses before her, served a public role in a public realm.

Concerning the current trend of some to demote Deborah from the public life of Israel, Christina Campbell rightly observes,

> Deborah's prophet/judgeship was not a private little cottage industry being practiced out of her home. In view of the text there can be little doubt that Deborah was the recognized, appointed leader/judge of

the Israelites at that time. I mention this fairly obvious fact only because of the persistent rejection or downplaying of Deborah's authority by traditional patriarchalists: Deborah does not fit into their male "headship" theory of God's economy.[11]

The example of Deborah confirms that neither God nor the ancient Hebrews found female leadership intrinsically abhorrent. On the contrary, a woman could—and did—exercise authority over the entire community, including men. The predominance of male judges does not mitigate the significance of God's choice of Deborah and her praiseworthy service in obedience to that call. We do Deborah and God a disservice when we suggest that she worked as Israel's judge only because no men were available. Rather, as Irene Foulkes explains, Deborah's story is much more significant: "In the earlier period of the Judges [before the rise of the monarchy] charismatic leaders like Deborah, with their strong personalities heightened by the gift of God, could find room for action."[12]

Women in the Prophetic Community. We have noted two instances of Israelite women whose political responsibilities apparently grew out of their role as prophets. In this prophetic ministry, Miriam and Deborah were joined by a number of other women. Female prophets seem to have been accepted without question in the Old Testament. Through Ezekiel, God denounced some false prophets in the land who happened to be women (Ezek 13:17-24; see also Neh 6:14). They did not sin by usurping the authority of an exclusively male office, but by prophesying contrary to the word of the Lord. The reference to false female prophets also suggests the ongoing presence of true female prophets, such as the unnamed woman whom Isaiah married (Is 8:3).

As we noted in our discussion of Miriam, women could likewise be heralds of the word of God (Ps 68:11), a task associated with the prophetic office. Consequently, as the Hebrew construction of Isaiah 40:9 indicates, the prophet could freely use the feminine form to designate the herald who would one day announce the good tidings of God's powerful arrival: "You [feminine] who bring good tidings to Zion, go up on a high mountain. You [feminine] who bring good tidings to Jerusalem, lift up your voice with a shout" (NIV).[13]

Perhaps the most widely known female prophet in Israelite history was Huldah (2 Kings 22:14-20). When King Josiah desired to hear the prophetic word following the discovery of the Book of the Law in the temple, he apparently did not seek out any of the leading male prophets of the day, such as Zephaniah (Zeph 1:1) and Jeremiah (Jer 1:2). Instead, he sent five prominent officials to Huldah, who declared the word of the Lord. In response to Huldah's oracle, the king led the people in an act of covenant renewal.

Nothing in the text suggests that Huldah acted in a manner different from the great male prophets. Nor in contrast to their public ministries, did she prophesy and teach only in private. The intent of the narrator can hardly be construed in the manner complementarians sometimes read the passage, namely, that Huldah exercised "her prophetic ministry in a way that did not obstruct male headship."[14] Instead, Huldah stands among the men and women who proclaimed the true word of God to the people of their day.

This brief survey suggests that despite male dominance among the Hebrews, the Old Testament faith instilled in Israel the seeds of an egalitarian strand unparalleled among surrounding nations. Nevertheless, not until the coming of Jesus did God act decisively to liberate men and women for full fellowship with himself and each other.

Women in Jesus' Ministry

Jesus gave no explicit teaching on the role of women in the church. In fact, he left no teaching at all concerning women as a class of people. This is not surprising, for he treated each woman he met as a person in her own right. Yet by observing Jesus in action and listening to his words we can deduce much about his attitude toward women.[15] In turn, the attitude of our Lord coupled with his liberating message formed the foundation for women's roles in the early church.

Scholars agree that in the context of the Judaism of his day, Jesus emerges as a unique, even a radical reformer of the widely-held attitudes toward women and their role in society.[16] C. G. Montefiore observes, "There can be little doubt that in Jesus' attitude towards women we have a highly original and significant feature of his life and teaching."[17] Likewise, in contrast to the religious leaders of his day, the Jesus of the Gospels was comfortable with women. As G. N. Stanton concludes, "he was able to mix freely and naturally with women of all sorts, and women followed and ministered to him."[18]

The gospel's liberation of women comes into full relief only when we view the ministry of Jesus and the early Christian community in light of the strictures against women prevalent in the ancient Near East.[19] From Galilee to Rome, the message of Jesus was a breath of fresh air that transformed the first-century world.

In nearly every ancient Mediterranean society, women possessed very little status indeed. The Greeks, for example, believed that women existed either to produce sons for their husbands or to provide sexual pleasure as courtesans. Women could not aspire to become teachers or philosophers,[20] although by the first century a few had gained this status. Similarly, women in ancient Rome lived under male authority, whether that of father or husband.

In traditional Mediterranean culture, the patriarchal order reflected the dichotomy between public and private life. The cultural ideal associated men with the public sphere. Men, therefore, actively engaged in commerce and politics, and socialized in public meeting places. Women, in contrast, belonged to the private sphere, and were largely confined to the home. Relegating women to the domestic sphere facilitated the enforcement of ancient standards of sexual purity. According to cultural anthropologist David Cohen, "The separation of women from men and the man's public sphere within this protected domain is the chief means by which sexual purity is both guarded and demonstrated to the community."[21]

Roman women were more visible in public and exercised more influence on commerce and politics than their sisters in Greek cities such as Athens. Nevertheless, even in the midst of this greater emancipation such women remained subject to the cultural ideal of the domestic woman. They were continually reminded of their primary responsibility to the household.[22]

In Jewish society, women enjoyed similar, perhaps slightly higher, status. During the intertestamental period, more restrictive attitudes overshadowed the egalitarian aspects of the Old Testament. The largely subordinate role women had played in the older patriarchal society hardened to become a clearly inferior status.

Some Jewish teachers considered women to be the source of sin and death in the world.[23] They taught that women are more sensual and less rational than men and therefore inferior.[24] Their low view of women allowed these teachers to cite women as examples of undesirable traits.[25] In addition, the fear of being seduced by women, whom they pictured as temptresses, led men to avoid social contact and conversation with them.[26]

Despite the Old Testament admonition that all Israelites hear the law (Deut 31:12; Josh 8:35), women received minimal religious instruction at best. Their role in Jewish worship was also restricted. In Herod's temple, they could not enter the sacred inner section.[27] Even in the synagogues, they were generally passive observers rather than active participants. Because a woman's primary function was domestic, men often treated them as having little to contribute to public life in general and religion in particular. No wonder Jewish men learned to pray, "Blessed art thou . . . who hast not made me a woman."[28]

Compared to women, first-century men enjoyed a privileged status. Nevertheless, the plight of women was not uniformly inferior, but varied according to locale. In cities such as Alexandria and Jerusalem, women lived in domestic seclusion, in keeping with the idea that home was the only appropriate place for women (and slaves).[29] Women in rural Palestine, in contrast, moved about in public with a certain degree of freedom.[30] A parallel situation emerged in the Roman world. Despite the male dominance of Roman society in general, certain matrons enjoyed great power and influence on politics and culture. They increasingly pursued personal interests outside the home, including commerce.

The greater freedom that some women enjoyed in certain sectors of society contributed to the advance of the gospel. Jesus himself received support from women (Lk 8:1-3). Later, merchants like Lydia and Priscilla played important roles in several Gentile churches (see Acts 16:11-15 and 18:1-3, 18-28).

Jesus' Attitude Toward Women. Jesus' dealings with women ran contrary to the cultural norms of his day; he viewed all people, whether male or female, as persons. Counter to rabbinic practice, our Lord freely associated with women. Jesus responded with compassion to the needy, whether male or female. He touched and was touched by women, even those who were ritually unclean (Mt 9:18-26) or whose morals were questionable (Lk 7:36-50). Jesus not only warmly received women who came to him, he considered women such as Lazarus's sisters, Mary and

Martha, and Mary Magdalene among his close friends. In so doing, he clearly demonstrated that men and women could intimately relate to each other on more than just a sexual level.

The strict separation of the sexes governing relationships in Jewish society paralleled the belief that women derived their identity from men. Jesus, however, taught that all persons find their true identity in relationship to God. Consequently, he did not perpetuate the widely held attitudes that favored men at the expense of women. He did not view women primarily within their culturally assigned roles of wife and mother. And he refused to consider women as the source of sexual temptation.

As James Hurley observes, "The foundation-stone of Jesus' attitude toward women was his vision of them as *persons* to whom and for whom he had come. He did not perceive them primarily in terms of their sex, age or marital status; he seems to have considered them in terms of their relation (or lack of one) to God."[31]

In contrast to the rabbis, who avoided even mentioning women,[32] Jesus did not limit his illustrations to male experiences but often clarified his teaching with incidents from women's lives. He characterized the divine joy over of a sinner's salvation through not only the image of a shepherd seeking a lost lamb but also the image of a woman finding a lost coin (Lk 15:3-10). Jesus appealed to women's experiences to exemplify persistence (Lk 18:1-8) and to admonish his followers to be watchful (Mt 25:1-13). He likewise pointed out certain women who exemplified the proper response to his message. For example, our Lord used the loving act of a forgiven prostitute to shame the inhospitable behavior of a Pharisee (Lk 7:36-50). And he singled out a destitute widow who contributed a small coin to the temple treasury to illustrate the heartfelt nature of true giving (Mk 12:41-44). Grant Osborne concludes from his study of the Gospels that Jesus set women "alongside men as models for true discipleship and kingdom ethics." In fact, "on many occasions Jesus not only set them alongside men but contrasted their greater piety and faith to the weaknesses of Jewish leaders and even his own disciples."[33]

Women Among the Disciples. Jesus perhaps most notably departed from cultural norms by including women among his followers. The Evangelists clearly indicate that throughout most of his ministry, Jesus was accompanied by several women, some of whom he had healed (Lk 8:1-3). These women contributed financially to the cause and provided for Jesus' needs (Mt 27:55-56; Mk 15:40-41). True, Jesus chose no women to serve within the special circle of the Twelve. In chapters six and seven we will look more closely at the significance of this choice as an eschatological act rather than as the foundation for the future administration of the church.[34] In the present context, we need only observe that the exclusion of women from the Twelve ought not to blind us to the importance of their presence among Jesus' followers.

In contrast to many rabbis who considered it inappropriate to instruct women, Jesus readily taught them. Perhaps the most obvious example is Mary of Bethany, who sat at Jesus' feet (Lk 10:39). In describing the scene, the Evangelist chooses terminology associated with rabbinic study (compare Acts 22:3), suggesting that Mary became Jesus' student.[35] By his response, Jesus overturned the culturally determined priorities for women. He rejected the Jewish notion that household maintenance constituted the only appropriate role for women in society. And he defied the practice of excluding women from the study of the Torah. Our Lord set aside the customary prejudices of his day and restored the Old Testament injunction that both men and women apply themselves to learning God's law (Lk 11:27-28).

As the master teacher, Jesus concerned himself with the spiritual development of his disciples. To accomplish this goal, he engaged in conversation with them. The Gospel writers indicate our Lord's willingness to include women in such theological discussions. In this manner, he awakened faith in the hearts of several women, including a Canaanite woman (Mt 15:21-28; Mk 7:24-30) and a woman from Samaria (Jn 4:1-42). The Evangelists emphasize the unusual and radical nature of Jesus' departure from cultural mores by taking note of how his disciples responded. In Samaria, they "were astonished that he was speaking with a woman" (Jn 4:27). As for the Canaanite woman, they "urged him" to send her away (Mt 15:23).

Jesus' female students bore the good fruit of his teaching. At Lazarus's tomb, Martha clearly affirmed Jesus' true identity: "I believe that you are the Messiah, the Son of God, the one coming into the world" (Jn 11:27). Martha's confession in John's Gospel functions as the narrative and theological equivalent of Peter's confession at Caesarea Philippi in the Synoptics (Mt 16:13-17; Mk 8:27-30; Lk 9:18-20).[36]

In reporting Mary's anointing of Jesus at Bethany, the Evangelists imply that Mary understood the true nature of Jesus' messiahship, a theological insight that Jesus' male disciples failed to grasp throughout his entire earthly ministry. This female follower seemed to realize that her Lord's vocation included death. On this basis, Jesus rebuked the disciples' grumbling against her, and he praised her action (Mt 26:6-13; Mk 14:3-9; Jn 12:1-8).

Perhaps our clearest glimpse at Jesus' close relationship with women comes at the time of his death. Whereas most of his male followers fled, an apparently large number of women remained at the crucifixion site (Mt 27:55-56; Mk 15:40-41). To the Evangelists, this made them the primary eyewitnesses to the event.[37]

At least two of the women also observed his hasty burial (Mt 27:57-61; Mk 15:42-47; Lk 23:50-56). Their concern to complete the burial rituals after the sabbath brought them to the tomb on Sunday. By taking the risk of going to the cemetery, these women were the first to learn of the empty tomb and to hear the good news of their Lord's resurrection.[38]

Although the Gospel writers all agree that women were the first to hear and experience firsthand the resurrection message, they do not elaborate on its importance. Consequently, scholars disagree about its theological significance. Some find in it the climax to God's elevation of women through the ministry of Christ. Others see the preeminence of the women at the resurrection as God's reward for the loyalty and love these followers showed our Lord.[39] Eduard Schweizer weaves these two ideas together by noting that "the very persons who in general held a rather despised position . . . were in this instance more persevering than the disciples. This feature delineates the new position of women in the fellowship of Jesus."[40] Other scholars, in contrast, are reluctant to find any theological importance beyond the simple fact that the women received the message first because they happened to be first at the tomb.[41]

Regardless of the significance given to their priority in receiving the resurrection message, the Gospel writers do give a certain preeminence to the women. The risen Lord apparently appeared first to the women (Mt 28:1-10), or to one of them, Mary Magdalene (Jn 20:10-18). The

Gospel writers agree that the women were the first to receive the command to proclaim the resurrection gospel and that they obeyed that command (Mt 28:7; Mk 16:7; Jn 20:17-18). For the Evangelists this meant that in God's new economy, men *and* women are credible witnesses and capable messengers of the risen Lord.

In the postresurrection community, women and men share in the proclamation of the good news. This new role for women forms a fitting climax to what developed throughout Jesus' life. Luke hints at this early on in Jesus' birth narrative, where both the prophet Anna and the devout Simeon announce the arrival of the Savior (Lk 2:25-38). Similarly, in the Fourth Gospel the Samaritan woman functions as an early credible witness to Jesus' identity (Jn 4:1-42).

Grant Osborne is surely on the right track in concluding,

> Jesus overturned Jewish views on the place of women (restricted to the home) by giving them an active role in his mission and even chose them to be the first recipients of a resurrection appearance. Women were the first ambassadors of the "age to come." As such they functioned as a "remnant" within Jesus' band of followers to call the others back to him.[42]

Osborne rightly places the significance of this new status within the broader work of God in the world: "The elevation of women to a ministerial role is a sign of the inbreaking kingdom, demonstrating that the old order has ceased and a new set of relationships has begun."[43]

The participation of women with men as witnesses and messengers of the resurrection gospel from the beginning may not settle all questions surrounding women's role in the church, but we dare not ignore its significance.[44]

Women in the Early Church

Early disciples united around a common confession of faith in Jesus as Messiah and a shared commitment to him as Lord. They sought to live out within the context of community the attitudes and character they had observed in Jesus' own life. By the power of the Holy Spirit these believers were to exemplify the mind of Christ in all their relationships.

How did the example of Jesus' relationship with women affect women's status and roles within the early church communities? In what ways did women serve in these churches? And as official roles became more structured, what offices were open to them?

The New Testament indicates that the gospel radically altered the position of women, elevating them to a partnership with men unparalleled in first-century society. Wherever the gospel went, women were among the first, foremost and most faithful converts. The gospel led them to engage in aspects of Christ's service that went beyond the cultural limitations of the day. As Ben Witherington III observes, "In the post-Easter community we find women assuming a greater variety of roles, some of which were specifically of a religious nature (e.g., the prophetesses of Acts 21:9), and some of which would have been forbidden to a Jewish woman (e.g., being a teacher of men in Acts 18:24-6)."[45]

The New Testament portrays women as full participants in the church from the beginning of its existence. They were fully present in the activities of the congregations. And they shared fully in the Spirit's endowment for service.

We depend on Luke's narrative in Acts for much of what we know about the early church community. As the curtain rises on part two of Luke's story, we find Jesus' female followers among those gathered in the upper room (Acts 1:14). Then as the early witnesses proclaim the good news, many who respond to the message and become part of the fledgling church are women. In fact, Luke is careful to place women at each stage in his narrative of the church's expansion: Jerusalem (Acts 5:14), Samaria (8:12) and cities of the Roman world like Philippi (16:13-15), Thessalonica (17:4), Berea (17:12), Athens (17:34) and Corinth (18:2).

Women particularly stand out in Luke's description of the founding of the Philippian church. Paul began his work there by speaking to some Jews who had gathered at a place of prayer—a group consisting solely of women (Acts 16:13). The first convert, Lydia, invited Paul to her home, which then became the meeting place for the believers (16:40). Luke's detail here draws a stark contrast between the new faith and the older Jewish order. Whereas a legitimate synagogue required the presence of men, a new congregation of Christian disciples could begin with a woman convert, and her home could shelter their gatherings.[46] This radical change, however, was merely the outworking of Jesus' own attitude. During our Lord's earthly ministry the testimony of a woman occasioned the entrance of the gospel into a Samaritan village (Jn 4:27-30, 39-42).

Not only did Luke include women in his history of the early church communities, he also takes care to show that women shared in the spiritual gifts of the church. His account of Pentecost forms the foundation for his inclusive perspective. Luke points out that women were present in the upper room as the believers waited in prayerful expectation for the fulfillment of Jesus' promise of divine power (Acts 1:14). Consequently, they were also in that place when the Spirit came. Luke's inclusion of Peter's sermon provides conclusive evidence that the Pentecost experience was shared by all—both male and female. To explain the strange phenomenon of people speaking in foreign languages, the apostle appealed to an important egalitarian prophecy from the Old Testament: "This is what was spoken by the prophet Joel: 'In the last days, God says, I will pour out my Spirit on all people. Your sons and daughters will prophesy' " (Acts 2:16-17 NIV).

Women's participation in the Pentecost event has radical and far-reaching implications. Not only did women receive Christ's commission as credible witnesses to the resurrection, but at Pentecost they also received the Spirit's power to carry out this central community responsibility. This means that women had received the same foundational qualifications for ministry as men in the New Testament church.[47]

The endowment of women for ministry finds confirmation in Luke's narrative of the activities and experiences of the community. All disciples—men and women—shared together in prayer, were filled with the Spirit and proclaimed the gospel message on Pentecost. In the same way, both men and women participated in subsequent prayer gatherings, experienced the fullness of the Spirit, and preached the Word of God with boldness (e.g., Acts 4:23-31).

Luke repeatedly cites the importance of women's ministry in the early church. Above all, women were bona fide witnesses who proclaimed the gospel, as we have already seen. What the narratives of Good Friday, Easter and Pentecost clearly indicate Luke's account of Peter's release from prison confirms by detail. The servant-girl Rhoda was the one who reported the miraculous presence of Peter at the door. At first the assembled believers rejected her report, but in the end her persistence won them over. In the story, Rhoda stands as an example of a woman whose witness proves trustworthy despite initial rejection (Acts 12:1-17). This account reminds us of the faithful testimony of the women who found the empty tomb on resurrection Sunday.[48]

Women in the Jerusalem church played such a vital role that they suffered persecution right alongside the men (Acts 8:3; 9:1-2). From the explicit reference to women, Witherington concludes, "This should imply to Luke's readers that the women were significant enough in number and/or importance to the cause of The Way that Saul did not think he could stop the movement without taking women as well as men prisoners."[49]

Women in Ministry

Women served important roles within the ministries of the early church, as we have seen in the Acts narratives. Although the New Testament as a whole focuses greater attention on individual men than on women, Luke includes examples of women involved in various dimensions of ministry. Most contemporary scholars do not think Luke included these stories as "filler" in a merely descriptive account of history, but as something much more profound. In the words of Witherington, "Their choice, position and content reveal a deliberate attempt on the author's part to indicate to his audience how things ought to be."[50]

Some ministries that women engaged in would not have shocked first-century society. For example, many women functioned as leaders in relief work, especially in aiding the needy. In Joppa, Peter encountered one such woman by the name of Tabitha (or Dorcas). According to the narrative, she provided material aid to many people but especially to the poor and perhaps to widows (Acts 9:36-43). Her ministry was so significant that Luke pairs her miraculous restoration with the healing of Aeneas (Acts 9:32-43). In fact, Tabitha's example may have been instrumental in the development of church offices that focused on service. Churches later commissioned a number of women to ministries reminiscent of Tabitha's.

In addition to aiding the needy, which some might consider the archetypical women's ministry, female believers served in more prominent roles in the early communities. One such role was patron to a congregation. Few ministries wielded greater influence in local churches than patrons. Unlike today's common practice of constructing church buildings, the early congregations generally gathered in homes for worship, exhortation and prayer. Often a fledgling church would be hosted by a wealthy convert (or patron), who provided material support and sometimes even certain social or political benefits to the group. Luke includes several examples of women who served as hosts to the early communities.

The Jerusalem congregation enjoyed the hospitality of Mary the mother of John Mark (Acts 12:12-17). She seems to have been a woman of some means, for her household included servants. And apparently the church regularly met at Mary's home, for we find Peter making his way there immediately after escaping from prison (Acts 12:12).

Another woman who served as an early-church patron was Lydia, who played a prominent role in the founding of the Philippian church. This successful merchant offered hospitality to the Christian evangelists upon the arrival of the gospel in the city (Acts 16:13-15). She then provided a meeting place for the fledgling community of believers (16:40). Both of these Lukan accounts clearly teach that women "aid both the intensive and extensive growth of the Christian community."[51]

We could (erroneously) conceive of the previous activities in which women served as limited to purely supportive, nonauthoritative roles. Several other functions, however, clearly move us into the realm of authoritative speaking. One such function was prophesying.[52]

Prophecy served to tie the believers to the Hebrew heritage, for the activity traces its roots to the Old Testament. At the same time, being a crucial manifestation of the gift of the Spirit, post-Pentecost prophecy was a distinctively Christian phenomenon. The importance of prophecy placed it first on the list of desirable spiritual gifts (1 Cor 14:1), even though prophets were not first in importance in the church (1 Cor 12:28).

Women clearly functioned as prophets in the New Testament communities. Luke, for example, reports that while en route to Jerusalem, Paul's company stayed in Caesarea "at the house of Philip the evangelist, one of the Seven. He had four unmarried daughters who prophesied" (Acts 21:8-9 NIV). Some scholars argue that because Luke tends to limit the designation *prophet* to church leaders, his description of

Philip's daughters as persons "who prophesied" suggests that they played a leadership role in the church.[53] However, the designation "unmarried" (literally, "virgin") may indicate that they were in their early to mid-teens. If so, it is unlikely that they had any leadership role in the church. In any case, for Luke, their involvement in prophesying clearly moved women such as Philip's daughters into the realm of authoritative utterance and beyond the traditional first-century roles of daughter, wife and mother.

The evidence from Paul's writings is even stronger. The apostle indicates that it was natural for women to pray and prophesy in public (1 Cor 11:5). In addition, he suggests that *prophet*, like *apostle* and other functional terms, designated an official status (1 Cor 12:28-29).

In addition, women functioned as teachers in the New Testament. A prime example of a woman teacher is Priscilla (whose given name was actually Prisca). In four out of six references to this married woman, Paul and Luke break with customary form by mentioning Priscilla before her husband, Aquila (Acts 18:18, 26; Rom 16:3; 2 Tim 4:19). This may mean that of the two, Priscilla enjoyed higher social rank.[54] Or perhaps she was more prominent in the church.[55] Whatever we conjecture as to why the biblical authors wrote in this fashion, we say too little if we pass over this unusual way of referring to a married couple by saying that "Luke may simply have wanted to give greater honor to the woman."[56] Such a comment overlooks the significance of the biblical authors' obvious departure from the norms of their day.

Priscilla's role as teacher emerges within the narrative of Apollos's visit to Ephesus (Acts 18:18-28). The account will not allow us to minimize her role in the teaching process. The narrator intentionally mentions her before her husband in connection with the instruction of Apollos: "When Priscilla and Aquila heard him [Apollos], they took him aside and explained the Way of God to him more accurately" (18:26). The reference to "Priscilla and Aquila" suggests that she was probably the primary instructor.

Nor should we minimize the depth of Priscilla and Aquila's teaching. In so far as Apollos was "well-versed in the scriptures" (18:24), their explaining of "the Way of God to him more accurately" must have been of sufficient expertise to warrant his acceptance.

Contrary to complementarian opinion, the text of Acts will not allow

us to transform this narrative into anything other than a clear indication of authoritative teaching by a woman in the church.[57] The text
gives no warrant to importing a distinction between private teaching
in a home and authoritative teaching in the church. To pass by this
incident as "*unofficial* guidance" as distinct from "*official* teaching leadership"[58] is to draw too fine a line between authoritative and so-called
nonauthoritative teaching among the people of God. As Witherington
concludes,

> The fact that this act took place in at least semi-privacy is probably
> not very significant in terms of its possible implications for correct
> church practice, since there is no indication that Luke was trying to
> avoid having Priscilla teach Apollos in a worship context.[59]

Finally, we should not overlook the significance of Priscilla's ongoing
teaching ministry. In Romans, Paul greets this couple as those "who
work with me in Christ Jesus" (16:3), suggesting that their instruction
of Apollos was no isolated incident. Priscilla's ministry was so important that she won the apostle Paul's commendation and gratitude, and
the gratitude of "all the churches of the Gentiles" (16:3). Nor was
Priscilla's ministry limited to other women. Rather, together with her
husband, she possessed sufficient biblical knowledge—and authority—
to instruct an important male evangelist. Witherington's conclusion is
illuminating: "By including this story, Luke reveals the new roles wom-
en ought to be assuming in his view in the Christian community." The
New Testament authors portrayed Priscilla as someone that Christians
ought to emulate.

Women as Coworkers. We have glimpsed at a few of the authoritative
roles women exercised in the early churches through examples of
women who functioned as prophets and teachers. The scattered references to Priscilla also introduce us to an equally important designation,
the *coworker.* Several biblical texts refer to women as workers in the
churches and coworkers with Paul.

Paul's favorite term for those who aided him in ministry was "coworker" *(synergos).* This term, together with its equivalent, "hard
worker" *(kopiōn),* appears to refer to a particular group of Christians.[60]
To understand the roles Paul's coworkers fulfilled we must remind
ourselves of the types of leadership that emerged in the developing
churches. Of first importance were the apostles, especially Paul, and

other recognized persons of reputation (such as Apollos). Paul also had traveling companions, emissaries and coworkers, who, like him, were involved in the work of several congregations (e.g., Timothy and Titus). Finally, each congregation came under the direction of its local leaders. The New Testament suggests some fluidity between the various groups: local leaders often became missionaries (Col 1:7-8; 4:12-13), and itinerants in turn settled in specific locations for a period of time (Phil 2:25-30; 4:18).

Within this loose structure, Paul's coworkers carried out a variety of functions. They assisted in composing letters (Rom 16:22; 1 Thess 1:1), carried apostolic messages to local churches (1 Cor 4:17; 16:10-11), sought to encourage the believers on Paul's behalf (1 Thess 3:2), reported to Paul the status of congregations under his care (1 Thess 3:6) and even occasionally hosted house churches (1 Cor 16:19).

In view of this wide range of ministry, it would be ludicrous to deny that Paul's coworkers possessed authority in the churches (1 Cor 16:17-18). Some of those whom he described as "hard workers" provided oversight to a local congregation, a role which included the task of admonition (1 Thess 5:12). Consequently, their leadership function obviously involved some form of authoritative speech, such as preaching and teaching.[61]

Paul readily spoke of women, as well as men, as his coworkers. He never cautioned his recipients to view only the men as possessing authority or being worthy of honor. Rather, his readers were to "submit to . . . everyone who joins in the work, and labors at it" (1 Cor 16:16 NIV).

Two women that Paul cited as his coworkers—Euodia and Syntyche (Phil 4:2-3)—ministered in the church at Philippi, which traced its founding to Lydia's conversion. Paul's reference to these two women raises the question of what type of ministry they pursued together with the apostle.

To understand the role Euodia and Syntyche played, we must consider what Paul meant when he said "they have struggled beside me in the work of the gospel" (Phil 4:3). According to W. Derek Thomas, the term *contended (synēthlēsan)* provides an important clue. This word "meant 'to contend,' as the athlete strained every muscle to achieve victory in the games. So, with equal dedication these women had contended with all zeal for the victory of the Gospel at Philippi." Thomas then draws this conclusion:

The Apostle would scarcely have used this strong word if they had merely "assisted him with material help" and hospitality, while remaining in the background. The word *sunethlesan* suggests a more active participation in the work of Paul, probably even a vocal declaration of the faith. How far this is true is admittedly a matter of conjecture; what can be said with certainty, however, is that they had contended with the Apostle in the cause of the Gospel and had gained a position of such influence as to make their present conflict a risk to the well-being of the church.[62]

Victor Pfitzner's research supports this conclusion: "The verb would seem to imply a more active role than the mere acceptance of the Apostle into their homes on the part of these women."[63]

A further clue lies in the phrase "in the gospel." As a description of the work these women carried out with Paul, the phrase may suggest an official ministry,[64] including an active role in preaching the gospel.[65] Whatever Euodia and Syntyche did, Paul ranks their work with that of men such as Clement. And he places them with "the rest of my fellow workers [*synergōn*], whose names are in the book of life" (Phil 4:3 NIV).

Paul mentions several other female coworkers in a lengthy greeting (Rom 16:1-16). Of the twenty-seven people cited by name here, six (or seven, if we include Junia) are women. The apostle gives a specific designation to several of these, including five (or six) of the women.

Prominent on the list are Aquila and Priscilla, who with Urbanus are called "fellow workers" (*synergous*). Mary and Persis are two women who Paul says "worked very hard" (*polla ekopiasen*). He calls Tryphaena and Tryphosa "workers in the Lord" (*kopiōsas en kyriō*). The last two women named, Phoebe and Junia, deserve lengthier comment.

Two aspects of these shorter designations stand out. First, Paul readily affirms the ministry of women with the same words of commendation that he uses for men, indicating a partnership of men and women in the ministry. Second, the terms Paul uses in this text suggest the participation of women in all dimensions of the ministry. In fact, his language is reminiscent of his description of his own hard work on behalf of others (compare Rom 16:6 with Gal 4:11). Some commentators see in these words reference to "the work of evangelism" and even to "apostolic tasks."[66] Ronald Fung, who favors a more traditional position on women in ministry, nevertheless concludes, "These considerations would seem to suggest that the 'labor' of these women for the church and for the Lord included, or at least may have included, the activities of preaching and teaching."[67]

Whatever their actual functions, Paul esteemed the labors of his female associates. In 1 Corinthians 16:16 (NIV) Paul instructs his readers "to submit . . . to everyone who joins in the work [synergounti], and labors at it [kopiōnti]." The apostle employs these same words to describe the work of his male and female friends. All believers—including men—were to honor these women as leaders and submit to their authority.

Despite Paul's commendations of these first-century women, complementarians tend merely to patronize them. Commenting on the apostle's glowing remarks about his Philippian coworkers, John Piper and Wayne Grudem declare,

> There is wonderful honor given to Euodia and Syntyche here for their ministry with Paul. But there are no compelling grounds for affirming that the nature of the ministry was contrary to the limitations that we argue are set forth in 1 Timothy 2:12 [i.e., barring women from exercising authority over, or teaching men].[68]

Women in Church Offices

We have noted the importance of women in the early communities and the significant roles they played. But did they serve as officers in local churches? And were they appointed to offices that entailed leadership, oversight and authoritative teaching? To answer this question, we must look first at church office structures in general, before inquiring about the specific positions that emerged in the first century.

Scholars are becoming increasingly aware of the practical and sociological factors that were at work in the development of church office structures.[69] Church leaders often emerged from those who were among the first converts and who, because of their financial means and social status, could act as patrons to the fledgling church (1 Cor 16:15-16).[70] Thus, we underestimate these sociological dynamics when we compare those who provided their homes as a meeting place for first-century churches to those who host a Bible study group today.[71]

Although early patrons primarily served a practical role, pastoral aspects were inseparable from their status.[72] The New Testament gives evidence that this role was not limited to men. Mary the mother of John Mark (Acts 12:12), Lydia (Acts 16:40), Priscilla together with Aquila (Rom 16:3-5), and perhaps Phoebe (Rom 16:1-2) all served as patrons of early churches.

Alvera Mickelsen may overstate the case in asserting, "In no instance is a man mentioned by name for a church office that does not also include women named for that same office."[73] But when placed in the broader context of how office structure developed in the fluid situation of the early churches, her conclusion that women served in various official capacities is correct.[74] Now let us look at the specific offices themselves.

Women as Deacons. During the first century the new Christian communities eventually developed a twofold office structure to provide leadership for God's people as they lived out the Lord's mandate. This structure was divided between leadership in oversight (bishops or elders) and leadership in service (deacons). We find in the New Testament indication that the early congregations appointed women to service ministries that we associate with the diaconate. Two texts are especially promising in this context.

Although in his Philippian epistle Paul greets the "bishops and deacons" (Phil 1:1), we find the clearest indication of office structure in the pastoral epistles. For this reason, we generally turn to 1 Timothy 3 for insight into the role of deacons. This text, however, does not unambiguously assert that women served as deacons.

In Paul's reference to women in 1 Timothy 3:11, the apostle does not use the word *deacon (diakonos)*. His choice of a feminine noun *(gynaikas)* opens the possibility that he was referring either to women office holders or, less likely, to the wives of male deacons. Even if we suppose that Paul meant women office holders, the exact nature of the office remains in question.

Some commentators see in the text evidence of a specifically female office (deaconesses), separate from, but parallel to, the deacons who were exclusively male. Others, however, point out that this conclusion reads a later development back into the first-century situation. They argue that the designation *deaconess* did not develop until the late third or early fourth century, at which time it indicated a role that differed greatly from that of first-century deacons.[75]

More probable is the suggestion that in the midst of Paul's discussion of the qualifications for deacons, the apostle suddenly singles out women serving in that capacity.[76] We can only conjecture as to why he refers to them in particular. Perhaps the apostle wants to remind his readers that service was open to women, even though in first-century culture their status was limited to the home. Or perhaps the fact that they may have been single or widowed would not have allowed them to fulfill the family qualifications which follow (1 Tim 3:12).[77]

Regardless of our conclusions, the ambiguity of the verse disqualifies Paul's injunctions to Timothy as a definitive example of women being admitted to the diaconate. A second text, however, is less ambiguous. In the lengthy greetings which close the epistle to the Romans, Paul commends to them Phoebe, "a *diakonos* of the church at Cenchreae" (Rom 16:1-2).

Before assuming that this designation refers to the office of deacon, we must look more closely at the term itself. The New Testament writers often use *diakonos* in accordance with its original, nontechnical meaning of "servant" (e.g., Mt 22:13; 23:11). Only later did the word become the designation for a church office (Phil 1:1; 1 Tim 3:8). The exegetical difficulty in the text before us is whether Paul intends to designate Phoebe as ministering in some official church capacity or merely to speak of her in more general terms, that is, as a servant to the congregation.[78]

On several occasions, Paul uses the word *diakonos* to describe his own ministry (1 Cor 3:5; Eph 3:7; Col 1:23). Elsewhere the term functions as a commendation of his coworkers, including Tychichus (Eph 6:21; Col 4:7), Epaphras (Col 1:7) and Timothy (1 Tim 4:6). In these texts, Paul is not referring to an office within a local congregation but to the more general idea of "servants of God" (e.g., 2 Cor 6:4).

The reference to Phoebe is unique, however, in two aspects. First, Paul refers to her using the specifically masculine noun form (*diakonos*), rather than some feminine alternative reflecting the more general idea of service. Second, the apostle places Phoebe's ministry within a specific congregation, for she is a *diakonos* "of the church at Cenchreae."[79] This is the only New Testament occurrence of the word followed by a genitive construction linking a person's service directly to a local church.

Usually the biblical writers use the genitive appellation to denote a broader application as a "minister of Christ" (Col 1:7; 1 Tim 4:6).

The idiosyncrasies of the apostle's commendation provide strong evidence that Paul intended to designate Phoebe as serving in some important official capacity in the Cenchrean church.[80] She was a deacon,[81] an office to which a congregation could appoint both men and women.

Paul held Phoebe in high esteem, as demonstrated by his request that the Roman church "help her in whatever she may require from you." To this end, he cites her work as a *prostatis* of many, including the apostle himself (Rom 16:2). Scholars are divided as to the significance of the feminine noun *prostatis* ("benefactor"), for which this is the only New Testament occurrence.[82] Some suggest that Phoebe had intervened with government authorities on behalf of Christians.[83] More commonly scholars appeal to the cognate terms, which suggest that she exercised leadership in the church.[84] We note, however, that Paul mentions Phoebe's activities as a *prostatis* in the context of people—including himself—and not a specific congregation.[85] Hence, it is unlikely that he refers here to a formal office[86] that entailed church oversight, such as a "ruling elder."[87] Nevertheless, Paul's commendation suggests that Phoebe was a person of great influence among the believers in Cenchreae; she was perhaps a wealthy patron. The apostle apparently anticipated that her influence and help would extend to his readers as well.[88]

Women as Elders or Bishops. Complementarians might welcome the conclusion that the early Christian communities appointed women to the diaconate, which would be in keeping with their perspective on a woman's place in God's order—those called to serving ministries. For complementarians, however, the possibility that women acted as elders is more problematic. Without question, women serving in this office would entail the exercise of authority that they would find incompatible with the male headship principle. Is there evidence that the early church appointed women elders? Or are complementarians correct in boldly asserting that nowhere in the New Testament did a woman serve as an elder?

The Case of Phoebe. Some egalitarians elevate Phoebe as the model female elder. As we have already noted, Paul refers to her as a *prostatis*, that is, a patron; a position that these interpreters claim must have entailed oversight in the Cenchrean church. We have already suggested, however, that this conclusion reads too much into the text. Are there other possible candidates?

The elimination of Phoebe from consideration seems to rob egalitarians of their clearest candidate. From her study, Mary Evans concludes, "There is no woman anywhere in the New Testament who is ever described as being either an elder or a bishop."[89] This seems to confirm the complementarian contention.

Evans and complementarians may be technically correct. With the possible exception of 1 Timothy 5:2, nowhere does a biblical author use either Greek designation for this office (*episkopos* or *presbyteros*) in conjunction with specific women. But this must be placed within the context of two other considerations. As Evans herself then adds,

> No man is ever described as being a bishop and the only men who are specifically referred to as elders are Peter (1 Peter 5:1) and the writer of 2 and 3 John, both of whom refer to themselves in this way.[90]

Consequently, we cannot build a case against women elders from the lack of personal designations in the texts.

In addition, the New Testament nowhere directly prohibits the appointment of women to this office. Consequently, persons who would bar women from the eldership on biblical grounds must develop their case from inferences.

Women in Church Leadership. Although the New Testament probably does not directly designate a specific woman as an elder or bishop, we do find women acting in the kind of leadership functions normally associated with this office. We have already spoken of the authority exercised in the wider Christian fellowship by women numbered among the prophets, teachers and apostolic coworkers. In addition to these examples, we have noted the more localized leadership of women who hosted house churches.

The New Testament provides ample evidence that local congregations regularly enjoyed the hospitality of women who thereby acted as patrons. Among those specifically named are Lydia (Acts 16:40), Priscilla (Rom 16:3-5; 1 Cor 16:19), Chloe (1 Cor 1:11) and Nympha (Col 4:15). One commentator suggests that five out of the six passages which mention house churches refer to women among the leaders.[91] As we have already seen, the New Testament indicates that serving as patron to a local congregation brought with it certain leadership responsibilities and authority (e.g., 1 Cor 16:15-16). There is no suggestion that the honor given to such persons was to be withheld whenever the host was a woman.

The *"Elect Lady."* Some might dismiss the above argument as mere inference. Therefore, we must ask, Is there a specific example that offers additional confirmation that women acted as congregational leaders? In this context, egalitarians occasionally cite the "co-elect woman" Peter perhaps mentions in the close of his first epistle (1 Pet 5:13).[92] More commonly mentioned, however, is the "elect lady" of the Johannine community. John the elder addresses his second epistle to "the elect lady and her children" (2 Jn 1).

The egalitarian use of this text hinges on the identity of the recipient of the letter. Is the epistle addressed to an individual or a congregation? Many commentators propose that "elect lady" is a metaphorical designation for an entire congregation. They find support for this interpretation in several details of the letter.[93] A. E. Brooke, for example, concludes that John's greeting, "whom I love in the truth, and not only I but also all who know the truth" (v. 1), reads more naturally if it is addressed to a community. The same holds for the greeting from "the children of your elect sister" (v. 13). Commentators likewise point to the shift in address from singular (vv. 4-5) to plural (vv. 6, 8, 10, 12) and back to singular (v. 13) as favoring the metaphorical view.[94]

Other commentators, in contrast, argue that the elect lady is a specific woman. They are divided, however, concerning the identity of her "children," as well as those of her "chosen sister" who sent their greetings. Some understand both as references to her blood relatives who were also believers.[95] Others see "children" (v. 1) as a metaphorical designation for the congregation that met in her house and that she served as leader.[96]

Several clues in the epistle suggest that its recipient may have been a woman church leader—a prominent patron of a Christian community, like Mary or Lydia—together with the congregation under her care. The word translated "lady" *(kyria)* fits best with this personal interpretation. The term is the feminine form of "lord" *(kyrios)*, which could connote a guardian, the master of a house or the head of a family. The personal interpretation is preferable in that the New Testament nowhere uses the word as a metaphor for a congregation.[97] This interpretation also fits best within the address itself. If "lady" refers to the church and not a female church leader, the greeting to "her children" is redundant. John's use elsewhere of "my children" to address the members of his community (1 Jn 2:1, 12-14; 3:7) suggests that in this text "her children" refers to the community under the watchful care of this leader, many of whom may have become believers through her witness.

In addition to the form of the address, the admonition to reject false teachers favors the suggestion that the letter was intended for the leader of a house church. Although the command is directed to the congregation as a whole, John's point is that they not admit a false teacher into the *house*, thereby cautioning against either providing lodging for or harboring within the fellowship such a person. In either case, a house church, which could both provide sanctuary as well as access to the gathering of believers, seems to be in view. Ultimately, the patron of the church, in whose house the *persona non grata* would need to gain entry, must take the lead in obeying the apostolic directive. In keeping with this, Brooke himself, who argues for the metaphorical understanding, admits that much of the contents of the epistle "might be regarded as advice needed by the leading member of a Church on whom the duty mainly fell of entertaining the strangers who visited it."[98]

To date, the exegetical question has not been answered definitively. There are good reasons to see in this epistle support for the contention that the early congregations had women leaders. But the exegetical case is admittedly inconclusive.

Women as Apostles. The New Testament documents clearly indicate that no office was as foundational to the advance of the gospel in the first century as the apostolate. Was this authoritative position closed to women? Or is there evidence that women were numbered with the apostles?

The search for a woman who bore the title *apostle* focuses on a somewhat obscure reference couched within the long greetings which close Paul's epistle to the Romans: "Greet Andronicus and Junia, my relatives who were in prison with me; they are prominent among the apostles, and they were in Christ before I was" (Rom 16:7). The question is: Was

Junia (or Junias according to some manuscripts) a woman? And if so, was she a member of the apostolate? Our attempt to resolve the identity and status of the person in Paul's greeting leads us through several exegetical difficulties.

In determining the status of Junia(s), we encounter immediately the task of determining what Paul means by the phrase "prominent among the apostles." Commentators have proposed two possibilities. These two people were either "well known by the apostles" or "outstanding as apostles." Either they were highly regarded by the early church leaders (the apostles),[99] or they were regarded as apostles themselves.[100]

Of the two, the latter interpretation appears to be the preferred interpretation[101] even among contemporary commentators who oppose women's ordination. James B. Hurley, for example, offers a terse rationale for this preference: "It is unlike Paul to make something like acquaintance with the apostles a matter of praise."[102] Piper and Grudem add this comment: "Paul himself is an apostle and would probably not refer to them in the third person."[103] "Prominent among the apostles" is also a more appropriate rendering of Paul's choice of words, *episemoi en*. As Sanday and Headlam argue, "*epissemos*, lit. 'stamped,' 'marked,' would be used of those who were selected from the Apostolic body as 'distinguished,' not of those known to the Apostolic body."[104]

Our conclusion raises the next question: What does Paul mean when he uses *apostle* to describe his friends? In the New Testament the word can denote several functions.[105] Arising out of the ministry of Jesus, an apostle could be a member of the Lord's twelve closest associates. Paul was obviously not implying that his two friends were numbered among the original Twelve. *Apostle* could also designate the wider circle of witnesses to the resurrection or those whom the risen Lord had directly commissioned to a special ministry (e.g., Paul himself). In so far as Andronicus and Junia(s) were believers prior to Paul, they may possibly have been among the many Jewish followers of Jesus to whom the risen Lord appeared prior to his ascension (cf. 1 Cor 15:6). Indeed, in keeping with this view, Origen's statement that Andronicus and Junia were among the seventy-two sent out by Jesus gained a large following among the church fathers.[106]

More likely, however, is the possibility that Paul used the appellation to place his two friends within a circle wider than either of the previous alternatives. *Apostle* could also function as an official designation (e.g., Eph 4:11), indicating persons such as Barnabas (e.g., Acts 14:1-7, 14) who were commissioned by a congregation and confirmed by the calling of the Holy Spirit to act on the local church's behalf in spreading the gospel.

Complementarians tend to favor a fourth alternative, an apostle as an emissary or missionary sent out by a church to perform specific tasks (2 Cor 8:23; Phil 2:25). Hence, Piper and Grudem assume without giving a rationale that Andronicus and Junia served "in some kind of itinerant ministry."[107]

Whatever their function may have been, it is difficult to avoid the conclusion that Andronicus and Junia exercised a certain authority within the church (e.g., 1 Cor 12:28). Even as itinerant missionaries sent out by a congregation, they would have engaged in authoritative preaching and teaching on behalf of the church. In fact, their influence was significant enough to gain the accolade "prominent among the apostles" from Paul himself. Complementarians, therefore, fail to reflect the dynamic of the first-century church when they dismiss the ministry of Andronicus and Junia as "significant but not necessarily in the category of an authoritative governor of the churches like Paul."[108] The congregations entrusted authoritative leadership to a wide variety of persons who ministered in their name or on their behalf.

The most controversial exegetical difficulty is the gender of the second person mentioned, Junia(s). The problem centers on the correct nominative form of the name, which in the text is in the accusative case *(Iounian)*. Was Paul's respected associate a woman (Junia) or a man (Junias)?

Several considerations favor the feminine, Junia. First, Junias is an unlikely candidate for the name of the person Paul greets.[109] Whereas Junia was a common name in the ancient Roman world, Junias appears to have been completely unknown. Supporters of this reading, therefore, theorize that Junias is an endearing contraction of a longer Latin name, possibly Junianus, Junianius or Junilius. However, as the use of Priscilla for Prisca illustrates, Latin names of endearment are normally lengthened forms, not shortened. Further, Paul's letters tend to avoid using familiar forms of Latin names, even when referring to the apostle's close associates, such as Silvanus (2 Cor 1:19; 1 Thess 1:1; 2 Thess 1:1) and Prisca (Rom 16:3; 1 Cor 16:19; 2 Tim 4:19). Second, questioning the gender of Junia(s) is a relatively recent addition. The presence of a circumflex accent in the Greek text, which indicates a contraction in the name, is a recent phenomenon. The earliest manuscripts had no accents. And from the time when they were added (in the ninth or tenth centuries) until the twentieth century, Greek New Testaments printed an acute accent, indicating a noun of the first declension, which is mainly feminine.

In contrast to the stormy contemporary debate, the gender of Junia was not an issue in the patristic era. In the second century, Origen assumed that Paul's friend was a woman.[110] The fourth-century church father John Chrysostom, who was no supporter of women bishops, expressed high regard for Junia: "Oh how great is the devotion of this woman, that she should be even counted worthy of the appellation of apostle."[111] Some contemporary scholars maintain that prior to the 1200s almost all commentators on this text regarded Junia as a female.[112]

Ray R. Schulz offers an even more pointed conclusion:

The problem of the Church Fathers cited above was not whether a male or female name is meant in Romans 16:7, nor whether or not Andronicus and Junia were apostles. They agreed on these matters. Their problem was how to accommodate this text alongside other New Testament texts which take a more negative attitude to the position of women in the church.[113]

Many evangelical scholars accept one of two popular options: (1) they dismiss the verse on the basis that the gender of Paul's friend is unknowable, or (2) they dogmatically read "Junias" into the text. We cannot help but wonder if these current options stem from a concern to smooth out the rough edges of a biblical text that strongly testifies to the presence of women leaders in the early church.

Assuming that Junia is indeed a woman, however, raises the question of her relationship to Andronicus. Some commentators suspect that these two apostles were married and therefore ministered in a manner similar to Aquila and Priscilla.[114] From this possibility several conclude that this couple (to whom they may add Aquila and Priscilla) exemplify the principle of a married woman engaging in ministry under the authority of her husband. This principle suggests that wives of church leaders may serve in ministries otherwise closed to women, especially single women.

This conjecture, however, runs against Paul's declaration that singleness places a women in a *better* position to engage in undivided service (1 Cor 7:34). In addition, the New Testament references to Priscilla and Aquila, which give greater prominence to the female member of this partnership, do not fit with the complementarians' picture of a woman serving under her husband's authority. In the same way, Paul's greeting indicates that Junia shared equally with Andronicus in the lofty designation *apostle*.

Complementarians are quick to cite ambiguities in the text as to the stature of Junia(s) in the church. They claim that these ambiguities eliminate the value of this reference as a clear example of a woman apostle, thereby cautioning us against reading too much into the text.[115] The greater danger, however, is to read too little into it.

Because the weight of evidence favors interpreting Junia as an authoritative apostle, Paul's greeting sufficiently opens the possibility that women served in this capacity. Consequently, we can no longer categorically deny that women fulfilled leadership roles in the early communities. Indeed, if the general tone of the New Testament best fits with an egalitarian understanding of church life—which we think it does—then this text, even with its difficulties, joins the others that suggest that there were women whose abilities, work and leadership won the acknowledgment of the apostle Paul himself.

Conclusion

We have surveyed the manifold ways women functioned in the ancient faith communities, beginning with Israel in the Old Testament and climaxing with the fellowship of those who sought to live out the attitudes and teachings of Jesus. The goal of biblical history is the establishment of a new people among whom outward distinctions no longer govern interpersonal relationships. The New Testament testifies that through Jesus of Nazareth, God has inaugurated just such a people. Consequently, within the company of Jesus' disciples all believers enjoy an equal status. Our new position "in Christ" transcends racial, socioeconomic and gender distinctions. The fundamental egalitarianism of the new reality Jesus established means that in principle every aspect of the church's ministry is open to believers without regard to these long-standing distinctions. Only specific injunctions from the New Testament barring certain classes of people from specific ministries would weigh against our *prima facie* openness to the participation of persons of any race, social standing or gender. This means that the burden of proof rests with those who claim that the Spirit overlooks the majority of the disciples of Christ when he endows God's people with gifts for authoritative ministry.

Complementarians, however, claim that Paul explicitly prohibited the full inclusion of women in church ministry. Therefore we must now turn our attention to a closer consideration of the apostle's teaching, including the texts that seem to move against the egalitarianism of salvation history.

FOUR

WOMEN
IN THE WRITINGS
OF PAUL

◆

O N SEVERAL OCCASIONS, PAUL TURNS his attention to the place and
function of women in the church. In our contemporary setting, sensi-
tized as it is to feminist concerns, the apostle's teaching has received
mixed reviews. Some have even gone so far as to dismiss him—and the
religion he espoused—as hopelessly misogynist.

Among evangelicals, Paul fares much better. Some evangelical feminists admit that some of the apostle's statements did limit the role of
women, but they nevertheless seek to salvage the biblical writer. Paul
Jewett, for example, claims that the apostle grasped "the essential truth
that the revelation of God in Christ radically affects the man/woman
relationship" but that he "did not press all the implications rigorously."[1]
Other thinkers explain the seemingly problematic texts as adaptations
to the cultural restraints of Paul's day. Or perhaps his negative injunctions were intended only for certain women in specific situations. Finally, certain evangelical scholars have completely rehabilitated Paul's
reputation, applauding the apostle as "one of the most revolutionary

writers in ancient times for the liberation of women, an outspoken voice for equality of men and women before God."[2]

Which of these pictures represents the "true historical Paul"? More specifically, how does Paul's teaching on the role of women in the church fit with the practice of the faith communities we explored in the previous chapter? And what is the significance of Paul's teaching for the church today?

To answer these questions, we must focus our attention on four statements in Paul's epistles. First we consider Paul's declaration of male and female unity in Christ (Gal 3:28). Then we explore Paul's teaching concerning the demeanor of women in church worship as found in long passages in 1 Corinthians (11:3-16; 14:34-36). Finally, we look at his apparent injunction against women in authoritative teaching offices (1 Tim 2:11-15).[3]

Paul's Charter of Equality

A central theme of the Pauline epistles is the unity of believers in Christ. Above all, Paul wants his readers to grasp the truth that God destroyed the barrier between Jew and Gentile (Gal 5:6; 6:15; Eph 2:11-22). Appealing to their new status in Christ, he repeatedly instructs the two groups to live in harmony with one another. The apostle's concern is not surprising, for as Richardson observes, "The single most pressing issue in Paul's churches was the problem of the relationship of Jew and Greek."[4]

Alongside Paul's teaching concerning the unity of Jew and Gentile, we often find him affirming the gospel's power to overcome the socio-economic differences that separate people into "slave" and "free" (1 Cor 12:13; Col 3:11). In his most expanded statement of the unifying implications of the gospel, Paul declares that in addition to racial and social distinctions, gender distinctions likewise give way to a new unity in Christ: "There is no longer Jew or Greek, there is no longer slave or free, there is no longer male and female; for all of you are one in Christ Jesus" (Gal 3:28).

Many scholars now believe that this far-reaching Pauline statement reflects an early baptismal formula.[5] The immediate context makes this connection clear: "As many of you as were baptized into Christ have clothed yourselves with Christ" (Gal 3:27). As new believers entered the baptismal waters, they may have articulated their newfound unity in Christ. Paul appeals to this baptismal formula to remind his readers that the "clothing" all believers share marks them with a "sameness" greater than any human distinctions. Believers, regardless of race, class or gender, possess the great benefits that come from union with Christ. They are all children of God (v. 26), as well as the offspring of Abraham and heirs of the promise (v. 29).

Scholars have also repeatedly noted the relationship between the Pauline declaration and several Jewish formulas which include similar threefold distinctions.[6] We find the most important of these contained in the morning prayer spoken by male Jews. In this prayer a man thanks God that he was not created a Gentile, a slave or a woman. As F. F. Bruce notes, the pious expressed such gratitude because these other persons "were disqualified from several religious privileges which were open to free Jewish males."[7]

While scholars agree on the central point of Paul's statement, they disagree over the apostle's intent. In Christ all believers enjoy an equal status before God, but the advent of salvation has obviously not eliminated all human distinctions. Even when we become believers, we retain our distinctive racial and social standing, and we continue to exist as male and female. What does this oneness in Christ mean, then, for relationships among believers who nevertheless differ in race, class and gender? Does Paul merely want us to affirm our unity before God in salvation, or should this theological truth also affect practical living within the Christian community? On this question, Paul's interpreters remain divided.

Complementarians generally limit the implications of Paul's declaration of equality in Christ to our *position* as redeemed persons. They see Galatians 3:28 as a statement of our soteriological position, but not of our soteriological function. In their understanding, rather than arguing for "social equality" between male and female, Paul merely declared our fundamental equality of "position" before God *(coram Deo)*.[8] As Robert Saucy explains, "The thrust of these statements is the truth that all are equally sons of God; all are equally clothed with Christ; all are equally heirs of the promise. Nothing whatsoever is said about all being equal functionally in the church or for that matter in the home or in the state."[9] Consequently, the declaration provides no foundation for egalitarian social relations within the body of Christ.[10]

Egalitarians, in contrast, see Galatians 3:28 as the foundation for a new social order in the church. It is Paul's "Magna Carta of Humanity,"[11] a charter of Christian equality. In their view this verse looms as the clearest statement of the apostle's own understanding of the role of women, thereby serving as an "Emancipation Proclamation for Women."[12] Egalitarians, therefore, assert that equality of soteriological *position* in Christ must receive an appropriate outworking in the *practice* of the church (and in society as well).[13] To Klyne Snodgrass, for example, this is "the most socially explosive text in the Bible." Responding to the complementarian claim that its scope is limited to our soteriological position, he adds, "There is nothing in the Christian faith that is merely coram Deo [before God]. All our faith engages all of our lives."[14]

Which of these two proposals comes closer to Paul's intent? The apostle devotes comparatively little attention to the practicalities of male-female relations in the church. But his writings do show us how he envisioned overcoming other distinctions, especially that of Jew and Gentile. The apostle expected the fledgling Christian communities to live out the implications of their unity in Christ, and in this aspect of the faith—as in so many others—he himself led the way. Perhaps Paul's instructions for racial and socioeconomic unity in the church will shed light on the implications of Galatians 3:28 for male-female relations.[15]

Neither Jew nor Gentile. No division troubled Paul more than the hostility between Jew and Gentile. In his thinking, the gospel itself was at stake in this controversy. The outcome of this debate would determine whether Christianity became a universal religion, intended for all the peoples of the world, or merely a Jewish sect. Paul's position in the controversy is clear: Jews could no longer demand that Gentiles follow Jewish legal stipulations. This meant that Jews could not require Gentile believers to convert to Judaism before they became followers of Christ.

At the heart of the struggle was circumcision. The Judaizers wanted to maintain this Old Testament rite as the sign of the new covenant, even though it had been replaced by baptism. Paul refused to acquiesce. He did not yield even to the demand that Titus be circumcised (Gal 2:3-5). The apostle's tenacity was rewarded at the Jerusalem council (Acts 15:1-35).[16]

The Judaizing faction within the church also stipulated that Christian converts must follow other laws, including dietary and sabbath regulations (Col 2:16). Here too Paul refused to acknowledge as authoritative the practices that had been "a shadow of what is to come" (v. 17). Finally, the "Judaizers" sought to maintain ritual purity by not eating with Gentile believers. In the heat of this controversy, Paul stood against Peter and other Jewish church leaders (Gal 2:11-14), arguing his point on the basis of their common belief that Jews and Gentiles are both justified by faith in Jesus Christ (2:15-21).

According to Stephen Lowe, Paul's passion for practical unity among Jews and Gentiles can be seen in the very structure of Romans and Ephesians. In each, the apostle first states the theological premise that Gentile believers share equal status with Jewish Christians and then spells out the practical significance of this status at the functional or social level. The bridge between theology and practice lies in the realm of spiritual giftedness, for equality in the distribution of gifts naturally leads to an equality in function. Because Gentiles receive the same gifts as Jews, they are equally eligible for leadership roles in the church.

Lowe concludes that Paul obviously "wished to see the two contrary groups manifest in social and ethical practice what was true about their relationship theologically."[17] Consequently,

> what is true of Gentiles at the level of soteriology (status) is operationalized at the ministry level (function). Simply to have in theory the privileges of equal status without the accompanying experiencing of that equal status would seem to have been insufficient from Paul's perspective.[18]

The implication for the unity of male and female readily follows: Paul "apparently saw some relationship between the issue of Gentile and female status or otherwise his statement in Gal. 3:28 does not make any sense."[19]

Paul does show a willingness to accommodate himself to cultural sensitivities when the situation demanded it. "Because of the Jews who lived in that area" (NIV), he circumcised Timothy (whose mother was Jewish) before taking him on his missionary journeys (Acts 16:3). Upon his return to Jerusalem, Paul followed the advice of the church leaders and joined four other men in ritual purification rites before entering the temple (Acts 21:26). In these cases, the apostle obeyed another principle, namely, his desire to give offense to no one, so that the gospel might be advanced (1 Cor 9:19-23). Nevertheless, in the matter of Jew-Gentile relations, Paul tolerates no split between theory and practice. The theological truth that Jews and Gentiles are one in Christ demands practical expression in the life of the church.

Neither Slave nor Free. Paul's passion for racial reconciliation in Galatians 3:28 is matched by his concern to overcome the socioeconomic distinctions between freeborn and slaves in the church. Paul eloquently expresses the practical implications of this concern in his epistle to Philemon. He admonishes Philemon, a Christian slave owner, to welcome back his runaway slave, Onesimus. But in sending Onesimus back to his owner, Paul did not intend to maintain the status quo of their relationship. Rather, he challenges Philemon to receive Onesimus "no longer as a slave, but better than a slave, as a dear brother. He is very dear to me but even dearer to you, both as a man and as a brother in the Lord" (Philem 1:16 NIV).

Some commentators contrast Paul's reserved address to Philemon with his forthright challenge to Peter in Antioch.[20] Whatever Paul's reason for his conciliatory tone in the letter, we ought not to miss the radical implications of his admonition.[21] Paul believed that the social order of slavery and the unity of all believers in Christ were fundamentally incompatible. From this radical base, Christianity subverted the Roman social order. As Harold Mattingly concludes, "Christianity made no attempt to abolish slavery at one blow, but it undermined its basis by admitting slaves into the same religious fellowship as their masters."[22]

Paul tempers his advice with a keen perception of the situation of first-century society. He calls on slaves not to revolt but to obey their masters in order to advance the gospel (Eph 6:5-8). He balances this teaching, however, with pointed demands that masters treat their slaves "in the same way" (v. 9 NIV). Nevertheless, the apostle advises slaves to gain their freedom if they can (1 Cor 7:21).[23]

Yet his chief concern is not with slavery in society, but with the unity of slave and freeborn in the church. Despite the continuance of socioeconomic discrimination in society, slaves in the church are to enjoy equal status with their free brothers and sisters. According to F. F. Bruce,

This could mean, for example, that someone who was a slave in the outside world might be entrusted with spiritual leadership in the church, and if the owner of the slave was a member of the same church, he would submit to that spiritual leadership.[24]

Neither Male nor Female. From the unity of Jew/Gentile and freeborn/ slave, Paul cites the final distinction to overcome in Christ—male and female. Because the apostle demands that the positional unity of the other groups be made evident in church life, we can anticipate that Paul intends that the unity of male and female have the same effect. Indeed, as Bruce concludes,

> No more restriction is implied in Paul's equalizing of the status of male and female in Christ than in his equalizing of the status of Jew and Gentile, or of slave and free person. If in ordinary life existence in Christ is manifested openly in church fellowship, then, if a Gentile may exercise spiritual leadership in church as freely as a Jew, or a slave as freely as a citizen, why not a woman as freely as a man?[25]

As we saw earlier, Paul himself led the way in the practice of this principle. He treated women with equal dignity and valued their contribution to the ministry of the gospel. For Paul the unity of believers from different racial and socioeconomic backgrounds carried implications for relationships within the Christian community. His desire to see the church implement these changes suggests that the unity of male and female in Christ must also affect community life. But is this confirmed by the apostle's statement in Galatians 3:28?

Many commentators note the subtle change in the connecting conjunction from the first and second pairs to the third: "neither Jew or Greek, slave or free" becomes "male and female." In addition, Paul avoids the customary words for man and woman (*anēr* and *gynē*) in favor of the more technical terms denoting the gender distinction, "male and female" (*arsēn kai thēlys*).[26] Scholars generally agree that this structure reflects the influence of the wording in the Greek translation (the Septuagint) of Genesis 1:27.[27] But they are divided as to the significance of Paul's use of this formula.

Perhaps the most widely held opinion is that the influence from the Septuagint has no interpretive significance. This is reflected in many English translations: "There is neither . . . male nor female" (NIV, cf.

KJV). Similarly, many scholars would agree with Fung that Paul's choice of terms indicates that he had "the relationship between the sexes (not specifically husband and wife) in view."[28]

Others, however, find Paul's direct quotation from the Old Testament crucial to the interpretation of the text. Some complementarians, for example, find in the appeal to Genesis 1:27 an indication that Paul meant to set the male-female relation apart from the other two. Whereas the others are human differentiations introduced after the Fall, "male and female" belongs to the creation order. Consequently their unity in Christ does not obliterate the functional distinctions which God himself placed in creation.

Our detailed development of woman in creation must wait until the next chapter. Here we need only observe that the complementarian claim that God intended a creation order consisting of a hierarchy of male over female is highly debatable. Further, evangelical egalitarians do not interpret Paul as saying that in Christ gender distinctions no longer exist. (Paul's Corinthian opponents drew this erroneous conclusion.) Rather, they argue that we must read the text in the light of Paul's central interest, namely, the reconciliation of divisions among humans by means of our participation in a common reconciliation with God. Consequently, the point of the text is that the old way of relating as male and female must give way to the new unity of all believers. Our position in Christ carries us beyond creation, not by destroying it but by lifting creation to God's redemptive intent.

More plausible than the complementarian explanation is Witherington's suggestion. He interprets Galatians 3:28 in light of Paul's argument against the Judaizers, who teach that circumcision and the observance of certain holy days are required for salvation. These regulations, which were permanent features of Jewish practice (even in early rabbinic texts), introduced into the church a similar discrimination against women (who could not be circumcised or participate in the festivals at times when they were ritually unclean). As a consequence, a woman gained status in the Jewish community primarily through marriage to a circumcised male and by bearing sons who would subsequently be circumcised.[29] Paul's response reads literally, "In Christ there is . . . not any male and female." Witherington expounds Paul's point: "Gentiles are not required to become Jews, nor females to become males (or be necessarily linked to males), before becoming part of the body of Christ."[30]

Although Witherington's interpretation follows a different path, it nevertheless leads to the egalitarian conclusion that Galatians 3:28 entails powerful implications for social relations. Paul's declaration meant that a female no longer needed to be attached to a male to have a place in the community. Women's roles need not be limited to wife and mother. As in Jesus' own teaching, the apostle's declaration opened the door to the ministry of women as women, including the ministry of single women.[31]

This interpretation of Galatians 3:28 coheres with other Pauline statements. In 1 Corinthians 7:34-35 the apostle overturns first-century social mores by elevating the service of single persons in the church. He thereby opens the way for women to assume roles in the Christian community other than wife and mother. Like men, women may remain single, if that is their gift, in order to concentrate wholly on the things of the Lord.

According to Paul, then, each person is to use his or her own ethnic background, social status or gender as the context in which—and a vehicle through which—to glorify God. These human distinctions are not obliterated in Christ. Rather, because they have no significance for a person's position *coram Deo*, they no longer provide the basis for functional differences within Christ's fellowship.

The Question of Hermeneutical Priority. Yet one question remains: Which Pauline text(s) carry hermeneutical priority in our attempt to understand Paul's teaching about women in the church? Are we to look to the egalitarian principle the apostle set forth in Galatians 3:28 as the foundation for our understanding of the apostle's own position? Or do we begin with those passages which seem to place limitations on the service of women (1 Cor 11:3-16; 14:34-35; 1 Tim 2:11-15) and understand the Galatians text in the light of such restrictions?[32]

Egalitarians often claim that Galatians 3:28 deserves hermeneutical priority. In this text, Paul articulates the overarching principle that in turn must inform community practice. The place of this text is confirmed by its location in the composition of the Pauline corpus. Because the apostle penned Galatians before setting down the stipulations concerning women's place in the church,[33] we must read these later texts against the background of the lofty ideal presented in the earlier epistle. Hence, F. F. Bruce concludes,

> Paul states the basic principle here; if restrictions on it are found elsewhere in the Pauline corpus . . . they are to be understood in relation to Gal. 3:28, and not *vice versa*. Attempts to find canon law [i.e., rules which ought to govern church practice in all cases] in Paul, or to base canon law on Paul, should be forestalled by a consideration of Paul's probable reaction to the very idea of canon law.[34]

With Bruce's admonition in mind, we turn to the texts that supposedly set forth restrictions on women's service in the church.

The egalitarian case may be overstated. Complementarians rightly remind us that Galatians 3:28 is a broad, general statement that occurs in a discussion of soteriology (God's work in salvation), not church practice. They correctly add that we must look to other, more specific examples of how Paul intends the church to work out this principle in practice.

Nevertheless, at this point egalitarians, and not complementarians, are on the right track. Complementarians read texts such as 1 Timothy 2:11-14 as giving a universal application to Paul's principle of church order. But if Paul ever acknowledged the ministry of a woman Christian leader—and we have noted several examples indicating that he not only acknowledged but actually supported women in ministry—then egalitarians are following Paul's own lead in their application of Galatians 3:28. And the seemingly restrictive texts complementarians cite, in turn, cannot be universal rules but Paul's attempts to counter the abuses of specific situations.

Women in Worship: Head Coverings

No first-century church appears to have caused Paul more difficulties than the unruly Corinthians. Their problems evoked a strong written response from the apostle, which we know as 1 Corinthians. In the middle chapters of this epistle, Paul turns to certain difficulties associated with the worship life of the congregation. His overall concern is that everything "be done decently and in order" (1 Cor 14:40) so that the saints could be built up in the faith and the gospel would not come into disrepute among outsiders. Within this larger section, the apostle devotes two short passages to the abuses that surrounded the activities of women in the public gatherings.

In the first text (1 Cor 11:3-16), Paul takes up the matter of head coverings. Nearly all scholars admit that Paul's advice is burdened with exegetical problems. In fact some scholars, exasperated by the debate, deny that Paul could have written these verses.[35] Although the case against Pauline authorship is not persuasive,[36] the text poses a great challenge to modern readers. As C. F. D. Moule quips, "St Paul's strictures . . . still await a really convincing explanation."[37]

The interpretive difficulties begin with the most fundamental aspects, for scholars cannot even agree as to the problem that Paul intended to correct.[38] Today many commentators favor the view that Paul's words were triggered by certain "emancipated" women in Corinth who were asserting their newfound equality with men in an improper manner. They were exercising active leadership in certain aspects of public worship without proper regard for propriety. In rebuking these women, Paul does not direct them to stop praying and prophesying in public, but cautions them to engage in these activities with due regard for norms governing proper attire.[39]

An alternative historical reconstruction describes the problem as emerging from the clash of cultures represented in the church. Well-to-do Roman women wore elaborate hairstyles in church gatherings without regard to the norms of female modesty among the lower classes, who in turn considered this immodest or even seductive.[40]

Whatever the problem Paul encountered in Corinth, our central concern lies in the abiding significance of the apostle's advice. Does his discussion incorporate transcultural principles limiting the role of women in the church? In our attempt to answer this question, we must raise certain exegetical questions which have bearing on our view of women's place in the church.

The Head Covering. Paul's advice to the Corinthians focuses on the propriety of head coverings for men and women. But what does the apostle have in mind when he commands women to cover their heads? At the heart of the question is the meaning of two expressions in the text (vv. 4-5). Paul notes that it is shameful for a man to pray or prophesy "with something on his head" *(kata kephalēs echōn)*, or literally, "having down from the head." A woman, in contrast, disgraces her head if she does so "with her head uncovered" *(akatakalyptō tē kephalē).*

Scholars are divided between two possible meanings.[41] Until recent years, most thought that Paul had in mind a material covering, whether a veil which covered the head including the face or a shawl that covered only the head.[42] Critics, however, mass several arguments against this position.[43]

Paul does not directly mention a veil *(kalymma)* in these verses but does speak about long hair (vv. 14-15), explaining that it is a disgrace for a man but the glory of a woman. Further, critics wonder why Paul would object to men wearing a material head covering, given that the practice was part of Jewish custom (e.g., Lev 16:4). A third point arises from Paul's subsequent use of a word denoting a material covering *(peribolaiou)*: "For long hair is given to her as a covering" (v. 15 NIV). Critics point out that the word translated "as" *(anti)* generally conveys the idea of replacement. It is used "in order to indicate that one person or thing is, or is to be, replaced by another."[44] If we follow its usual translation, "in place of" or "instead of," the verse then reads, "For long hair is given to her in place of a covering."

Perhaps the most detrimental criticism appeals to the Jewishness of the custom. It appears that the veiling of women was no longer generally practiced in first-century Greco-Roman society, but was a distinctly Eastern practice by that time.[45] Jewish piety may have dictated that women wear a shawl over their heads when out of doors,[46] a custom particularly prevalent in cities such as Jerusalem.[47] In Greco-Roman circles, whether or not women pulled their shawls over their heads was a matter of indifference, although a head covering would have been customary in certain situations, including participation in religious rituals.[48] The coiffure of women, in contrast, was of great concern in Gentile circles, for braided and decorated hair was a sign of rank and dignity.[49] Critics argue that these cultural considerations make it unlikely that Paul would have insisted that Gentile women in Corinth follow a distinctively Jewish practice. Such an injunction would have been contrary to his own stated abhorrence for imposing Jewish religious scruples (such as circumcision) on Gentile believers.

Arguments such as these have led a growing number of scholars—but by no means the majority—to conclude that the apostle is concerned about hairstyles. Hurley finds an interpretive key in the Greek translation of an Old Testament reference to a suspected adulteress

(Num 5:18). This woman was accused of signaling her repudiation of her husband by leaving her hair loose. The term used in the Septuagint (*apokalypsei*) to translate the Hebrew original is closely related to the word found in 1 Corinthians 11:5, 13 (*akatakalyptos*).[50] Consequently, the apostle's remarks must be directed toward women "having long hair coming down from the head."[51] Specifically, he objects to long, loosed hair that falls down on the back, preferring that women follow the usual custom of piling their hair on top of their heads.

This interpretation is also not without problems. For example, it appears to pose a contradiction to New Testament injunctions against braided hair (1 Tim 2:9; cf. 1 Pet 3:3). Would Paul have advocated the kind of feminine hairstyles that he and Peter elsewhere criticized?[52]

A related question addresses the purpose of the head covering. According to the traditional view, Paul commands women to wear a head covering (i.e., a veil or shawl) as a sign of submission to their husbands. In this way Paul reaffirms in the church a hierarchical social order he supposedly found in creation.[53]

Many recent commentators, however, reject the traditional interpretation. A few scholars consider verses 3-6 to be in opposition to verses 8-16 (with verse 7 being transitional). They claim that the second section (vv. 8-16) contains Paul's own egalitarian view and should be set against the opening verses (vv. 3-6), in which Paul merely repeats the hierarchical arguments of the Corinthians.[54] According to this interpretation, Paul issues no personal directive in the opening verses of the text. He merely states what was the case, not what ought to be the case: cultural norms declare that it is a shame for women in church not to wear their hair bound up and beautified in the Greek manner. In the second section we find Paul's own conclusion: hair lengths for men and women are matters of indifference.[55] Proponents of this interpretation appeal to Paul's closing comment, "We have no other practice—nor do the churches of God" (v. 16 NIV). The word translated "other" (*toiautēn*) generally means "such."[56] Hence, the apostle concludes that entire discussion by saying that the Corinthian custom, namely, the strict demand pertaining to head covering, is inconsistent with the practice of the churches with which Paul is familiar.[57]

A more widely held alternative finds concern for acceptable cultural practice in Paul's discussion. Women must dress or wear their hair in a manner becoming to their sex. According to J. Keir Howard, the apostle condemns women "for not having their hair neatly arranged in a style becoming to their femininity."[58] Similarly, Jerome Murphy-O'Connor suggests that Paul was concerned with the distinction between the sexes, not discrimination. He is not demanding that women wear veils as a sign of their subordination to men, but that they have well-ordered hair instead of loose, untidy hair, and that men have short hair.[59]

A final interpretation places Paul's discussion in the context of his struggle against cultic religious rituals. Elisabeth Schüssler Fiorenza, for example, suggests that Paul is warning against a practice common in the cults of Dionysus, Cybele, Pythia and the Sibyl, where "unbound hair was necessary for a woman to produce an effective magical incantation" and thus was "a mark of true prophecy."[60] According to the Greek ecstatic model, prophetic behavior was a divine madness or possession by a deity, the spirit of which would enter the worshiper, who would then be in a state of *enthousiasmos* ("having the god within"). These cultic practices apparently carried cultural overtones in the hierarchically structured first-century world.[61] Because of their confinement within a male-dominated society, women in the Greco-Roman world were attracted to ecstatic forms of religion in which controls were deliberately breached, social roles were inverted or blurred, and such behavior was legitimated by the claim that these women were under the control of a god.[62] In some ecstatic cults, possession by the deity was symbolized by the casting off of head covering, the loosening and probable shaking or tossing of the hair, and the exchange of clothing between men and women.[63] Paul was concerned that the Corinthian Christians not be identified with this cultic worship.

The debates among the scholars clearly indicate that we can no longer simply assume that Paul had a material veil in view.

The Word "Head." A second exegetical problem focuses on Paul's use of *head (kephalē)* in a statement in which he offers three examples of headship: "The head of every man is Christ, and the head of the woman is man, and the head of Christ is God" (1 Cor 11:3 NIV). In keeping with the idea that the apostle here argues for a hierarchy of male over female, commentators traditionally interpreted *head* as "having authority over."[64] In recent years, however, attempts to maintain the older view have come under intense attack. Scholars have introduced alternative suggestions, some arguing that it designates "beginning"[65] or "source"[66] and others offering "preeminence,"[67] that is, the one to whom is due prominence, honor, respect.[68]

In their search for the meaning of *head*, commentators find linguistic considerations important. What was the meaning of *kephalē* in Paul's day, as evidenced by other ancient Greek literature? What meaning does Paul attach to the word elsewhere in his writings (for example, 1 Cor 12:21-27; Eph 1:15-23; 4:15-16; 5:22-24; Col 1:18; 2:9-10; 2:18-19)? Can we gain insight into the apostle's understanding of headship from his statements concerning Christ's relationship to God (such as 1 Cor 3:23; 15:28) or marriage (Eph 5:22-33)? How was *kephalē* understood in the Hellenistic world as reflected in the Septuagint? Of special importance is the use of *kephalē* to translate the Hebrew word *ro'sh*, which refers to the ruler of a society (as in Judg 10:18).

In addition to linguistic considerations, scholars look within the text itself for hints to the meaning of *head*. In this context, Paul's citation of the creation story (1 Cor 11:9) is a focal point of controversy. The traditional view interprets the apostle's appeal to the order and purpose of woman's creation as the foundation for the subordination of woman to man.[69] Critics counter, however, by noting that Paul himself does not explicitly draw this conclusion in the text, nor do the creation narratives in themselves offer support for the subordination of women.[70]

Bolstered by these considerations, egalitarians offer several alternatives to the traditional interpretation. Evans, for example, suggests that Paul appeals to differences in the creation of male and female in order to emphasize that woman, who was created different from man, can therefore worship as a woman, without needing to imitate man.[71] More often noted is the apostle's care in designating woman as "the glory of man." Perhaps Paul's point is that women be properly adorned so as not to distract worshipers from God's image by attracting attention to themselves.[72]

However they understand these verses, egalitarians emphasize what seems to be Paul's antihierarchical declarations in the second part of the text. Crucial to their case is a newer interpretation of *authority (exousia)* in Paul's statement "The woman ought to have a sign of authority on her head" (v. 10 NIV). According to the traditional interpretation, Paul is directing the woman to wear a head covering as a sign of man's authority over her. (This is reflected in the New International Version by the addition of the words *sign of*, which are not in the Greek text.) A growing chorus of scholars,[73] including several complementarians,[74] argue on linguistic grounds that Paul is referring to an authority possessed by the woman herself. The Greek term simply cannot be interpreted here as referring to a head covering, because every Pauline use of *exousia* designates "an abstract reality, or one who has that abstract reality." In view of this finding, the text ought to read, "A woman ought to have authority [that is, liberty, right or control] over her head."[75]

What Paul means by saying, in effect, "A woman ought to exercise authority over her head," remains an open question. Many exegetes would agree with Kenneth T. Wilson: "Specifically it is her authority to participate in the worship of the church. In the synagogue women were not allowed to speak, but now in Christ they have freedom or authority to speak in worship." But then Wilson sneaks his complementarian view into the verse: "Thus the woman should wear a sign of her authority in order to allow her to have the freedom and authority to pray and prophesy in the presence of the man who is 'head' over her."[76] A more likely suggestion is that Paul here affirms a woman's right to determine how she should dress her head for worship.[77] Even though scholars differ on the significance of this reference, we cannot miss the egalitarianism that this freedom entails.

Paul also reveals his egalitarian commitments when he sets forth the reciprocal nature of the male-female relationship in verses 11 and 12. An exegetical question arises, however, in the statement "Woman is not independent of man, nor is man independent of woman" (NIV). The rendering "independent of" is itself an interpretation. The underlying Greek term *(chōris)* generally means "without," "apart from" or "without relation to." Paul's comment, therefore, is literally, "Neither is woman without relation to man, nor is man without relation to woman in the Lord." Appealing to her discovery that the term frequently means "different from," Fiorenza renders the verse "In the Lord woman is not different from man nor man from woman."[78] If she is correct, Paul reiterates here the basic egalitarianism he set forth in Galatians 3:28.

The way we translate the verse, however, does not affect the fundamental egalitarianism Paul here asserts and the significance of the foundation on which he constructs it (v. 12). Through his appeal to the reciprocal relation of male and female in original creation and human birth, the apostle provides a contextual correction for the understanding of headship he stated earlier. The derivation of woman from man and man from woman together with their common origin in God speak of a mutuality of source. The statement lacks any overtones of "authority over."

Finally, the debate over the meaning of *head* has also raised a crucial theological issue: the connection—if any—between subordination and inferiority. Some egalitarians object to the complementarian interpretation of *head* as "authority over" on the grounds that it requires that we not only view woman as subordinate to man but also view Christ as subordinate to God. By making the Son inferior to the Father, this interpretation introduces a heretical subordinationism into the Trinity.[79]

Complementarians are quick to respond to this challenge. They remind their critics that the position of the church throughout its history has been that the subordination of the Son to the Father in the Trinity is functional and not ontological; consequently, functional subordination need not imply ontological inferiority.[80]

Insofar as the subordinate Son and Spirit share fully in deity with the Father, the complementarian argument is technically correct. Nevertheless, it fails to see the crucial difference between the person-centered subordination in the Trinity and the group-oriented subordination of the hierarchical view of male-female relations. Our model of the trinitarian structure arises from the historical life of Jesus. It consists of the voluntary submission of one specific person (the Son) to another specific person (the Father) on the basis of personal mission and for the sake of accomplishing the goals of both. This salvation-historical subordination, in turn, points to an eternal ground, namely, in the eternal generation of the Son (and the eternal spiration of the Spirit), to use the terminology of the patristic church. The subordination of individual persons within the one Trinity is quite different from a social order that encodes the subordination of one group (women/wives) to another group (men/husbands) apart from considerations of the abilities, giftedness or mission of the individuals involved.

Scholars have not been able to reach a consensus as to what type of headship Paul has in mind in this text. Elsewhere the apostle does bring together male headship, however he may have understood it, and female submission (Eph 5:23-24). But he plainly indicates that this refers to marriage, and that the overarching principle for relationships among God's people is mutual submission (Eph 5:21). In his discussion of head coverings, Paul does not use the word *submission*. And as we saw, although the term *authority* does occur, it likely refers to the authority of the woman herself, and not the authority of man over woman. Finally, Paul's obvious egalitarianism of male and female "in the Lord" (that is, in the context of Christ's church) must form the foundation for our understanding of his view of the relationship between the sexes, as he himself declares in the context of marriage earlier in the epistle (1 Cor 7:4) and in his discussion of Christian conduct in Ephesians.

Paul's Transcultural Principles. In the midst of the controversy surrounding the interpretation of this text in 1 Corinthians 11, what principles can we draw from the apostle's discussion? Paul obviously assumes that women, together with men, will be actively and vocally involved in public worship, specifically that they have the prerogative to pray and prophesy. The apostle's intent is not to hinder this practice, but merely to regulate the way in which men and women exercise the prerogative in the Corinthian church. There is good reason to conclude that Paul's pervasive concern for evangelism is also operative here. Believers must always act with a sense of propriety which prevents their conduct from becoming a source of offense to those outside the faith.

Most commentators agree that the first-century expression of propriety—whether it be covering the head or how hair is worn—is not binding on us today.[81] But does this mean that the text entails no principles for contemporary Christians?

Complementarians conclude that the apostle also instructs women to be characterized by a specific attitude in public gatherings. They argue that the text reflects a transcultural ordering of male over female which eliminates women from leadership roles in the church.[82] Schreiner speaks for many in asserting,

Women can pray and prophesy in public, but they must do so with a demeanor and attitude that supports male headship because in that culture wearing a head covering communicated a submissive demeanor and feminine adornment. Thus, Paul does not forbid women to participate in public worship, yet he does insist that in their participation they should evidence a demeanor that is humble and submissive to male leadership.[83]

The problems with this conclusion, however, go beyond the questionable exegetical foundation upon which it rests. The principle of male headship as understood by complementarians poses a grave difficulty for working out its practical implications within our culture. Complementarians argue that the head covering was a sign of submission to male headship. But once the head covering is disregarded (as merely a first-century cultural expression), the difficulty of finding a contemporary cultural alternative emerges. With what material sign should women today signify their subordinate position?

Even more problematic is the difficulty of determining exactly how the hierarchical social order fits into our church context. The complementarian position appeals to Paul's statement "The head of the woman is man." But to whom does this statement refer? The most obvious answer is to interpret it as a generic principle referring to all women and men: in the church every man is the head of every woman.[84] Most complementarians, however, would not go so far as to conclude that each woman must always "give evidence to a demeanor that is humble and submissive" to every man in the congregation. Some suggest instead that each woman must submit to those men in the church who are in authority over the flock. But in this case Paul's injunction would carry little significance. All members of the congregation—not only women—are to submit to the authority of their elders. Why single out the women?

Considerations such as these lead some scholars to yet a third possibility. Generally when complementarians invoke male headship, they have the marital relationship in mind. Hence Fung concludes that Paul's statement announces "the general principle of the headship of man in relation to woman, a principle which finds its primary application and obvious illustration in the specific husband-wife relationship."[85] In this case the timeless principle is that a married woman must exercise her public gifts conscious of her marital status. This seems plausible when we remember that according to Jewish custom a woman who appeared in public with her head uncovered could be regarded as holding her marriage oath in contempt and thus giving her husband legitimate grounds for divorce.[86] In following this cultural norm, women not only avoid giving offense to Jews but also safeguard Christian marriage from possible reproach.[87]

Our discussion leads to an important conclusion. Lying behind 1 Corinthians 11:3-16 is a radical assumption: that women prayed and prophesied in the public gatherings of the early community. Paul affirms, then, the prerogatives God had already given women in the Old Testament. These privileges had been suppressed by Judaism, but were restored in Christ through his Spirit. Thus all Christians, without regard to gender, share in the one Spirit (1 Cor 12:13) who sovereignly bestows gifts on all (1 Cor 12:7). Hence in a social context that marginalized women, the gospel restored their freedom to participate in worship as full partners with men, even to the point of being the vehicles through whom the Spirit brings authoritative communications to the entire community.

The text therefore does not lay a foundation for eliminating women from leadership in the church. Paul places no restrictions on the breadth of women's use of their gifts in public worship. He speaks only to the demeanor in which women are to serve, as those mindful of cultural sensibilities concerning male-female relations. The apostle cautions the Corinthians lest the manner in which women ministered might violate cultural norms and therefore bring the gospel into ill repute.

Women in Worship: Silence

Paul's injunction about head coverings sought to regulate the use of spiritual gifts in accordance with cultural norms. His subsequent directive that women be silent (1 Cor 14:33-40) appears to govern their more general conduct during congregational gatherings.

These instructions come near the end of the longer discussion of corporate worship which begins with the injunction about head coverings (1 Cor 11—14). In this final chapter of the section, Paul focuses his attention on the conduct of three specific groups: those who speak in tongues, prophets and women. Fiorenza notes that in order to counteract abuses, the apostle enjoins each group to silence, gives to each a concrete application of the command and provides a rationale for his instruction.[88] Thereby the apostle seeks to transform the noisy confusion of the Corinthian worship into a harmonious masterpiece that will glorify God and edify the church.[89]

Despite the simplicity of Paul's overarching goal, the text itself is an exegetical minefield. In an attempt to determine the implications of the apostle's advice for the contemporary issue of women in ministry, we must step gingerly through the difficulties the text poses.

The interpretive challenge arises at the most foundational point, namely, the integrity of the verses themselves and their place in the flow of the chapter. Several distinctive features contribute to this problem. A number of early (largely Western) manuscripts place 1 Corinthians 14:34-35 after 14:40, and one codex even consigns them to the margin. Another factor is the flow of the chapter. Scholars have pointed out that the short discussion of women (vv. 34-35) appears to interrupt Paul's argument, which flows more smoothly without it.

The connection of the text to its context is complicated by certain internal features. Does the phrase "as in all the churches of the saints" (v. 33) introduce the command that women keep silent (NRSV, NIV)? Or does it conclude the previous topic: "For God is not the author of confusion, but of peace, as in all the churches of the saints" (KJV)?[90] Further, what is the significance of the particle (ē) with which Paul introduces the rhetorical questions aimed at his opponents (v. 36)? This particle remains untranslated in the NIV but is rendered "What!" in the KJV. Also problematic is the masculine gender of the second-person plural pronouns (hymōn, hymas) which Paul uses to address his opponents in these questions (v. 36). Is he speaking only to the men of the congregation, or to all church members? In either case, however, the use of the masculine pronouns indicates that the apostle does not direct the rhetorical questions solely to the women. As Hurley concludes, "It is not, and indeed cannot be, his closing blast against women who speak in the church."[91]

Difficulties such as these have evoked several proposals from egalitarians. Some conclude that Paul is not the author of the command silencing women. Recently, evangelical scholar Gordon Fee joined many critical commentators in arguing persuasively that the injunctions concerning women (vv. 34-35) were not from the apostle's own pen, but are an interpolation into the chapter.[92] If this conjecture is correct, we can dispense with the two verses as carrying no authority for the church. Another possibility is that the statements directing women to keep silent represent the teaching of Paul's opponents, which he quotes from the Corinthian correspondence to him. The rhetorical questions (v. 36) introduced by the exclamation "What!" form Paul's refutation of the ban on women's vocal participation in worship.[93]

Other egalitarians acknowledge the injunctions as Pauline but do not interpret them as silencing women. Perhaps they are not in their rightful place in the text, and being out of context they erroneously appear to be a prohibition against women's participation in worship.[94] Or perhaps the rhetorical questions are not specifically directed against women. Instead they may form part of Paul's conclusion to the entire chapter—a kind of climax to the series of commands to silence he addresses to various groups.[95] Then again, Paul may be addressing a specific problem within the Corinthian church (such as women who habitually disrupt worship meetings with their questions).

Despite the problems we noted above, most evangelical scholars accept the integrity of 1 Corinthians 14:34-35. The words did come from Paul, and they belong where they occur in our Bibles. Therefore, our focus will be on how we are to understand the apostle's words in the context of his discussion of prophecy and Corinthian worship.[96]

Paul's Appeal to the Law. As a foundation for enjoining the women to be silent, the apostle appeals to the law. The significance of this injunction for the contemporary issue of women in ministry will be determined in part by our understanding of the nature of this law *(nomos)*. Concerning this, however, scholars are also divided.

Some maintain that the apostle rests his case on the oral law (the Old Testament as interpreted by the Jewish religious teachers).[97] Specifically, Paul appeals to the oral tradition of his day which stipulated that out of respect for the congregation, women should be silent in synagogue worship.[98] Proponents point to other examples in which Paul uses the term in this manner (Acts 22:3; Rom 2:17-20; Eph 2:15; Phil 3:5-6). They note that in the Pauline literature *law* is a broad term. It encompasses the "whole of Israel's sacred traditions,"[99] which can even include the Jewish religion.[100]

Others assert that Paul appeals to Roman law. Advocates understand the Greek verb *(hypotassesthōsan)* to mean "they must control themselves," rather than the usual translation, "they must be in submission." The basis for his command lay in the "law," understood as the legal efforts of Greco-Roman society to control ecstatic female behavior.[101] Although this suggestion may offer a hint as to the apostle's meaning, critics are not convinced. They note that Paul never uses *law* to refer to Roman sanctions. Nor is there evidence that he employs the verb to enjoin self-control.[102]

A more plausible suggestion than either of these alternatives is that Paul is appealing to the Old Testament law (as in Rom 3:19; 1 Cor 9:8).[103] Indeed, *nomos* can be understood as a rough Greek equivalent for "Torah."[104] But exactly which law did he have in mind? Where does the Old Testament command women to be in submission to men?

The most common interpretation claims that Paul invokes a general Old Testament principle of male headship involved in the order of creation.[105] In support of this claim many proponents cite God's statement to Eve after the Fall (Gen 3:16). We will speak to this argument at length in the next chapter. Here we need only remark that this interpretation can hardly be correct.[106] As many scholars note, God's pronouncement to Eve is neither a command nor a divinely invoked curse on women, but a predictive warning or a description of life after the Fall. Further, God declares that Eve will desire her husband, not be subordinate to him. Other advocates appeal to the creation of Adam before Eve (Gen 2:20-24).[107] However, as we will also explore in greater detail in the next chapter, the Genesis narrator does not conclude from the order of creation that women must be silent or subordinate.

Perhaps Paul's appeal to the law is not intended to subordinate women to men in general, but to require women's subordination to men in worship meetings in particular, as reflected by their silence.[108] Nowhere does the Old Testament command women to be silent in worship. Nevertheless, the ancient authors did enjoin submission and silence in certain contexts. This attitude reflects respect for God (Is 41:1; Hab 2:20; Zech 2:13), for those in authority (Judg 3:19) and for wise persons noted for their knowledge and counsel (Job 29:21). In addition, God himself imposes silence on someone who speaks insolently to a righteous person (Ps 31:17-18).[109] Although Paul may have this Old

Testament principle of submission in view, the question remains as to why the apostle specifically enjoins the subordination of women.

The Corinthian Problem and Paul's Response. The central interpretive difficulty remains the reasons behind the injunctions to women's subordination. Is Paul primarily or exclusively addressing the Corinthian situation, or does he set down a universally binding injunction for the church in all settings? Does the command pertain only to wives or does it encompass all women? Scholars offer several proposals.[110]

Complementarians generally interpret this text as a universally binding prohibition encompassing all women. Fung, for example, argues that its similarity to other transcultural injunctions (compare 1 Cor 14:33 with 7:17 and 16:1) suggests that this command "represents a standard procedure in the Pauline communities,"[111] for it is a specific application of the creation order governing male-female relationships.

Some complementarians draw from the text a prohibition against women's engaging in any form of speaking in the context of church worship.[112] This interpretation has been influential throughout church history.[113] From Tertullian to Thomas Aquinas, commentators concluded that women could not even sing or pray audibly among men. Although the Reformers relaxed some of these restrictions,[114] as late as the 1890s certain Presbyterians still forbade women's singing in worship.[115] And well into the twentieth century many Protestants remained convinced that the injunction prohibited women from voting in church meetings.[116]

Despite its lengthy pedigree in the history of exegesis, the strict interpretation of Paul's injunction entails several problems. It appears to contradict the apostle's earlier assumption that women prayed and prophesied openly in the church (1 Cor 11:3-16). In fact, it carries far-reaching implications for how we understand all of Paul's instructions about orderly worship in chapters 12—14. For if we accept the traditional complementarian view of universally binding silence for women in church, all these instructions must by necessity exclude women.

Contemporary complementarians offer several solutions to the apparent contradiction to the wider context posed by the stricter interpretation of 1 Corinthians 14:34-35.[118] Some make this text the rule that should govern our understanding of 1 Corinthians 11:3-16, concluding thereby that women's praying and prophesying is an exceptional and specifically Corinthian phenomenon which Paul himself does not favor.[119]

Others maintain that the two texts address different situations. Perhaps Paul has different settings in view, allowing women to participate in informal gatherings but demanding that they remain silent in formal church meetings.[120] Or perhaps he is speaking about different women. Women who have received charismatic gifts can prophesy, whereas the ordinary female members of the congregation must remain silent.[121]

The most widely held solution, however, proposes that Paul's intent in both texts is the same (to forbid acts that violate the headship principle), but the two passages speak of different activities. This, of course, raises the question of what exactly Paul deems contrary to the headship principle in the latter text. On this matter proponents are divided.

Perhaps Paul prohibits women from speaking in the case of directly inspired speech (praying, prophesying, speaking in tongues), whether or not such speech comes from women who have special edifying gifts[122] or are in a Spirit-inspired state.[123] A more reasonable suggestion is that Paul wants to prohibit women's involvement in certain aspects of inspired speech, the most obvious being prophecy. But in his earlier discussion Paul already acknowledged the freedom of women to engage in this activity. Consequently, a growing number of complementarians claim that Paul means to bar women from participating in the evaluation of prophetic utterances.[124] However, if we interpret the text as banning all women from involvement, it remains an unsatisfactory response. The New Testament associates the evaluation of prophecy with "discernment of the spirits," but there is no indication that this gift is limited to men. Nor does the New Testament suggest that asking questions (the apparent difficulty Paul addresses in the text) is the means of testing prophecies.[125] Considerations such as these lead one proponent of this view to admit, "Why the principle of headship/subordination is considered to be violated by the one activity [evaluation of prophecy] and not by the other two [prayer and prophecy] is not evident from the Corinthian passages themselves."[126]

Some complementarians surmise that Paul banned women from the careful weighing of prophecies because that activity fell under the ministerial function and therefore constituted the exercise of a church-recognized teaching authority over men.[127] The apostle is in effect also barring women from preaching or teaching in the church.[128] However, there is nothing in the context of the Corinthian epistle to support a ban on the latter activities.[129] On the contrary, Paul's explanatory command "Let them ask their husbands at home" indicates that he is primarily concerned with women interrupting teaching, not women engaged in teaching. In addition, nothing in the epistle suggests that preaching and teaching, which Paul seems to associate with prophecy, are gender-specific gifts.[130] In the end, the entire case for this view seems to rest on interpreting this text in the light of a complementarian understanding of another Pauline passage (1 Tim 2:11-15), which was written to combat a problem that arose in a different time and place.

One final variation of this view deserves mention. Perhaps Paul is addressing only the wives whose husbands were Christians and not women in general (hence Paul's admonition, "let them ask their husbands at home"). Indeed, the word Paul used (*gynē*) can be translated either "woman" or "wife." If this view is correct, then Paul may intend to prohibit a wife from participating with her husband in prophetic ministries that involve her publicly testing his message. Such an act would violate the creation order prescribing the relation of a wife to her husband.[131] Or the apostle may want to prohibit a wife from taking part in public discussions of prophecies made by her own husband.[132]

Despite the attractiveness of this proposal, it has not captured a large following. Paul's explanation "For it is shameful for a woman to speak in church" indicates that he is addressing an issue that includes women in general, not merely wives.

In contrast to complementarians, egalitarians understand the text as an apostolic response to a local problem. But what is the Corinthian abuse which the apostle seeks to correct? Some scholars theorize that certain women were eager to engage in charismatic activities (such as speaking in tongues) in an unacceptable manner.[133] But this proposal does not fit well with Paul's directive that women inquire of their husbands at home (v. 35). Perhaps Paul directs this injunction to certain wives who sought equality with their husbands as teachers in the congregation, speaking in "inspired" languages and claiming to introduce new revelations which they were unwilling to submit to the assembly's assessment and correction.[134]

The most widely held view among egalitarians claims that the problem in Corinth focused on certain women who were asking many questions that disrupted the worship services. As to the details, however, proponents offer various accounts. The women may have been recent converts who were hungry to know more about their new faith,[136] or perhaps they were uneducated women voicing irrelevant questions.[136] The interruptions may have occurred during formal teaching sessions, which were conducted in the form of orderly discussion and argument,[137] or perhaps the women were interrupting either the Scripture exposition in the services or the evaluation of prophetic messages.[139] They may have themselves been prophets, who were entitled to weigh the prophetic utterances verbally.[140]

Regardless of the actual details, the results were the same. The adamant questoning resulted in chaos. In response, Paul rules the women out of order. The church worship service is not the proper setting for their questions, for it results in chaos and offends the cultural sensibilities of the day (being "shameful," v. 35). These women should ask their own husbands at home (v. 35).[141] Perhaps Paul's intent is that husbands, who in first-century society were better educated, assume some responsibility for the catechetical learning of their less educated wives.[142]

The apostle's advice finds a parallel in his response to those who were abusing the Lord's Supper: they should "eat at home" (1 Cor 11:22, 34). His command does not forbid all eating in the church. (They were to eat the Lord's Supper, for example.) Rather, Paul's point is that it is better to eat at home than to disrupt the community by the way one eats at church. In the same way, the problem with women asking questions during worship services does not indicate that their attempts to learn were wrong but that their timing was a problem.

If this was the underlying problem Paul addressed, then the egalitarian interpretation follows. As Witherington declares,

I conclude that a creation order or family order problem was not at issue in this passage but rather a church order problem caused by some women in the congregation. Paul corrects the abuse not by banning women from ever speaking in worship, but by silencing their particular abuse of speech and redirecting their questions to another time and place. Paul does wish the women to learn the answers to their questions. This passage in no way contradicts 1

Cor. 11.5, nor any other passage which suggests that women can teach, preach, pray, or prophesy in or outside the churches.[145]

As a response to a local problem, Paul's injunction may have implications for similar situations today. But we cannot appeal to this text as providing the foundation for prohibiting women in ministry. Howard correctly concludes, "Sadly, what was a particular and local admonition in respect of a particular and local situation has become consistently interpreted by many sections of the Church as a general ban and thus the women members of the congregation have been denied their Christian rights."[146]

Our discussion suggests that neither of the two Pauline texts that speak to the conduct of women in worship forms a basis for prohibiting women from serving in any aspect of church ministry. Mary Evans's conclusion is therefore appropriate:

> Thus, Paul, in the passages where the position of woman in worship is considered, shows clearly that sexual differentiation is part of God's creation, and rejects any false identification of the sexes. A woman will worship as a woman, and a man will worship as a man. Nevertheless, there is very little to suggest that Paul advocated specific differences in the activities of men and women as such when the church met together for worship.[147]

Women in Authority

For the foundational Pauline statement relegating women to subordinate roles in the church, most complementarians do not turn to 1 Corinthians 11:3-16 or 1 Corinthians 14:34-36, but to 1 Timothy 2:11-15. Like the other texts we have reviewed, however, Paul's injunction against women's teaching or exercising authority over men is an exegetical challenge.

Many commentators, whether complementarian or egalitarian, note the occasional nature of the three Pastoral Epistles, including 1 Timothy.[148] Paul does not intend to establish a blueprint for church structure, but to deal with the circumstances that the church (and especially Paul's associate Timothy) faced in Ephesus. His advice concerning women was not triggered by questions arising in our day, but by the conduct in worship assemblies of the first-century church.[149] For this reason, before we can draw conclusions from this passage for the role of women in the church today, we must try to understand Paul's message for his original readers.

The Context of Paul's Discussion. As with the other Pauline statements we have perused, the primary goal is to find uncontested transcultural principles guiding the role of women in church ministry. Before launching into the text itself, however, we must touch on the social and historical setting of the text.

Although commentators offer several historical reconstructions of the situation Paul addresses,[150] they are in general agreement that the apostle's words were evoked by difficulties that centered on the women of the church. Perhaps certain Ephesian women were attempting to gain improper authority over men in the worship assembly.[151] Maybe some of them were teaching heresy, and Paul wants to prevent them from using the worship assembly for that purpose.[152] Or the Ephesian women may have been doctrinally naive, and for this reason they were more susceptible to false teaching.[153]

Whatever the actual situation, it occurred in the context of a city known as a center of pagan religion. Ephesus boasted the largest temple in Asia Minor, which was dedicated to Artemis, the goddess of fertility. The rites surrounding this place of worship endangered the purity of the church. Alvera Mickelsen explains the connection:

> In Ephesus with its huge temple to the goddess Artemis were hundreds of sacred priestesses who probably also served as sacred prostitutes. There were also hundreds of *hetaerae*, the most educated of Greek women who were the regular companions and often the extramarital sexual partners of upper-class Greek men. Possibly some of these women had been converted and were wearing their suggestive and expensive clothing to church. Since *hetaerae* were often respected teachers of men in Greece (many are named in Greek literature), they would be more likely to become teachers after they became part of the church.[154]

The Ephesian church was wracked by the influence of false teachers who espoused a proto-Gnostic form of Jewish Christianity.[155] They probably proclaimed a dualism that led to either libertine or ascetic approaches to physical existence (1 Tim 4:1-8). These teachers propagated myths and genealogies (1 Tim 6:3-5), as well as godless chatter (6:20-21).

These false teachers were especially successful at influencing the women of Ephesus (2 Tim 3:1-9). Younger widows were plagued by sexual problems (1 Tim 5:6, 11-16). The women were weak in faith and susceptible to evil desires (2 Tim 3:6-7), and they were immodest in dress (1 Tim 2:9-10). Women were probably among the perpetrators of the old wives' tales (1 Tim 4:7) and myths (1 Tim 1:3; note the generic indefinite pronoun *tisin*)[156] that competed with Christian truth.

In the face of this challenge, Paul is concerned that his associates guard orthodoxy by promoting the "knowledge of the truth" (1 Tim 2:4; 2 Tim 2:25; 3:7; Tit 1:1). The apostle's main purpose, therefore, is to assist a church suffering from heretical teachings[157] perpetrated by persons who aspired to be teachers but did not have the prerequisite understanding (1 Tim 1:7). To this end, Paul emphasizes the need for good teaching (1 Tim 1:3-11, 18-20; 4:1-7, 16; 6:20-21). Hence orthodox teaching—not the preservation of male headship—appears to be uppermost in Paul's mind as he writes his injunction concerning women.[158]

In the context of dealing with problems of heresy, Paul turns his attention to the worship life of the Ephesian church (1 Tim 2:1-10) and the role of women in the fellowship. The problems in public worship included the men of the congregation whose conduct dishonored the gospel. In response, the apostle commanded them to pray "without anger or argument" (1 Tim 2:8). The dishonorable demeanor of men found a parallel in the immodesty of the women (vv. 9-10).

Scholars are divided as to whether the apostle directs his command toward women's apparel itself—"I also want women to dress modestly, with decency and propriety" (1 Tim 2:9 NIV)—or toward women's demeanor in prayer—"Likewise I want women to pray in modest apparel, to adorn themselves in modesty and chastity."[159] According to the latter view the two commands address parallel problems that arose during public prayer: "Perhaps the men at Ephesus had a tendency to use the opportunity given by public prayer to further their own quarrels and the women had a tendency to show off."[160] In either case, Paul's concern for propriety led him to speak to the issue of women and teaching authority within the church.

Some readers find in 1 Timothy 2:11-12 a series of injunctions (women should learn in silence, be in subjection, not teach and not exercise authority over men). However, Paul issues only one command: "Let a woman learn" (v. 11). The other phrases set the parameters of the directive. In issuing the command, Paul chooses a word *(manthanō)* that encompasses learning through practical experience (1 Tim 5:4) or, as in this case,[161] through more formal instruction (2 Tim 3:7, 10-17). The term likewise includes learning through inquiry[162] and even refers to study like that of a rabbinic school (as in Jn 7:15).[163] As we noted earlier, the idea that women should be educated at all was a radical notion in the first century.

Paul's injunction incorporates the radical ideal that women learn. Yet its central purpose is not to enjoin the church to teach women (this is assumed) but to describe the demeanor in which such learning was to occur. Consequently, the apostle adds to the command two descriptive phrases.

The women are to "learn in silence." Despite the negative connotations this phrase brings to our ears, in the first century "silence" *(hēsychia)* was a positive attribute. It did not necessarily entail "not speaking," as is evident in Paul's use of the word earlier in the chapter (1 Tim 2:2; compare 2 Thess 3:12). Rather, it implied respect or lack of disagreement (as in Acts 11:18; 21:14). As a result, the rabbis and the early church fathers deemed quietness appropriate for rabbinical students, wise persons and even leaders.[164] Spencer summarizes the significance of the term for this verse: "Consequently, when Paul commands that women learn in silence he is commanding them to be students who respect and affirm their teacher's convictions."[165]

The women are likewise to learn "with full submission" (1 Tim 2:11). Complementarians see in this phrase another Pauline injunction of female submission to male authority.[166] Egalitarians, however, note that the apostle did not instruct the women to be in submission to either their husbands or male church leadership. Rather than pointing to marriage or to a patriarchal church social order, the phrase is synonymous with Paul's other descriptive word, "in silence." With both of these statements, Paul is enjoining an attitude of receptivity.

Some commentators suggest that Paul intends that this demeanor be directed toward Christ himself.[167] It is more likely, however, that the apostle has a more specific object in mind. These women had been learning in submission to false teachers (2 Tim 3:6). In response, he commands them to submit instead to orthodox teaching[168] or (by extension) to the authority of the true teachers.[169] The orthodox teachers Paul has in mind are probably men, but could include certain older women in the church as well (Tit 2:3-5).

After setting down a positive command concerning the proper demeanor of female learners, Paul outlines the situation he opposes. Thereby he provides the parameters for the involvement of the women in church life. Specifically, the apostle denies the women in his readership the prerogative of teaching and exercising authority over men.

Paul's statement immediately raises a crucial exegetical question. Some scholars, complementarians and egalitarians alike,[170] argue that Paul intends to prohibit two distinct activities. Others understand the second part of the prohibition as qualifying or explaining the specific aspect of the teaching activity that Paul forbids.[171]

Those who see two prohibitions in 1 Timothy 2:12 connect the object "a man" solely with the second verb, "to have authority over."[172] They note that this Greek verb requires its direct object in the genitive case, whereas "to teach" requires the accusative. Because "man" is in the genitive case, it is the object only of "to have authority over" and not "to teach."[173] They likewise claim that "a man" is too far removed from "to teach" to be understood as qualifying the meaning of that verb.[174]

Critics counter that the New Testament contains exceptions to the grammatical rule proponents cite (see Acts 8:21, where the same construction is present).[175] In addition, they point out that in 1 Timothy, "teach" (*didaskō*) is always accompanied by another verb (1 Tim 1:3-4; 4:11; 6:2b). This suggests that the second verb ("to have authority over") qualifies the teaching Paul has in mind.[176]

The Prohibition of Teaching. Regardless of whether we find one or two directives in Paul's injunction, we are faced with the question of the meaning of the prohibition. Most interpreters agree that the teaching activity discussed here (*didaskō*) refers to the doctrinal instruction of groups of Christians,[177] including "the careful transmission of the tradition concerning Jesus Christ and the authoritative proclamation of God's will to believers in light of that tradition," to use Douglas Moo's definition.

Complementarians find in this verse a permanent apostolic prohibition barring all women from the official teaching office of the church, that is, the office of elder-teacher. They claim that Paul's directive is in keeping with the biblical creation order of male headship and female submission. Critics however, are not convinced. They chastise complementarians for basing their argument on inference, noting that in the text Paul discusses an activity not an office.[179]

Egalitarians see indications in the text that the apostle does not intend to set down a permanent prohibition. Important in this context is the grammatical shift that occurs between the command, "Let a woman learn" and Paul's declarative statement "I permit no woman to teach." On the basis of his choice of the present active indicative (epitrepō) rather than the imperative, egalitarians conclude that Paul is not voicing a timeless command, but a temporary directive applicable to a specific situation: "I am not presently allowing." They find support for this conclusion in the general use of the Greek word. There are not examples in the Septuagint or the New Testament where this verb in the present active indicative first-person singular implies a perpetual injunction; rather, it involves a timely and specific prohibition[180] (e.g., Gen 39:6; Esther 9:14; Job 32:14).[181] Complementarians, however, respond by citing other present active indicative verbs which have the force of ongoing, customary rule (1 Cor 14:34; 1 Tim 2:1, 8).[182]

Some egalitarians find additional support for the temporary character of the prohibition in Paul's use of the word but (de) to join the two verses: "Let the women learn . . . but I am not [currently] permitting them to teach." They argue that the problem was not women teaching in general (Tit 2:3-4), or even women teaching men (2 Tim 1:5; 3:14-15), but that certain women were putting themselves in the position of teachers before they had been properly taught (1 Tim 1:7). Paul temporarily bars women from teaching in keeping with the close connection he makes between possessing wisdom or knowledge and being actively involved in the teaching and admonishing role in the church.[183] That the ban will one day be lifted, however, is indicated by Paul's instruction to Timothy to entrust sound doctrine to persons who in turn could teach others. Like other texts in which the apostle admonishes Christians to teach each other (1 Cor 14:26; Col 3:16; cf. Heb 5:12), he gives no hint that the teaching is to carry gender restrictions (note the use of the gender-inclusive Greek term anthrōpos rather than the specifically male word anēr).

Although egalitarians agree that the ban was temporary, they differ with each other as to the actual persons against whom Paul aims his injunction. Several scholars suggest that the apostle set down a general ban against women teachers.

Paul's temporary injunction may have been motivated by the associations that first-century Ephesians would have made between the presence of any women teachers in the church and false teaching. Bruce Barron explains:

> It is not simply that some women are teaching error. Rather, the placing of any women, whether qualified or not, in authority may be undesirably reinforcing pagan cultural baggage. The proto-gnostics may have been associating female leadership in their own congregation with the perpetual female dominance that their distortion of the Eve and Adam story embodied for them. To quash this error and its obvious threat to Timothy's authority as appointed overseer of the Ephesus congregation, Paul excludes all women from leadership. The limitations thus placed temporarily on genuinely gifted women are less harmful to the congregation than the confusion fostered by the existence of women leaders in this gnostic context would be.[184]

Perhaps the general ban was based on cultural sensitivities. Indeed, the Mediterranean cultural ideal was that of the domesticated woman; a woman's place was in the home, not in the public sphere. The cultural ideal resulted in widespread criticism of various religious sects which elevated the status of women, claiming that these cults produced immorality and sedition.[185] In view of these cultural sensitivities, the New Testament writers restrict the involvement of women in the public sphere of the church. Just as Paul willingly gave up his freedom for the sake of the gospel (1 Cor 9:7-23), so also he calls on women to give up their freedom in the interests of the Christian witness in the non-Christian world.[186] Especially offensive in first-century society were women teachers.[187] Therefore, Paul's advice is that in the hostile cultural climate women refrain from aspiring to the teaching office in the church.[188]

Another alternative sees the ban as arising out of the low level of education among first-century women, rather than cultural sensitivities. Paul's declaration is a general statement applying to the Ephesian women until their educational level is sufficiently raised that they can discern truth and error.

Other egalitarians understand Paul's declaration as a temporary ban that involves only the women in Ephesus, rather than women universally.[189] The most likely historical reconstruction concludes that Paul is intent on silencing the Ephesian women because they were involved in heresy.[190] As Spencer explains, "Women were learning unorthodox doctrines and probably also propagating unorthodox teachings. No wonder Paul commands they learn while not allowing them to teach."[191]

The Prohibition Against Exercising Authority. In the same breath as Paul speaks about women and teaching, he deals with women and the exercise of authority over men. Commentators are generally aware that rather than choosing the common verbs for the exercise of authority (*exousiazō*) or of power (*kyrieuō*), the apostle uses a word that is found nowhere else in the New Testament (*authenteō*). They differ, however, as to the significance of this *hapax legomenon*—this single New Testament occurrence of the word.

Egalitarians appeal to the strong connotations that are normally associated with the verb in other early writings.[192] For example, from their studies of the cult of the feminine as primal source, Richard and Catherine Clark Kroeger concluded that Paul's directive should read, "I do not permit woman to represent herself as originator of man."[193]

Typically, egalitarians appeal to the root meaning of the verb *authenteō* ("to commit a murder"). On this basis they suggest that Paul uses the word in the sense of "to have full power or authority over."[194] They conclude that in this context it denotes a negative situation, the exercise of self-willed, arbitrary behavior.[195] As Witherington asserts, in order to correct the abuses in the Ephesian church, "Paul was saying that women are not to 'rule over,' 'master,' or 'play the despot' over men."[196]

Other scholars contest this egalitarian understanding of *authenteō*. Some appeal to surveys of the extrabiblical uses of the term, which indicate that the verb could also be used in a neutral, nonpejorative sense of "have authority over."[197] Although technically correct, such surveys tend to overlook the chief consideration—that is, the most common meaning of the word in Paul's day. Recent studies indicate that in the first century *authenteō* was more likely to carry negative than neutral or positive connotations. In fact, Andrew C. Perriman declares that the passive idea of "having authority" was actually a later development in the meaning of *authenteō*. At the time of Paul the verb carried two closely related meanings: "instigating or perpetrating a crime" and "the active wielding of influence (with respect to a person) or the initiation of an action."[198] Similarly, Timothy J. Harris concludes from his study of the occurrences of the verb close to the New Testament period that it meant "to hold sway or use power, to be dominant." In itself it never meant "to be an official" or "to be authorized."[199] Leland Wilshire confirms this general position:

> The meaning of *authentein* in 1 Tim. 2:12 may not be "exercising authority" or even "holding sway or using power," or "being dominant." The issue may be (compressing a complex meaning into two words) "instigating violence."[200]

Of course, the context must be the final arbiter in determining the meaning of words. Nevertheless, the fact that Paul uses an unusual term that generally carried negative connotations, rather than the more prevalent neutral verbs, should predispose us to anticipate a negative meaning. With this in view, Perriman finds in the apostle's statement an overlapping of two contexts, the Ephesian situation and the biblical story of Adam and Eve: "Eve did not have authority, but in her action became responsible for—became the cause of—Adam's transgression. In the light of these associations the connotation of 'perpetrating a crime' is fully appropriate."[201]

It may be that Paul's prohibitions against women teaching in 1 Timothy 2:11-12 established important boundaries within which women could maximize their learning. With this in mind, Spencer offers a plausible summary of the intent of these two verses:

> Women are to be calm and to have restraint and respect and affirm their teachers rather than to engage in an autocratic authority which destroys its subjects. Paul here is not prohibiting women from preaching nor praying nor having an edifying authority nor pastoring. He is simply prohibiting them from teaching and using their authority in a destructive way.[202]

Although the apostle intends his directives specifically for the women in Ephesus who were causing problems, the principles of the text hold true for any similar situations in which unlearned women are usurping authority over those who are the true teachers in the community.

After establishing the boundaries surrounding his instructions, the apostle gives an explanation for his commands in verses 13 and 14. Our understanding of Paul's statements will be determined in part by what we think he is explaining. Some scholars suggest that the apostle's directives (v. 12) are actually parenthetical, so that he intends these statements (vv. 13-14) to indicate why women were to learn in submissiveness.[203] The more general understanding, however, connects Paul's explanation with the immediately preceding verse or perhaps with both verses as a unit. In either case, the explanation provides the final basis for determining whether the apostle's ban was temporary or permanent.

The Kroegers find in these verses the biblical support for their theory that Paul has a specific Ephesian problem in view, namely, a Gnostic heresy which glorified Eve.[204] The Gnostic myths elevated Eve as existing prior to Adam, and they spoke of the higher powers (or God) as deceiving Adam into believing that he was created first. These heretical stories also presented the serpent in a positive light as the one who brought true knowledge to Eve, who then enlightened Adam. The Gnostic mythology did not relegate Eve to the distant past, but gave her a continuing importance as the one who could communicate mystic knowledge and enlighten humanity.[205] The believers in Ephesus were apparently turning away from the truth and believing this mythology (2 Tim 4:4). They were being duped by the foolish talk of false teachers (1 Tim 1:6) and old women, who led young widows to turn to Satan (1 Tim 4:7; 5:15). Paul's statements, therefore, are "an emphatic appeal to orthodoxy and the traditional biblical account."[206]

Complementarians, in contrast, find in Paul's explanation the proof that his directives permanently prohibit women from the authoritative office. They argue that the apostle constructs the foundation of his prohibition upon the events of the opening chapters of Genesis and not culture-specific realities such as the lower educational status of women. According to Piper and Grudem, for example, creation and not education was the issue. Hence they assert, "Not even well-educated Priscilla, nor any other well-educated women in Ephesus, were allowed to teach men in the public assembly of the church."[207] Paul's appeal to creation and the Fall means that his argument "does not allow the introduction of 'new cultural factors' which would have caused him to make other applications of his principles."[208]

Egalitarians are quick to raise objections to this argument. Some critics point out that complementarians assume that the word which begins the verse *(gar)* introduces the reason for the prohibition and therefore is to be translated "for" or "because." However, the word may also introduce an example (thus being translated "for example").[209] This reading interprets Paul as intending that the remaining verses of the section be read together as a historical illustration. His goal is to teach women not to emulate Eve, but to follow the behavior with which the text concludes.[210]

According to complementarians, Paul offers two arguments to show why a woman should not teach or have authority over a man. First, Paul grounds the prohibition in the order of creation: God created Adam, then Eve. Douglas Moo draws the obvious conclusion:

> The woman's being created after man, as his helper, shows the position of submission that God intended as inherent in the woman's relation to the man, a submission that is violated if a woman teaches doctrine or exercises authority over a man.[211]

Some egalitarians counter this interpretation by arguing that being created first does not necessarily entail headship or superiority. For a lucid example, they often point to the first creation narrative, in which humans appear after the animals.

Certain complementarians offer an ingenious response to this counterexample. They note that Paul is not appealing to first creation, but to the ancient understanding of the right of the firstborn, that is, to the status of the eldest as carrying particular responsibilities and authority in the family.[212] The formation of Adam prior to Eve meant that he would carry the responsibilities and authority of the firstborn. However, the idea of the responsibility and prerogatives of the firstborn is not present in the second creation narrative. Even Hurley, one of the architects of the complementarian rebuttal, is forced to admit, "The actual text of Genesis makes clear the prior formation of Adam, but does not discuss its implications as such."[213]

To fill this void, some complementarians appeal to the creation of the woman as the helper of the man. This argument likewise runs aground on the shoals of Old Testament exegesis. As we will see in the next chapter, the Hebrew word translated "helper" does not imply the idea of subordination, but designates the female as the one who rescues the man from his loneliness.

In the end, Hurley is forced to find the principle of the firstborn in Adam's role as the one who names his wife. But he fails to note that the actual naming occurred only after the Fall (Gen 3:20). Rather than an act of naming, Adam's joyful cry upon seeing his partner for the first time, "This one shall be called Woman" (Gen 2:23), reveals his understanding that Eve's femaleness (ʾiššâh) complements his maleness (ʾîš).

Even if the idea of firstborn prerogative were in the Genesis narrative, that alone would not substantiate the claim that Paul has this principle in view. In Hebrew tradition the firstborn did carry the most significant status in the family (e.g., Gen 38:27-30). But already in the Old Testament, God shows that he does not necessarily follow this human ordinance, for he chose Jacob, not Esau (Gen 25:21-26).

In Romans Paul cites this passage from Genesis as a precedent for God's gracious reversal in his dealings with humankind (Rom 9:10-13). In fact, rather than appealing to Adam's firstborn status as the basis for a permanent male-dominated hierarchy, Paul declares that in Christ the creation order of woman coming *from* man is balanced by women giving birth *to* men (1 Cor 11:11-12). These precedents in the Pauline literature lead E. Margaret Howe to wonder, "It is hard to imagine, then, why the priority in time reflected in the second creation narrative would carry the significance attributed to it in 1 Timothy 2:13."[214]

In addition to their appeal to the order of creation, complementarians generally find a second argument in Paul's explanation in support of their universal prohibition against women in authoritative teaching positions. Since the apostle bases his case on the Fall, where Eve was deceived and consequently sinned first, complementarians conclude that women should be prohibited from teaching men.

Complementarians do not all agree on the implications of this aspect of the Genesis narrative. Some suggest that the Fall establishes the "general truth" that a woman is more easily deceived than a man. Consequently, women cannot be trusted to teach,[215] nor should they take the lead in settling Christian doctrine or practice.[216] Others join egalitarians in rejecting this conclusion.[217] Indeed, there is no indication that Paul considers the inclination to being deceived a specifically fe-

teristic. On the contrary, on another occasion he uses the illustration of Eve's deception to express his fear that the Corinthians—both male and female—were being led astray in a similar manner (2 Cor 11:3).[218]

Aware of such criticisms, Hurley seeks to harmonize Paul's appeal to the Fall with his citing of the order of creation. Hurley offers this paraphrase of Paul's point:

> The man, upon whom lay responsibility for leadership in the home and in religious matters, was prepared by God to discern the serpent's lies. The woman was not appointed religious leader and was not prepared to discern them. She was taken in. Christian worship involves re-establishing the creational relationship in the time before the return of Christ.[219]

Paul, however, does not argue in this fashion. Does Hurley want us to believe that Paul is teaching that women, by their God-given nature, are unable to discern the lies of Satan? Where do we read that the apostle dismisses women from such responsibility? Must we now read the apostolic admonitions that the Christian community discern truth, test the spirits and so forth as addressed solely to men, or at least as implying that men must take the lead?

Egalitarians fundamentally reject any appeal to Eve's sin as the basis for limiting women's ministry. They note that the Bible never presents Eve, in contrast to Adam, as the source of sin in the world. On the contrary, if either of the two is to be singled out, it is Adam whom the biblical writers present as culpable (e.g., Rom 5:12-21; 1 Cor 15:21-22).

Unconvinced by the various complementarian proposals, some egalitarians have put forth an alternative interpretation of 1 Timothy 1:13-14. Taking a cue from the illustrative force of the introductory word *for (gar)*,[220] they view Paul's appeal to the Genesis narrative as typological;[221] the story of Adam and Eve provided the apostle with a powerful analogy to the situation in the church (cf. 2 Cor 11:3).

Paul's concern about deception and the perpetration of deception by false teachers (1 Tim 1:3-11; 4:1-5; 5:15) motivated his allusion to the Genesis story. The point of his appeal to the narrative is not that Eve sinned but that the transgression came through deception. As Perriman explains, "Rather than claiming that men are less likely to be deceived, Paul chose references from Genesis to illustrate the disastrous consequences of a woman accepting and passing on false teaching."[222] The women of Ephesus reminded Paul of the plight of the woman in Eden. Eve was deceived into believing certain erroneous statements, which she in turn passed on to Adam. In a similar manner the Ephesian women were susceptible to the deceit of the false teachers and to involvement in propagating their heretical beliefs.[223] Consequently, the apostle commanded that these women refrain from teaching and reverently learn from true teachers.

Some egalitarians reject the assumption that Paul presents two arguments, one from creation and the other from the Fall. Rather, the point of his explanation is that the one who was created second fell first. Perhaps Paul is suggesting that Eve's later creation provides a clue to why she was deceived. She was not present in the Garden when God gave Adam the command; thereby Eve serves as an analogy to the Ephesian women who are inadequately educated.[224] Or Paul's point may be that the one who was created to be a blessing to Adam led him into sin.[225]

Regardless of which interpretation ultimately gains a scholarly consensus, the complementarian case for the universal exclusion of women from the teaching office based on Paul's alleged appeal to the primacy of Adam in creation and the primacy of Eve in the Fall is fragile indeed.

Paul concludes his discussion of 1 Timothy 1 by holding out hope for the Ephesian women. Verse 15 has proved to be an interpretive riddle for commentators, who have proposed a host of solutions.[226]

In general, complementarians see this verse as Paul's way of enjoining women to accept their God-assigned place, whether that be the specific role of Christian motherhood[227] or the more general role of subordination to their husbands.[228] Many conclude that the apostle has spiritual salvation in view here. Ann Bowman's interpretation is typical: women

> will experience salvation in the eschatological sense, which includes the judgment of works and receiving of rewards. Women are to fulfil their proper role in life, a concept summarized by "childbearing." This figure of speech refers to the general scope of activities in which Christian women are to be involved.[229]

Critics point out that this interpretation paints a vastly different portrait of the apostle Paul than the one we find in the Corinthian epistles. In Paul's earlier Corinthian letter, the apostle articulates his preference for the single state not only for himself but for men and women in the congregation.

Aware of this difficulty, some complementarians favor a slightly altered version of the more typical proposal. They suggest that Paul addresses those wives who were aspiring to leave their role as mothers in order to take on the full-time position of teaching elder in the church. To combat this, Paul argues that

a wife's role as a mother is paramount and should not be abandoned for the sake of the office of *episkopos*. Let such a woman understand that her path to salvation means accepting the role of Christian motherhood.[230]

A second important complementarian perspective interprets Paul's assertion as suggesting that women are saved by the birth of the Christ child.[231] Proponents point to certain grammatical features of the verse. The passive construction (*dia* with the genitive), which indicates intermediate or indirect agency, suggests that "the childbearing" is the medium through which the original agent (God) acts. Furthermore, the verb is singular (*sōthēsetai*), not plural, likely referring back to Eve as the type or analogy for the women in Ephesus.

Proponents suggest that the "childbearing" is a veiled reference to Mary's giving birth to Jesus. Just as Eve—the one who sinned for she had been deceived—is the negative example whom the Ephesian women were following, so Mary—whose quiet obedience was instrumental in the birth of the Savior—is the positive example whom they should be emulating. When Paul adds the condition ("provided they continue in faith and love and holiness, with modesty"), he switches to the plural, clearly referring to the Ephesian women. Although the Ephesian women may be the contemporary embodiment of Eve in her sin, God will save them (together with their mother Eve) as they (in keeping with the good example of Mary) travel the true path rather than follow the heretical teachers.

Other scholars reject both of these interpretations in favor of a host of alternatives. Perhaps Paul promises that women will be brought safely through childbirth if they are faithful believers.[232] Or he may mean that women (or the women in Ephesus causing the problems) are to work out their salvation (e.g., Phil 2:12-13) by being married, having children and helping them to continue in faith, love and holiness.[233] A related interpretation places the apostolic statement in the context of the Gnostic disparaging of marriage and the childbearing function. Paul affirms the validity of women within their role as childbearers. He has in view the woman who remains in faith, love and hope, equating her "earthly function of bearing children with her eschatological or salvific reward."[234] Thus the apostle affirms that "woman can be saved while she still possesses that distinctive which most decisively sets her apart from man."[235]

Regardless of the correct interpretation of this difficult verse, we ought not to lose sight of its central purpose in the passage. Paul adds it in order to qualify the meaning he draws from the story of Eve. Whatever result followed for women because of her sin, it is no longer in effect for Christ's female disciples.[236] We must note as well that our interpretation of Paul's expression of hope does not directly affect our understanding of the role of women in the church.

To conclude: Paul proposes a twofold solution to the problem of women involved in false teaching. In the short term, he prohibits them from teaching and usurping authority over the men, who were their teachers. But the long-range answer requires that they be properly taught: "Let a woman learn in silence and full submission." Unlearned women continue to be vulnerable to false teaching, but as they gain biblical knowledge and understanding they can become mature believers equipped to teach (Tit 2:3-5). Spencer sums up the implications of this text for the contemporary issue of women in ministry:

> The passage of 1 Timothy 2:11-15 does not suggest opposition by Paul to the ordination of women. . . . Paul never meant for women to remain at the beginning stage of growth exemplified by women at Ephesus. It was his design to have them mature as heirs according to God's promise (Gal 3:26-29).[237]

How Do We Respond?

As our survey has indicated, recent studies have produced no consensus among evangelical scholars on the issue of women in ministry. How should we respond to the present impasse? And what ministry roles should women fulfill while we wait for a consensus?

Even though scholars have not come to a consensus on the issue, the discussion of the biblical texts to date has led to one significant conclusion. In view of the practice of the early church, the burden of proof now rests on those who would bar women from full participation with men in all dimensions of the gospel ministry. This conclusion has been affirmed even by some thinkers who prefer to limit women's involvement. J. I. Packer, for example, commenting at the conclusion of the Evangelical Colloquium on Women and the Bible (1984), offers this appraisal:

> While it would be inept euphoria to claim that all the exegetical questions tackled have now been finally resolved, I think the New Testament papers in particular make it evident that the burden of proof regarding the exclusion of women from the office of teaching and ruling within the congregation now lies on those who maintain the exclusion rather than on those who challenge it.[238]

In a subsequent article in *Christianity Today*, Packer suggests that since we are presently unsure of how Paul would apply these texts in our culture, we should give the apostle "the benefit of that doubt and retain his restriction on women exercising authority on Christ's behalf over men in the church."[239] Egalitarians, in contrast, believe that following Packer's principle would lead us to act in the opposite manner.[240] As we noted in the previous chapter, the apostle's own actions indicate that he valued and promoted the involvement—even the leadership—of his female associates, whom God had called to the gospel ministry. Therefore, giving Paul the "benefit of the doubt" means that we follow his lead and welcome the ministry and leadership of gifted women, until (and unless) the exegetical debate leads us clearly to conclude that God does not call women into positions of authority.

James Sigountos and Myron Shank offer this telling appraisal: "On exegetical grounds there is no a priori reason not to ordain women. The question to be answered, then, is whether societal perception of women's activities would prevent them from being effective ministers or would bring the gospel into disrepute."[241]

Sigountos and Shank move us from exegesis to practical considerations. That jump, however, is too great. We must first come to grips with the theological issues that are at stake in the question of women in ministry. Our discussion of the Pauline texts indicates that at the heart of the complementarian position is a foundational theological conviction. Ultimately, the complementarians' biblical arguments rest on the assumption that God has placed within creation the principle of male headship. To the discussion of this theological postulate, therefore, we must now turn.

FIVE

WOMEN
IN CREATION

◆

THE ISSUE OF WOMEN IN MINISTRY remains explosive and divisive. As a result, some Christians ask, Why push the matter? For the sake of peace, why not abandon the quest for women in ministry? We are convinced that the question of women in ministry cannot be abandoned because it is central to the gospel. Positions taken on this issue reveal one's deeper theological understanding or fundamental vision about the nature of God, the intent of God's program in the world and who we are as the people of God.

Because of the underlying theological commitments at stake, we cannot expect to settle the question of women in ministry by appeal to specific biblical texts. Rather, we must move beyond isolated passages of Scripture to speak about broader theological themes. It is ultimately in the context of foundational doctrinal commitments that the biblical texts find their cohesion.

In 1975, Paul King Jewett concluded that opponents of the ordination of women marshaled three basic theological arguments:

Those who would deny women full access to the sacred office of the ministry have argued that there are some deep and significant reasons "in the very nature of things" why men, and only men, should be ministers in the church of Christ. These reasons, whether elaborated in a Roman Catholic or in a Protestant frame of reference, finally reduce to three: the nature of woman, the nature of the ministerial office, and the nature of God himself.[1]

Jewett's remark is as perceptive today as it was then. Theological discussions of woman's role in the church tend to focus on only a few central considerations. At issue in the discussion are matters pertaining to the creation of man and woman, the nature of the church and the function of the ordained ministry.

In the following chapters we turn our attention to the theological issues that surround these topics. Fundamental evangelical theological convictions stand at the heart of the question of women in ministry. Specifically, a biblical understanding of creation, the community of Christ and the ordained offices all lead to the conclusion that women ought to be full participants with men in all dimensions of church life and ministry.

The central theological argument set forth by those opposed to the ordination of women concerns the authority inherent in the ministerial office: the ordained minister carries a spiritual authority and a leadership role which can only be exercised by a man. The foundations of this argument go deeper than a theology of ministry to certain bedrock convictions about creation itself. Ultimately, advocates assert, no woman can properly exercise leadership and authority in the church because women were created to be subordinate to men.

In this chapter we explore this foundational thesis. What is God's design for woman? If we take for granted that women and men should work together, then what roles can we properly assume to express our fundamental mutuality? This question is crucial. If the Bible teaches that God intends women to be subordinate to men in all dimensions of life, then we cannot anticipate that the Holy Spirit will call women to positions of leadership in the church.

The Bible may, however, lead us instead to more egalitarian conclusions. Perhaps God did not intend for men to lead and rule while women follow in subordinate roles. Maybe God wants women and men to serve together, apart from any preordained hierarchical arrangement based on sexual distinctions. If so, we should expect that the Spirit will choose both men and women to lead the church. Indeed, if God places women on equal footing with men, we should not be surprised when women sense a call to any area of ministry in Christ's community.

To understand God's intent for woman, we must carefully consider two major areas of Christian theology: the nature of God and humankind as created by God.

Woman and the Nature of God

Our foundational theological convictions as Christians focus on God. Therefore, it should not be surprising that we look first to our understanding of the nature of God to guide our thinking about the Christian life and practice, including the role of women in ministry. Specifically we ask: How is God connected to the human distinctions, male and female? Does Christ's subordination to God provide any insight into the male-female relationship? And what significance might the uniquely Christian understanding of God as triune have for the place of women in the church?

Gender and God. Some theologians advocate limiting the pastoral office to men because the Bible teaches that God is more like the male than the female. Proponents of this view believe that certain Scripture references clearly show that the female cannot bear the divine image to the same degree as the male (e.g., 1 Cor 11:7). Or they appeal to the preponderance of male imagery for God in the Bible. In the Old Testament, for example, God is the Lord of the universe, the King over all the earth, the Father of humankind and the Husband of Israel.[2] In addition to the use of specifically masculine images for God, the Bible ascribes activities to God in a seemingly masculine manner, for he enters into this world from a position of transcendence. Thus in creation God speaks the universe into existence; in redemption God sends his Son into the world; and in salvation God places the Holy Spirit in the hearts of his people.[3] The case for divine masculinity is strengthened by the consistent use of male pronouns by the biblical writers to refer to God.

Because an ordained minister stands in the place of God—or represents God to the congregation—opponents of the ordination of women conclude that a woman cannot properly fulfill the pastoral office. C. S. Lewis speaks for many when he says, "To us a priest is primarily a representative, a double representative, who represents us to God and God to us. . . . We have no objection to a woman doing the first: the whole difficulty is about the second."[4]

Proponents of this argument often claim that their views are confirmed in the incarnation. Many who oppose the ordination of women find theological significance in the incontestable fact that Jesus was male, not female. The Word of God became incarnate as a man—not a woman—indicating that God is more male than female. In keeping with the incarnation of the Son as male, the earthly Jesus appointed only men to act as his special emissaries. To this day our Lord remains consistent, the argument concludes, by commissioning only males to represent him in the church.

In some ecclesiastical traditions this representative function lies at the heart of the ordained office. Pastors (or priests) are Christ's representatives, standing for Christ at the altar during the celebration of the liturgy. For Christians in these traditions, any suggestion that the gender of the priest is irrelevant is tantamount to a docetic denial of the humanity of Christ in the historical givenness of revelation.[5]

At first glance the argument from the maleness of God (or of Christ) to the necessity of male leaders appears to have merit. Jesus, the revelation of God, was a man. And the biblical writers generally do use male imagery when speaking about God. Yet the move from male imagery to a male God is ill-founded. It goes beyond the intent of the authors of Scripture. Old Testament scholar Phyllis Trible, for example, notes that in spite of the strong preponderance of the masculine gender in metaphors and other imagery describing God, "there is a strong consensus that the Old Testament regards Yahweh as non-sexual."[6] In fact, one significant point of difference between Old Testament faith and the religions of other ancient Near Eastern peoples was the Hebrew desacralizing of sexuality. In the biblical writings Yahweh is not a male god who has a goddess at his side, as in other ancient religions; Yahweh alone is God.[7]

In the minds of the ancient Hebrew prophets, God could not have a specific gender, such as being a male deity. The reason for this can be traced back to the Old Testament doctrine of creation. Rather than needing to infuse the earth with fertility each spring (by some means of divine sexual activity), God gave fertility to the earth when he made it. As Pamela J. Scalise explains, "Sexuality is a means by which fertility has been granted by God from the beginning (Gen. 1:28). In Israelite faith, therefore, fertility did not depend on the sexuality of the gods, so Israel did not represent sexual activity among the gods in her worship."[8]

Gretchen Gaebelein Hull draws out the implications of this finding for the question of ordination:

> So teaching that an ordained clergy must be male, because only males can harmoniously and effectively represent God the Father and God the Son, proves too much. In spite of any protestations to the contrary, people who affirm this position do indeed end up with a male God—a larger than life masculine deity. They have fallen into the trap of confining God to their image.[9]

If God is not male, why do the biblical writers portray God in male images? Some feminists look to the social conditions of the ancient world for the explanation as to why the masculine images took precedence over the feminine. Stephen C. Barton, for example, states, "The predominance of masculine images of God in both Scripture and tradition has to do with the patriarchal structure of the societies in and for which those images were developed, not with the gender of God."[10] While Barton's explanation may have some merit, it is ultimately unsatisfactory, for it appeals solely to the social setting of the Bible. A more helpful approach also seeks to understand what God may be trying to communicate to us through the use of male imagery.

Building from the findings of biblical scholars, most Christian theologians conclude that there are no sexual distinctions in God. Rather, the only differentiations present within the divine reality are the personal distinctions that lie at the heart of God as triune. This central truth about the nature of God—namely, that he is personal—demands the use of personal pronouns. Substitution of the neuter term *it* when speaking of God would reduce God to an impersonal reality. The crucial personal dimension requires that humans refer to God by using personal pronouns, which can only be masculine or feminine. In neither case is the gender-specific aspect of the pronoun the chief focus of its use. Instead, the personal connotation is crucial.

Paul Jewett correctly states, "We construe the masculine language about God analogically, not literally, when we interpret Scripture. The univocal element in the analogy is the *personal*, not the *sexual*, meaning of the language."[11] He then draws the obvious conclusion: "Because the language about God is analogical, the personal pronouns used of God— he, his, him, himself—in Scripture, theology, and devotion are to be understood *generically*, not specifically."[12]

Yet the male orientation of the biblical designations for God runs deeper than the use of personal (male) pronouns. Repeatedly the biblical authors use male images and concepts to describe God. The most vital of these is the New Testament designation of God as Father. This leads us to ask, Does not God's fatherhood mean that he is male? And what about the maleness of the Second Person of the Trinity—God the Son?

Most theologians agree that we ought to avoid understanding *Father* as designating God as a male deity. Rather, the word is merely the best image available for conveying a dimension of the divine reality that God wants us to understand. Barton correctly pinpoints one central aspect of this revelation: "The Christian doctrine of God as 'Father' is an analogical way of describing the providence of God and our sense of God's care for the whole of creation. It has nothing to do with God's gender, for God is beyond gender."[13] Above all, calling God "Father" reminds us of the close relationship Jesus enjoyed with God and of his invitation to share in that special filial bond.

In a similar manner *Son* is also a metaphor. The early church fathers apparently clearly perceived the metaphorical nature of these designations. Madeleine Boucher explains:

The early Christian theologians understood perfectly well that names such as "Father" and "Son" were metaphors, and inadequate for describing God. For the theologians of the late first and second centuries, the metaphor "Father" simply referred to God considered as creator and author of all things. . . . For the early theologians, the metaphor "Son" was intended to assert only two points: that the Second Person is "like" the First, and that the Second Person is "from" the First rather than "from" nothing (that is, uncreated). The metaphors were not pressed beyond this. They were not taken to express sexual character whether in the divine Nature or in any of the Persons.[14]

Adherents of high church traditions, however, may not find this argument conclusive. They do not necessarily view the clergy as representing God the Father. Rather, priests or pastors provide an image of Christ, and specifically, Christ in his humanity. The Roman Catholic scholar Sara Butler summarizes the implication: "It is not helpful therefore, to argue that the Second Person of the Trinity is beyond sexuality and may, therefore, be represented by either males or females. It is in his humanity that Christ stands among us as our mediator, and his humanity is male."[15]

This argument raises the question of who can properly represent Christ, especially at the Eucharist. We must postpone our discussion of this topic until chapter six. In the present context, we note that God's transcendence of male and female sexual distinctions does not mean that the use of sexual metaphors to speak about God is of no significance. The richness and prevalence of the biblical imagery demand that we take these metaphors seriously.

As recent studies show, the widespread use of male images indicates that God relates to the world primarily in a manner analogous to the human male. God is ultimately transcendent, creating the world as a reality outside himself. In emphasizing male images, the ancient Hebrews set their understanding of God apart from that of the surrounding nations. Rather than a Mother Goddess who brings forth creation as a child is brought forth from the womb, the Old Testament writers teach that God created by fiat a universe that is external to God.[16] Classical theologians have spoken of this as *creatio ex nihilo*.

At the same time the primacy of divine transcendence does not mean that God stands aloof and distant from the creation. Not only is God the transcendent one who like a monarch exercises sovereign power, but God is also immanent in the universe as one who nurtures and cares for it. To communicate this dimension of God's relationship to creation, the biblical authors portray God through feminine images. The nurturing motif is present in various ways. For example, according to the first creation account, at the foundation of the world the Spirit of God hovered over the primeval waters (Gen 1:2).

God's nurturing is likewise expressed through feminine relational metaphors that focus on the mother-offspring relationship. God is pictured as one who like a mother protects, cares for and nurtures her offspring.[17] The Old Testament writers view the mother bird as a particularly helpful image of the divine care God's people enjoy. God cares for Israel "as an eagle stirs up its nest, and hovers over its young; as it spreads its wings, takes them up, and bears them aloft on its pinions" (Deut 32:11). In keeping with this imagery, the Hebrew poets repeatedly speak of the refuge available "in the shadow of your wings" (Ps 17:8; 36:7; 57:1; 61:4; 63:7; 91:4). This Old Testament image adds poignancy to Jesus' lament over Jerusalem: "How often have I desired to gather your children together as a hen gathers her brood under her wings, but you were not willing" (Mt 23:37).

At times the metaphor of maternal nurture conveys the divine compassion for people who have forsaken their God. Isaiah, for example, who presents God as lamenting, "I reared children and brought them up, but they have rebelled against me" (Is 1:2), declares, "For the LORD has comforted his people, and will have [motherly] compassion on his suffering ones" (Is 49:13). The maternal allusion is evident in God's subsequent exclamation through the prophet: "Can a woman forget her nursing child or show no compassion for the child of her womb? Even these may forget, yet I will not forget you!" (v. 15).

The parental heart of God, especially in its maternal aspect, forms an important imagery in Hosea as well:

When Israel was a child, I loved him, and out of Egypt I called my son. . . . It was I who taught Ephraim to walk, I took them up in my arms; . . . I led them with cords of human kindness, with bands of love. I was to them like those who lift infants to their cheeks. I bent down to them and fed them. (Hos 11:1-4)

Maternal and conjugal imagery unite in the opening chapters of Hosea as well. The child of the prophet's unfaithful wife is Lo-ruhamah, which Samuel Terrien claims means "the one for whom there is no motherly love."[18] In contrast to this unloved state, God's renewal, according to Hosea's vision, will extend motherly compassion to Lo-ruhamah (2:23).

Terrien notes that the Hebrew term translated "pity," "compassion" or "love" was etymologically linked to *womb* and that the word for "grace" originally meant "maternal yearning." While we must not put too much stock in conclusions built on etymology, Terrien is surely correct in seeing at least a parental, if not a specifically maternal, aspect of the Hebrew understanding of God at work in the Old Testament reflections on experiences of the gracious compassion of God. Even Paul, who as a male could never have experienced the maternal dimension of parenting, speaks of his relationship to converts in imagery reminiscent of the Old Testament metaphor of the divine maternal care of God's people: "But we were gentle among you, like a mother caring for her little children" (1 Thess 2:7 NIV). These images illumine God's tender care for us (see also Is 49:13-15; 66:13).[19]

The presence of both maternal and paternal metaphors in the Bible has sparked the use of such imagery in evangelical devotional literature. Hannah Whitall Smith, for example, writes,

> God is not only father. He is mother as well, and we have all of us known mothers whose love and tenderness has been without bound or limit. And it is very certain that the God who created them both, and who is Himself father and mother in one, could never have created earthly fathers and mothers who were more tender and more loving than He is Himself.[20]

The use of imagery for God which arises out of human sexuality leads to an important conclusion. God is not merely beyond male and female. Rather, God's relationship to creation takes on both male and female dimensions. Thereby, God forms the foundation for the distinctively male and female dimensions of human existence. As a consequence, a true perception of the divine nature requires the contribution of both men and women.

The importance of both male and female for an adequate picture of God has important ramifications for the church. It indicates the importance of the full partnership of both men and women in ministry, in order that we may understand and portray what God is like. Aída Besançon Spencer capsulizes the situation:

> If we want people to mature in God's image, it is *imperative* that we have women and men to model all aspects of God's nature. Women and men are needed to participate at every level of theological practice and discussion so that God's full counsel can become apparent.[21]

The full participation of women and men is crucial, in order that we might continually remind one another of, as well as show to the world, an accurate and complete picture of the God we serve.

Christ's Subordination and Women's Subordination. Women and men must serve together in the church so that God's people may more adequately perceive the breadth of the divine nature. Although God is neither male nor female, God's relationship to us includes both maternal and paternal characteristics. God therefore provides the basis for human sexual distinctions.

By drawing this conclusion, however, we are not indicating in what manner women and men should serve together in the church. Opponents of women in leadership assert that only men may lead. They argue that God intends women always to serve as subordinates to men. For their position these scholars appeal to the subordinate relationship of the Son (and the Holy Spirit) to the Father, which, they claim, indicates the "ultimacy of patriarchy in the domains of both created and uncreated being."[22] In this manner they offer an important rebuttal to a claim central to the egalitarian proposal.

Biblical feminists often equate subordination with inferiority. They claim that the subordination of women implies that women are inferior to men, which contradicts clear biblical evidence to the equality of all persons. In response, complementarians generally assert that women are subordinate in function only and that such subordination does not necessitate inferiority. To support their conclusion, they appeal to the subordination of Jesus Christ to God, or that of the eternal Son to the Father. The Son's subservience to the Father provides the ultimate example that a person may be subordinate in function while remaining ontologically equal to another.

In this manner complementarians rebut the suggestion that the subordinationism they advocate is based on a christological heresy. Appealing to Paul's declaration that "God is the head of Christ" (1 Cor 11:3; compare 15:28), Thomas R. Schreiner explains that the traditional position

> would only be heresy if one asserted that there was an ontological difference (a difference in nature or being) between Father and Son. The point is not that the Son is essentially inferior to the Father. Rather, the Son willingly submits Himself to the Father's authority. The difference between the members of the Trinity is a functional one, not an essential one.[23]

The implication for the relationship between woman and man is obvious:

> In the order of creation Adam is first and Eve is created out of his side. Furthermore she is created for him and not vice versa. Paul argues that the head of every man is Christ and the head of the woman is man (1 Cor. 11:3). Headship is clear and involves both authority and obedience. It is precisely here that the protest of the feminist movement is most vehement and it is exactly here that we must digest the fact that there is in the relationship of the Father and the Son both authority and obedience. These features do not mar the relationship which is sublime and beautiful. Why should the fact of submission and obedience by the Son to the Father provoke criticism?[24]

This argument, as cogent as it may seem, draws more from Christ's example than it should. In essence, the argument erroneously claims that a voluntary, temporal and personal subordination provides the basis for the necessary and permanent submission of one group to another. Several considerations highlight this.

First, we note that Christ's relationship to the Father was the temporary submission of one divine person to another in the economy of salvation. We can readily understand how such a functional submission of one person to another reveals no ontological subordination. But the situation changes when complementarians claim that each member of a group of persons necessarily must submit to the leadership of each member of another group solely on the basis of gender.

Longenecker pinpoints the problem involved: the traditional position "that advocates women's spiritual equality but societal subordination—venerable though it may be—leaves unresolved the question of how one can speak of a *necessary* subordination of status without also implying a *necessary* inferiority of person." He then explains the difficulty: "The emphasis here is on 'necessary.' Certainly society requires order, with some people functioning as overseers and others as subordinates. But that one gender necessarily must have the one place and the other gender the other place is another matter."[25]

Second, the complementarian argument improperly equates differences in gender, which are biologically determined, with functional differences arising from spiritual gifts and the Spirit's call. We readily acknowledge that Christ's redemptive subordination applies to functional differences among Christians which the Spirit inaugurates. The Holy Spirit bestows various gifts on individuals within the community of Christ in accordance with his own sovereign will and purpose. He calls certain people to serve in leadership roles while others serve in subordinate roles. The New Testament writers admonish the people of God to submit to the leadership of those who have been placed in office among them. Yet leaders are not ontologically superior to those endowed with other gifts, for all are equal in the sight of God.

Hence Christ's example applies to the functional differences that the Spirit introduces when he calls individual believers to certain areas of service and bestows on them the necessary spiritual gifts for carrying out that service. Believers with gifts other than leadership can willingly acknowledge the role of their leaders while knowing that these functional differences do not indicate differences in worth or status before God. Complementarians, however, extend the application of Christ's example to a quite different realm—that of gender. Rather than individuals submitting to other individuals on the basis of differing spiritual gifts, the complementarian position requires that all women submit to all men solely on the basis of gender.

Third, the complementarian argument misunderstands the intent of Christ's example. Nowhere does the New Testament assert that the Son's obedience to the Father is a model of how one gender (women) should relate to the other (men). Instead, Jesus' use of *Abba* demonstrates the intimacy and mutuality of the Son's relationship to the Father.[26] Jesus' obedience to the One he called "Abba" serves as the model for how all human beings—male or female—should live in obedience to God.[27] In addition, Jesus' example illustrates the proper attitude that all Christians, regardless of gender, should have toward one another. Rather than fighting to establish lines of authority and submission, we are to live in mutual submission to one another (Eph 5:21). This requires that we take on an attitude of humble self-sacrifice and service (see, for example, Phil 2:1-10).

Finally, the argument from Christ's example often overlooks the deeper dynamic of mutual dependence within the Trinity. Jesus willingly submitted himself to the One he called "Abba." Thereby he reveals that the Son is subordinate to the Father within the eternal Trinity. At the same time the Father is dependent on the Son for his deity. In sending his Son into the world, the Father entrusted his own reign—indeed his own deity—to the Son (for example, Lk 10:22).[28] Likewise, the Father is dependent on the Son for his title as the Father. As Irenaeus pointed out in the second century, without the Son the Father is not the Father of the Son. Hence the subordination of the Son to the Father must be balanced by the subordination of the Father to the Son.

Complementarians readily cite the Son's obedience to the Father as a theological foundation for the subordination of women to men. In so doing they appeal to a linear or asymmetrical model of the triune God, which pictures authority as flowing from the Father to the Son (and finally to the Spirit). This linear theological model, in turn, suggests a linear model of human relationships. Just as authority flows from the Father to the Son, so also the male has authority over the female.

The classical asymmetrical understanding of the trinitarian relations is increasingly coming under attack today, even by otherwise classically oriented theologians.[29] Indeed, because the Father is also dependent on the Son, a more nuanced, somewhat symmetrical model offers a better picture of God.

Consequently, we cannot set up the example of Christ's subordination to the Father alone—and hence a linear model of God—as definitive for the male-female relationship. Rather, the subordination of the Son to the Father must always be balanced with the dependency of the Father on the Son. The application of such a balanced model of the Trinity leads to an emphasis on mutual dependence and the interdependency of male and female, just as Paul concludes in 1 Corinthians 11:11-12.

The subordination of Christ is, therefore, an important model for human relationships. But subordination by itself does not adequately describe the fullness of the relationship between the Father and the Son. The mutual dependence of the two trinitarian persons suggests that woman and man are likewise mutually dependent. Rather than barring women from leadership roles in the church, therefore, this example encourages mutuality at all levels in the life of Christ's community.

The Significance of God as Triune. The appeal to the example of Christ leads us to consider further the nature of God as the foundation for human relationships. Rather than providing us with a model for a male-dominated hierarchy, the mutual dependence of the Father and the Son suggests the mutual subordination of men and women to each other. When we look more closely, we discover that the central Christian conception of God—the doctrine of the Trinity—leads us to affirm the importance of the inclusion of women in all aspects of the church's ministry.

Much of Christian theology throughout history has been dominated by an emphasis on the oneness of the transcendent God. According to this view, God is the powerful, solitary sovereign over the world. God is Father, Lord or King. Because God was characterized by these supposedly "male" traits, he was best represented by males. Hence as God's representatives, priests (or pastors) should be male. The clergy symbolized God in his abstract essence and rulership.

The twentieth century, however, witnessed a renewed awareness that God is triune and consequently fundamentally relational. God is the social Trinity, for the one God is Father, Son and Holy Spirit. Consequently, we must begin our discussion of the representational function of church leaders with the Trinity. God is relational, the community of the three trinitarian persons. If church leaders represent God in any manner, they must represent this triune, relational God.

The doctrine of the Trinity reminds us that the eternal God is not a solitary, undifferentiated reality. On the contrary, God is Father, Son and Spirit—a unity-in-diversity. It is not surprising, therefore, that when God fashions the pinnacle of creation, a unity-in-diversity—humankind as male and female—emerges.

Mutuality is an essential aspect of the eternal Godhead, as we see in the relationship between the Father and the Son. The primary movement within the Godhead is the Father's eternal generation of the Son. As the church father Origen declared, from all eternity the Father begets the Son in one eternal act. But this dynamic not only generates the Son, it also constitutes the Father. Hence the First and Second Persons of the Trinity enjoy a mutuality of roles in salvation history and in their eternal relationship.

Our life together as God's people, including how we organize ourselves for the work of the kingdom, will in many ways reflect our understanding of the nature of God. Our central theological affirmation is that the one God is Father, Son and Holy Spirit. This declaration should shine forth in our relationships to each other so that, like the triune God, we as the community of faith exhibit unity-in-diversity and mutuality. Just as Jesus' life reveals a mutuality of relationship between the Father and the Son, so also our corporate life as God's people should express the mutuality we are redeemed to enjoy.[30]

For this reason, ecclesiastical structures that function according to a male-dominated hierarchy or chain-of-command model simply cannot offer an adequate picture of the triune God. Rather, the conception of God as triune is best symbolized in an organization that fosters the cooperation of women and men in all dimensions of church life.

Woman as the Creation of God

A discussion of women's roles in the church must consider not only the nature of God but also the nature of woman and man. At its heart, the case against the full participation of women rests on the supposition that God ordained a fundamental order in the church which places woman in subordination to man. The basis for this subordination in function, proponents argue, lies not only in the nature of God but also in creation.[31] God created the male with the role of leadership and the female to be subordinate.[32]

Many egalitarians acknowledge that in the present age the male-female relationship regularly assumes a hierarchical form. In the family, society and the church, the male often rules over the submissive female. But egalitarians assert that such restrictions do not reflect God's original intent in creation. Rather they are the result of the Fall. Alvera Mickelsen succinctly states the central question: "Are restricted roles for men and women in church, family and society God-ordained, or are they the result of sin and/or cultural influences?"[33]

Posing the question in this manner places us in the midst of a debate that has simmered in the church since the Reformation. The two great Reformers, Martin Luther and John Calvin, came to somewhat different positions as to the source of woman's subordinate position. Calvin suggested that even though "gentle subjection" became "servitude" through the Fall, woman's subjection to man nevertheless is part of God's ordering of creation.[34] Luther, in contrast, indicated that woman's subordinate role came as the result of the Fall and sin.[35] We must explore this question more closely.

The Essence of Maleness and Femaleness. Foundational to the anthropological discussion is the question of whether we may properly speak of an essential distinction between male and female. If gender differences lie deeper than roles in reproduction, then perhaps we should anticipate that God intends men and women to fulfill different roles in church life. Indeed, complementarians often argue from the premise of an essential difference between male and female to conclude that men and women must assume different responsibilities in the family and church.

But wherein lies the difference between male and female? Complementarians claim that above all the God-given gender distinctions operate in the realm of leadership. The nature of manhood and womanhood dictates that males lead and females follow or submit to this leadership. John Piper's definitions capsulize the complementarian position: "At the heart of mature masculinity is a sense of benevolent responsibility to lead, provide for and protect women in ways appropriate to a man's differing relationships."[36] In the same way, "at the heart of mature femininity is a freeing disposition to affirm, receive and nurture strength and leadership from worthy men in ways appropriate to a woman's differing relationships."[37]

This understanding of the essence of manhood and womanhood translates into defined roles in human relationships. Man is to lead, woman to support; man is to initiate, woman to enable; man is to take responsibility for the well-being of woman, woman to take responsibility for helping man.[38]

Although complementarians see marriage as the primary context in which these differing realities operate, they claim that the dynamic of leadership and submission has its counterpart in the church.[39] Men are to lead the people of God, and women are to support male leaders. If this is so, it follows naturally that the church cannot place women in leadership positions. James I. Packer explains:

> Presbyters are set apart for a role of authoritative pastoral leadership. But this role is for manly men rather than womanly women, according to the creation pattern that redemption restores. Paternal pastoral oversight, which is of the essence of the presbyterial role, is not a task for which women are naturally fitted by their Maker.[40]

In the past egalitarians tended to counter the complementarian position by denying any distinction between male and female. This position, often termed "androgyny," declares that there is only one fundamental human essence. Essential humanity lies beyond, and also encompasses, the sexual distinctions of male and female. Proponents of androgyny assert that apart from the obvious differences in reproduction, no fundamental distinctions exist between males and females. Hence sexuality is external to our essential being, for maleness and femaleness have no bearing on our fundamental humanness. All persons, regardless of sex, share the one human asexual essence. In the words of the Roman Catholic scholar George Tavard, "Men and women are complementary in sexual activity, yet identically human in everything else."[41]

The implication of androgyny is far-reaching. It means that assigning gender roles to men and women (except for their differing functions in conception and birth) is purely arbitrary. In contrast to the traditional model of male-female relationships that envisioned definite and fixed roles, proponents of the androgynous understanding call for the eradication of all gender-based distinctions.[42]

Although the androgyny model provides a much-needed corrective to the traditional view with its focus on inherent gender roles, it is a flawed theory. Insofar as this viewpoint posits some ultimate humanness beyond existence as male and female, at its basis lies a denial of all sexually based distinctions.[43] However, there are important distinctions between the sexes.[44] Humans can exist only as male and female. And this primary sexual distinction is deeper than mere physical features related to reproduction.

The assertion that certain basic distinctions between the sexes do exist has gained support through recent anthropological research. One widely held conclusion sees men as being more linear and rational,[45] whereas women are oriented to a network of relationships embedded within the social context. Carol Gilligan, for example, maintains that women tend to define their identity through relationships of intimacy and care rather than through assertion and aggression.[46] Janet Spence and Robert Helmreich offer a similar description of this distinction, suggesting that the core properties of femininity can be conceptualized as a "sense of communion" and those of masculinity as a "sense of agency."[47] In a textbook intended for use in university social science courses, Milton Diamond and Arno Karlen succinctly summarize other distinctions noted by contemporary researchers:

It is fact, not social stereotype, that men virtually everywhere are sexually more active and aggressive than women, and that if either sex is to have more than one sexual partner, it is likely to be men. And in all known societies, men have greater authority than women both inside and outside the home. Images of power and success as masculine seem deeply rooted in the minds of both men and women, in our society and probably in virtually all others.[48]

Despite earlier attempts to minimize the importance of our different procreative capacities, it now appears that the distinct functions of male and female in this process affect the distinctive outlook of each of the sexes toward the world. A case in point are the differences noted by anthropologists, for several of these distinctions may readily be linked to our differing roles in childbearing. Only the female has the capacity to nurture developing life within herself, whereas the male must always nurture externally.

The basic difference between the sexes suggested by recent research in the human sciences functions beyond the reproductive dimension of life. Current discussions in neuropsychology, for example, suggest that men and women also think differently, even dream differently.[49] This difference in the way of thinking is due to the differing stages of brain development in boys as compared with girls.[50] Women, it is purported, are more readily able to use simultaneously both "left brain" (verbal, logical and analytical) and "right brain" (emotional, intuitive, creative and holistic) functions.[51] As a result, women are apparently more capable of holistic reasoning, whereas men tend to be more analytical.[52]

It is not surprising, then, that some distinction in roles between men and women arises.[53] Lisa Sowle Cahill offers a helpful summary of the relationship between sex-specific physiological differences and gender roles:

It appears that different physical characteristics, deriving at least in part from their reproductive roles, may create in men and women a tendency toward certain emotional (nurturing, aggressive) or cognitive (verbal, visual) capacities, which may in turn influence the ways they fulfill various social relationships. This is not to say, however, that emotional and cognitive traits vary greatly between the sexes or are manifested in comparable degrees by every member of each sex; or that the fact that males and females may fulfill certain roles somewhat differently implies that each sex can fulfill only a certain set of social roles, much less the devaluing of one sort of role or set of roles, and the subordination of it to that of the opposite sex.[54] In the light of contemporary findings, the simple definitions of masculinity and femininity offered by complementarians like Piper ring hollow. Yet the way forward is not to deny that reality of essential distinctions between male and female. Men and women do view the world differently, and they do bring differing skills to the task of Christian ministry. However, these differences do not bar women from leadership positions in the church, as complementarians claim. On the contrary, differences between the sexes compel us to encourage women and men to serve together at all levels of church life. Only then can the people of God benefit fully from the divinely created distinctions between male and female.

The thesis that sexual distinctions demand the full participation of women and men in all aspects of church life can be valid only if the complementarian claim that at creation God ordained a hierarchy of men over women proves untrue. Therefore we must look more closely at the story narrated in the opening chapters of the Bible.

Male and Female in Genesis 2. Although complementarians do not ignore the opening chapter of the Bible, it is in the second creation account that they find the definitive picture of God's intent for male and female. Genesis 1:26-28 provides only the preamble for the more complete picture disclosed in Genesis 2. Raymond C. Ortlund Jr. expounds a complementarian view of the relationship between the two texts: "God's naming of the race 'man' whispers male headship, which Moses will bring forward boldly in chapter two."[55]

Complementarians find in Genesis 2 clear indication that their position reflects God's design for creation. The timeless truth of the text, they argue, is the "natural subordination of woman to man . . . in the divine order of creation."[56] The Danvers Statement, drafted in December 1987 by the Council on Biblical Manhood and Womanhood, affirms that "distinctions in masculine and feminine roles are ordained by God as part of the created order, and should find an echo in every human heart."[57]

Proponents of the complementarian view find the subordination established in Genesis 2 subsequently confirmed throughout the Bible. Consequently, eliminating women from church leadership roles follows naturally: "The choice of the all-male apostolate is the result or expression of the principle of . . . the subordination of the woman in the church. The principle of woman's subordination in the church is buttressed by biblical history from beginning to end."[58]

Complementarians offer four main arguments to support the claim that Genesis 2 teaches subordination: woman was created after man, woman was created from man, woman was named by man, and woman was created for man.[59] From such arguments they conclude that women should not lead men. Elisabeth Elliot puts the matter in sharp relief: "The church must choose between the ordination and the subordination of women. Which does God command? If subordination is the command of God, ordination is excluded. It is a contradiction."[60]

The Genesis 2 narrative clearly shows God creating man first (Gen 2:18-23). For complementarians, the implication is obvious: hierarchy is inherent in the order of creation—the man first, then the woman. The woman therefore is to be subordinate to the man not only in marriage but also in the church. As Elliot declares, "The exclusion of women from ordination is based on the order established in creation. . . . The man Adam was created first."[61]

Complementarians claim that their interpretation of the creation order gains additional credence from the New Testament. Paul appeals to the creation order to substantiate his teaching about the role of women in the church: "Indeed, man was not made from woman, but woman from man. Neither was man created for the sake of woman, but woman for the sake of man" (1 Cor 11:8-9; see also 1 Tim 2:13). According to complementarians, the apostle believed that the creation narrative taught the subordination of women.

Viewed in its own context, the creation narrative does not explicitly indicate that a hierarchy of male over female was part of God's original intention.[62] In fact, we could also read the story in a manner that sees the woman as the more important of the two characters. The first creation narrative is governed by the principle of the ascending order of creation, the highest creation of God appearing last. Applying this axiom to the second account yields the conclusion that being created second places the woman above, not below, the man.[63]

Such a reading is invalid, of course, for it fails to take into consideration the different intentions of the two creation narratives. In contrast to the first story, which highlights the ascending order of creation leading to humankind and the divine sabbath, the second narrative focuses on God's provision in response to human solitude. The central figure in Genesis 2 is clearly the man. And the alleviation of his solitude is the goal that leads to divine action, as God brings the animals to Adam and then creates the woman.

The assertion that woman, as the final creation of God, is the highest creature may be fallacious, but it nevertheless points to an important truth. The narrative of Genesis 2 presents the woman as the one who saves the man from his loneliness. In so doing she does indeed function in the story as the crown of creation.[64]

In addition to portraying the woman as created after the man, the second creation narrative indicates that the woman derives her existence from the man. Complementarians argue that this clearly shows that God designed woman to be subordinate to man.

Egalitarian exegetes, however, deny that the narrator intends to teach a hierarchical ordering within creation. Rather, the significance of the text probably rests elsewhere. For example, God may have made woman from man in order to indicate that she alone of all the creatures is a fit companion for the man. Further, as the narrator's comment about marriage suggests, the story of the creation of two from one flesh may serve to explain the reciprocal movement of the marriage bond, in which the two become one. Finally, the narrator may intend by this act to emphasize the similarity between the male and the female, which allows the woman to be a "helper of his like."[65]

These alternative suggestions greatly weaken the complementarian claim that the creation narrative teaches subordination. In fact, the narrator's concluding editorial comment may indicate the exact opposite: "For this reason a man will leave his father and mother and be united to his wife" (Gen 2:24 NIV). This comment is the reverse of what we would anticipate in a patriarchal context, where the woman forsakes her parental home in order to join her husband.[66]

Complementarians also attach great importance to the man's naming his wife (Gen 2:23). They argue that in the Old Testament context, naming another indicates authority over another. As Ortlund explains,

"God charged the man with naming the creatures and gave him the freedom to exercise his own judgment in each case. In doing so, Adam brought the earthly creation under his dominion. This royal prerogative extended to Adam's naming of his helper."[67]

Several considerations, however, suggest that explanations such as Ortlund's read more into the text than the narrator intended.[68] First, the idea of authority over another is not always in view in Old Testament texts where a person names another. Second, the usual Hebrew construction for the act of naming is not present in the Genesis 2:23 text. Phyllis Trible points out that in order to denote naming, the Hebrew verb "call" must be followed by an actual name, as in Genesis 3:20 where "Adam named his wife Eve" (NIV).[69] In the Genesis 2:23 text, however, no actual name is present, only the designation *woman* (literally, "female").[70] Consequently, whatever occurred in the Garden, it was not the exercise of authority that may be indicated elsewhere in the Old Testament. Third, the narrator does not state that the man did in fact name his wife when God brought her to him, rather only that he recognized her as his counterpart (the "female" who was taken from the "male"). It is not until after the Fall that Adam calls her Eve (Gen 3:20).[71] In the Genesis 2 narrative he simply addresses her with the accolade *female.*

Mary Stewart Van Leeuwen correctly concludes, "The classic Hebrew naming formula (the one used by Adam when he 'named' the animals) consists of *calling* a person, an animal or a place *by name*. Upon seeing Eve for the first time, Adam does not 'call her by name'—he merely calls or recognizes her as 'woman' [better: female]."[72]

On the basis of these considerations, we conclude with Old Testament scholar Trible, "In calling the woman, the man is not establishing power over her, but rejoicing in their mutuality. . . . The man's poem . . . does not determine who the woman is, but rather delights in what God has already done in creating sexuality."[73]

Perhaps the central plank in the complementarian platform comes from God's expressed intention in creating the woman. She was to be a "suitable helper" for the man (Gen 2:18, 20). The divine declaration leads complementarians to assert that woman was created for the man's sake. Creation "for man," they conclude, means that God intends woman to be subordinate to man.

Complementarians find confirmation for this interpretation of Genesis 2 in Paul's teaching in 1 Corinthians 11:9. In the words of Elliot, "Paul called for the subjection of women. He pointed to the order of creation: quite simply, woman was made for man. Man was not made for woman."[74] In this manner the order of creation demands the leadership of man and the subordination of woman as the helper of man. As Ortlund explains, "A man, just by virtue of his manhood, is called to lead for God. A woman, just by virtue of her womanhood, is called to help for God."[75]

The debate over Genesis 2 verses 18 and 20 hinges on the meaning of the phrase 'ēzer kenegdô (helper fit). Egalitarians not only dispute the complementarian claim that helper means "subordinate," but they also claim that the Hebrew designation clearly indicates the equality of the sexes. Alvera Mickelsen, for example, notes that in the Bible the word 'ēzer (translated "helper") is never used of a subordinate. Of its twenty appearances in the Old Testament (in addition to the Genesis reference), seventeen are references to God as our helper. (The other three refer to a military ally.) Rather than indicating that God is secondary or subordinate to us, speaking of God as our helper acknowledges that he is our strength or power.[76] Similarly, the Hebrew word kenegdô indicates equality. On the basis of an examination of all the Old Testament uses of these words, Semitic language specialist David Freedman concludes, "When God creates Eve from Adam's rib, His intent is that she will be—unlike the animals—'a power (or strength) equal to him.' "[77]

Complementarians remain unconvinced by the egalitarian interpretation. Yet they do not provide a convincing refutation of it. At best, John Piper can offer only an unconvincing, seemingly contrived response. He admits that "the word [helper] itself does not imply anything about rank or authority." Then he claims (without substantiation) that in the text "God teaches us that the woman is a man's 'helper' in the sense of a loyal and suitable assistant in the life of the garden."[78] Not only is Piper's contention self-contradictory, but it assumes the point to be proved. The issue that separates complementarians and egalitarians is whether being a helper naturally entails subordination (or assistantship).

Egalitarians have satisfactorily shown that the Hebrew words do not require us to view the woman as man's assistant. Consequently, we ought not to read subordination into the comment in Genesis 2:18, 20 (nor into the Pauline commentary on this text in 1 Corinthians 11). Instead, the narrator's intent is precisely the opposite. As we noted earlier, the creation of woman "for man" or as his "helper" means that she rescues him from his solitude. Rather than being cast in a subservient role, she is thereby elevated in the narrative as the crowning achievement of God's saving intent for life in the Garden.

Male, Female and the Fall

We have been surveying answers to the question, What is the source of man's rule over women? Complementarians claim that subordination is an order of creation. Egalitarians, in contrast, argue that it is a result of the Fall. Some complementarians, however, also appeal to the Fall, finding confirmation of male headship in the story in Genesis 3.

The complementarian appeal to the story of the Fall focuses on the nature of Eve's sin. The woman's primary error, they assert, was not eating the forbidden fruit. Rather, her failure began as a circumvention of her husband's rightful role. According to the complementarians' reading of the text, the main focus of the tempter's assault was not God's prohibition as such but the divinely ordained male-female relationship. Old Testament scholar Ray Ortlund Jr. explains: "Satan struck at Adam's headship. His words had the effect of inviting Eve to assume primary responsibility at the moment of temptation. . . . Presumably, she really believed she could manage the partnership to both Adam's and her own advantage, if she would only assert herself."[79] Ortlund then adds that Adam acquiesced to her transgression, for he failed to assert his rightful role: "Eve usurped Adam's headship and led the way into sin. And Adam, who (it seems) had stood by passively, allowing the deception to progress without decisive intervention— Adam, for his part, abandoned his post as head."[80]

This reading of the text may seem plausible, but upon further reflection we discover that the proposal has little basis in the text itself. In seeking to set forth a psychological interpretation of the Fall, Ortlund goes beyond the explicit point of the narrative. He imports into the text his own understanding of what motivated our first parents to sin. In so doing he directs our attention away from the tempter's assault on God's prohibition to the fanciful suggestion that the problem originated in a male-female role reversal.

Ortlund does not deny that Adam and Eve transgressed the divine command. But in his treatment this aspect is clearly of less importance than the transgression of the gender roles that complementarians mine from the order of creation. Hence in commenting on the curse found in Genesis 3:17, Ortlund concludes, "Adam sinned at two levels. At one level, he defied the plain and simple command of 2:17. That is obvious. But God goes deeper. At another level, Adam sinned by 'listening to his wife.' He abandoned his headship."[81]

Egalitarians view the Fall in a very different light. They see God's intent in the creation narrative as one of male and female equality and complementarity, which precludes subordination. Genesis 3, in turn, recites the effects of sin on the original equitable relationship between the sexes.

Proponents of the egalitarian reading point to several important aspects of the narrative. Against the long-standing tradition that places the greater burden for the Fall on the woman (and hence forms a basis for the exclusion of women from church leadership), egalitarians note that the narrator does not assign more blame to the woman than to the man. Both discover their nakedness simultaneously; both sew fig leaves for coverings, and both hide from God. God, in turn, holds each accountable and addresses each as responsible.

Central to the egalitarian interpretation is God's statement to the woman, "Your desire shall be for your husband, and he shall rule over you" (Gen 3:16). According to egalitarians, the narrator clearly intends for us to understand this statement as a reference to what resulted from sin, and not as a structure of creation. The narrator here gives us a general picture of the post-Fall state of affairs, not a command as to what either must be or should be. God declares that the advent of sin will bring changes in the relationship of the sexes.

The announced change is especially pronounced within marriage. As a direct consequence of the sin of the first human pair, the husband will now rule over the wife. Rather than being a prescription for the proper ordering of male and female, therefore, the dynamic of rulership and subordination is a description of the present reality of life after the Fall. The woman's desire will be for her husband; the husband will rule over her.

But why did the Fall lead to male rather than female dominance? A clue may lie in God's statement to Adam: "Cursed is the ground because of you; through painful toil you will eat of it all the days of your life. It will produce thorns and thistles for you, and you will eat the plants of the fields. By the sweat of your brow you will eat your food" (Gen 3:17-19 NIV).

The anthropological research of Peggy Reeves Sanday indicates that in addition to biological sexual distinctions, the nature of the environment in which a society develops influences male and female roles. A hostile environment, she argues, readily leads to male domination, whereas relative equality between the sexes is most frequently found when the environment is beneficent.[82] Indeed, in the biblical narrative, human sin results in both a hostile environment (a cursed ground) and male dominance.

Many exegetes—both complementarians and egalitarians—understand the divine pronouncements to the man and the woman as curses. The egalitarian use of this to support their position, however, has left them open to a rejoinder by complementarians such as that voiced by Robert Saucy:

Contrary to this interpretation . . . the Scriptures ground the relationship between man and woman in God's good creation before the Fall. To be sure sin has brought discord into this order as it has in all of God's cosmos. Harshness and self-centered injustice have frequently replaced the divinely intended operational principle of love. But sin is never cited as the cause of the order itself. God's statement to fallen woman in Genesis 3:16 that her husband would rule over her is not the source of the order, nor is it ever cited in later Scripture as such. It rather points to the fact that with the entrance of sin and the obvious disruption of the man-woman order in the Fall, the divine order remains but sin's effect will now be experienced within the order.[83]

Saucy is correct in suggesting that the divine declarations to the man and the woman are not the immediate source of the hierarchy of the sexes, at least not in the sense of being curses that necessitate male dominance. Certain exegetes such as Mary Evans, in fact, suggest that God's statements are not curses in the strict sense:

It is a common assumption that Genesis 3:16 describes the punishment of the woman, the curse of God on her, with Genesis 3:17-19 similarly being the curse of God on the man. In fact, as a closer reading makes apparent, it is only the serpent, in verse 14, and the ground, in verse 17, that are described as cursed; neither the woman nor the man is described as under God's curse.[84]

Evans draws her conclusion from the work of Old Testament scholar Claus Westermann. Westermann sees the punishment of the first couple as consisting of their expulsion from the Garden, ensuring their removal from access to the tree of life and their consequent death, just as God had warned. If the point of the expulsion was to bar them from the tree of life (see Gen 3:24), then the purpose of verses 14-19 is to develop what it means for them to be driven out of the presence of God. These verses, in Westermann's words, "simply describe the actual state of man separated from God."[85]

If Westermann is correct, both an adverse environment and gender hierarchy are consequences of human sin, not necessary conditions of human life. They describe the state of humankind produced by the Fall and our separation from God. As we have seen above, the egalitarian position is not dependent on viewing the divine pronouncements to our first parents as curses in the strict sense. Westermann's conclusions complement our interpretation.

One final objection remains. Does not Paul's commentary on the creation-Fall narrative (1 Tim 2:11-15) discredit the egalitarian view as outlined here? Women are not to teach or have authority over men, the apostle declares, "for Adam was formed first, then Eve; and Adam was not deceived, but the woman was deceived and became a transgressor" (vv. 13-14).

The complementarian reading of this Pauline text assumes that the apostle offers two independent arguments for the prohibition against women teaching in authoritative positions—Eve was created second, and Eve sinned first. We do better, however, by seeing only one argument in the text. The author does not appeal to the creation of the first two humans and the order of their Fall as two isolated events, as would be the case if the verse were setting forth two arguments. Rather, for the apostle it is the relationship between the two events (creation and Fall) that is important. Specifically, he notes the *reversal* in order between creation and Fall. The one who was second in creation became the first in sin. Thus the point of the verse is that rather than fulfilling God's intention to complete the creation of humanity by delivering the male from his solitude, the female actually became the agent of the opposite result. She led him into the bondage that brought a more profound loneliness—alienation from God, each other and creation. Understood in this way, the point of the text is the same as that found in Genesis 3. The hierarchy between the sexes is an outworking of the Fall, in that Eve fell into sin first. The last creation of God is the first to transgress and therefore now will be ruled by the one who followed her into sin. But only with Adam's transgression is the Fall of humankind complete.[86]

To this statement, however, must be added the promise of salvation inherent in Genesis 3 and explicit in the New Testament. The toil of the woman will bring salvation, for through the process of giving birth, the Savior comes. And the role of Adam in the completion of the human fall into sin offers Paul the basis for his appropriation of this act as a typology between the willing transgression of the first Adam and the chosen obedience of the second, Christ (Rom 5:18-21).

Because male domination is not a morally binding injunction—a result of the Fall and not an order of creation—we can anticipate that the new creation will include the reshaping of male-female relationships. With the coming of the Savior, the effects of the Fall can be overcome. Christ's redemption includes liberation from hierarchy as the fundamental principle for male-female relationships.

Male and Female in the Divine Image

Finally, our exploration of woman in creation must consider the biblical understanding of the divine image. Specifically, we must ask, Are men and women equally created in the image of God?

Our first inclination may be to wonder whether this question deserves mention. How could anyone deny that both women and men are created in the divine image? Yet not all participants in the discussion offer an unqualified affirmation of this principle. Complementarians, including members of the Danvers group, conclude that in the final analysis men more completely reflect the divine image than do women.[87]

In constructing an understanding of the image of God, John M. Frame, for example, begins with God's lordship defined as control, authority and presence. It is not surprising, then, that he views the man as the more complete image-bearer and the better expression of the divine sovereignty: "As a vassal lord, Adam is to extend God's *control* over the world. . . . He has the right to name the animals, an exercise of *authority* in ancient thinking. . . . And he is to 'fill' the earth with his *presence.*"[88] What Frame says here in subtle form, Roger Beckwith states bluntly: "The image of God is in man directly, but in woman indirectly."[89] Hence, while not denying that women possess the divine image, some complementarians nevertheless subordinate woman to man in this important aspect of being human.

In response to the qualified understanding of complementarians, egalitarians affirm unequivocally that male and female are equally created in the image of God. They base their position on the first creation account (Gen 1:26-28). They see this text clearly declaring that male and female share equally the image of God, in that God gave to both identical responsibilities.[90] In Reformed theological terms, the Creator charged humankind—male and female—with the "cultural mandate."

In this controversy the egalitarian position may claim the better exegetical foundation. God does command humans, whom he created male and female, to be fruitful and have stewardship over the earth (Gen 1:26-28). But despite its exegetical advantage, the egalitarian position often shares a debilitating liability with the complementarian interpretation. Both readily operate from a misunderstanding of the image of God, namely, that the divine image is an individual possession. Egalitarians and complementarians alike speak of individuals as participants in the divine image. The resultant debate between them merely focuses on the question on the extent to which women possess the image of God.

In contrast to both positions, however, the image of God is primarily a relational concept. Ultimately we reflect God's image in relationship. Thus, the *imago Dei* is not primarily an individual possession but a corporate or social reality, present among humans-in-relationship or in "community."[91]

The creation narratives themselves point to the communal nature of the divine image.[92] Implicit in Genesis 1:26-28 and more explicit in the second creation narrative is the theme that God creates the first human pair in order that humans may enjoy community with each other. More specifically, the creation of the woman is designed to deliver the man from his isolation. This primal community of male and female then becomes expansive. It produces the offspring that arise from the sexual union of husband and wife, and it eventually gives rise to the development of societies. What begins in the primal Garden comes to completion at the consummation of history. God's will for his creation is the establishment of a human society in which his children enjoy perfect fellowship with each other, the created world and the Creator.

We should not be surprised that the image of God ultimately focuses on community. For the doctrine of the Trinity makes clear that throughout all eternity God is community, the fellowship of the three Persons who constitute the triune God. As the first creation narrative declares, when God created humankind, God built into creatures—created male and female—the unity-in-diversity and mutuality that characterize the eternal divine reality. Consequently, neither the male as such nor the isolated human is the image of God. Instead humans-in-relation or humans-in-community ultimately reflect the *imago Dei*. Such human fellowship encompasses diversity and illustrates mutuality.

Because humans reflect the nature of God through fellowship, each person participates in the image of God only within the context of life in community with others. Only in fellowship with others can we show forth what God is like, for God is the community of love—the eternal relationship between the Father, Son and Holy Spirit. In short, God's creation of humankind in the divine image means that human beings—male and female—should reflect the relational dynamic of the God whose representation we are called to be.

The social nature of our creation in the divine image emerges in the realm of gender relations. The *imago Dei* includes man in fellowship with woman. As we noted earlier, men and women are different in ways that are more fundamental than simply their roles in the reproductive process. The differences lie even in the basic ways in which we view ourselves and the world. Men and women think differently; they approach the world differently. These fundamentally different outlooks toward others, life and the world mean that each sex needs the other in order to fulfill the various dimensions of human life.

This understanding of the divine image constitutes a strong foundation for affirming the participation of men and women in all areas of church life. Because we are the image of God only as we share together in community, we must welcome the participation and contributions of all individuals, both male and female. Because men and women have unique contributions to make, the church must value the contributions of both sexes to the fulfillment of its task. No congregation can genuinely expect to complete the mandate given by the Lord if its structures allow only the male voice to be heard in planning and decision-making. The wisdom and insights of male and female are equally important to the ongoing ministry of God's people, for each gender's perspectives and experiences reflect quite different approaches to life.

We have explored God's intent for woman as seen in her creation as a unique being and as a participant in the human task of reflecting the divine image. This divine intent provides a theological foundation for the full inclusion of both male and female in all dimensions of the life of the church. What God has placed in creation is carried to a higher level in redemption. Therefore we now turn to the ecclesiological foundation for women in ministry.

SIX

WOMEN IN THE CHURCH & THE PRIESTHOOD

◆

T HE THEOLOGICAL ARGUMENT PROPOSED by opponents of the ordination of women draws from a specific understanding of the nature of the ministerial office. Complementarians claim that ordained ministers exercise roles that are solely the prerogative of men, cradling this argument in a specific understanding of the church (ecclesiology). Ultimately the people of God cannot set apart women for ministry, because the church is structured hierarchically. Men provide leadership, and women offer support. When correctly ordered, church structure reflects the roles complementarians find in creation.

In this chapter we explore this ecclesiological thesis. Does Christ intend the church to be a hierarchy in which only men fill the various leadership offices? And granted that women and men are to work together, how do we best express this mutuality within Christ's community?

We now wade into the ecclesiological debate, which remains a watershed issue. If the Bible indicates that Christ intends women to be subordinate to men within his fellowship, the Holy Spirit cannot call women to the ordained office. If the biblical model of the church is more egalitarian, however, we would expect the Spirit to lead both men and women into ministries in all aspects of church life.

In exploring the question of God's intent for woman in the church, we will consider three major aspects of Christian ecclesiology. First, we must set our discussion within its proper theological context, studying God's ultimate goal for the church within his overarching plan for creation. Next we focus on the implications of the church as a priesthood of believers: Who are to serve as priests? Finally, we raise the question of the ordained office itself: Does Christ intend that his people set apart certain persons for specific tasks in the church?

New Creation and the Church

In our discussion of God's purpose for woman in creation we concluded that male domination is a result of the Fall and not an order of creation. Women and men together share the *imago Dei*, and this divine image is a social reality. We concluded that considerations such as these suggest that God intends for women and men to serve together in all aspects of church life. What we found implicit in creation we now claim is explicit in the biblical vision of the new creation.

The phrase "new creation" refers to the goal of God's action in the world as described in the Bible. Although inaugurated in a final sense in the earthly ministry of Christ, God's purpose for creation reaches its culmination only at our Lord's return. Because God's *telos* determines the mandate we are called to fulfill, this vision forms the ultimate foundation for an ecclesiological exploration into the question of women in ministry. Therefore, we must look at this biblical vision and its implications for the ordination of women.

New Creation: God's Goal for His World. God's ultimate goal for human history is to establish community in the highest sense. This goal permeates the narrative of redemptive history from beginning to end. This vision begins in the past with the narrative of the primordial Garden, in which God says, "It is not good for the man to be alone" (Gen 2:18 NIV). The grand fulfillment of God's program, however, does not lie in the past, but in the future. The drama of the Bible climaxes with the marvelous hope of the new creation, the vision of white-robed multitudes inhabiting the new earth.

Encompassing this biblical vision of community is God's desire to dwell among a redeemed people. This was Yahweh's intention when he entered into covenant with Israel. He delivered Israel out of slavery in order that they might be his people (Ex 20:2-3) and that Yahweh himself might dwell among them. In the fullness of time Jesus came as Immanuel—God with us (Mt 1:22-23). Jesus, the divine Word, became flesh and "tabernacled" among humankind (Jn 1:14). In turn, Jesus spoke of another Comforter who would be present among his disciples (Jn 14:15-27). His promise was fulfilled at Pentecost with the coming of the Holy Spirit.

The biblical hope of a new creation envisions community in the fullest sense. At present, humanity is divided into groupings based on ethnic, socioeconomic and gender distinctions. But God intends to unite them into one new humanity. God's desire is that this reconciled people experience community with each other and enjoy the presence of their redeemer God on the renewed earth.

In the book of Revelation, John anticipates the new order as a human society, a city (Rev 21:9-21). In this city all the peoples of the new earth live together in peace, and nature fulfills its purpose of providing nourishment for all earthly inhabitants (Rev 22:1-4). But most glorious of all, in that city God himself dwells with its inhabitants (Rev 21:1-5; 22:1-5).

The Church in God's Plan. God's goal of establishing community sets the context for a biblical understanding of the church. God intends to bring glory to himself by establishing a reconciled people who reflect to all creation the character of their Creator and Redeemer. Our full participation in God's new community awaits the eschatological transformation of human life in the kingdom of God. Nevertheless, the New Testament announces that we can partake of that eschatological fellowship now. According to the New Testament writers, the focus of this present experience is the community of Christ, the church.

In the light of God's ultimate goal, Christ established the church. In the midst of a broken world, our Lord calls us to mirror as much as possible that ideal community of love which reflects his own character. Hence the church is to be the community of God—a fellowship of persons who are bound together by the love present among them through the power of God's Spirit and who seek thereby to show forth what God is like.

As an eschatological people, the church is the historical sign of an eternal community—the fellowship of those who seek to reflect in the present the future reality of God's reign. Our participation in the church, therefore, means that even now we can live in accordance with the goal God has for us. We can reflect, at least in part, God's character. As we do, we are the image of God.

We discover the theological link between the image of God and the church as the expression of the eschatological human community in the New Testament metaphor of the church as Christ's body. According to the New Testament, Christ is the fullness of the image of God (2 Cor 4:4; Col 1:15; Heb 1:3). As Christ's body the church shares in his relationship to God, and by extension in our Lord's status as the *imago Dei*. Through our connection with Christ we have the responsibility and privilege of reflecting the nature of the triune God. And as a result of this relationship the Holy Spirit is now transforming the members of the church into the image of God in Christ (1 Cor 15:42-49; 2 Cor 3:18; Col 3:5-11).

The Biblical Vision of Community and the Church. The vision of God's plan as inaugurated in Christ forms the heart of the New Testament conception of human relationships. With the coming of the Savior, a new era has dawned, one in which the effects of the Fall no longer need to dominate human living. The biblical writers declare that in Christ the old ways of structuring interpersonal relationships have been superseded. Our Lord has inaugurated God's intention for humankind and the entire creation.

Christ's community is to be not only the sign but also the foretaste of the future reality that God is bringing to pass. The New Testament declares that our Lord has relativized the old distinctions between humans, which people tend to find so important. The church is to be the community in which such differences do not constitute the foundation of identity and activity. Because we are Christ's community, we can no longer relate to one another on the basis of the old social distinctions.

Nearly all theologians—including contemporary complementarians—agree that this principle applies to structures that appeal to ethnic distinctions or economic standing.[1] Human societies may elevate social status as determinative of personal identity and worth, but this attitude should find no place in the church. In keeping with Jesus' teaching, James warns against giving preferential treatment to the rich (Jas 2:1-13). Likewise, Paul commanded Philemon to treat his slave Onesimus as a brother in the Lord, thereby undermining slavery as a social order (Philem 15-16; see also 1 Tim 6:1-2).

For many, it is less evident that this principle also applies to social structures based on gender distinctions. Complementarians do not agree with egalitarians that hierarchical relationships based on gender distinctions are comparable to those based on social class or race. In defense of this distinction they declare that in contrast to class and race, the principle of male headship and female submission is rooted in creation, was not abolished in redemption and is never indicted in the Bible.[2]

According to egalitarians, the complementarian argument takes too narrow a view of the scriptural teaching on gender. Gender-based discrimination runs counter to the entire thrust of the biblical vision of God's intention for creation. In the old order, people readily discriminate on the basis of sex. Christ's redemptive work, however, frees us from the role of hierarchy as the fundamental principle for male-female relationships. Just as our Lord's teachings undermine racial and socioeconomic discrimination, so also his followers should no longer use gender as a basis for determining responsibilities within the fellowship.

The radically egalitarian situation of the new era can clearly be seen in Peter's declaration that women and men are coheirs of the gracious gift of salvation (1 Pet 3:7). But egalitarians most frequently appeal to what Klyne R. Snodgrass calls "the most socially explosive text in the Bible"—the apostle Paul's declaration that "there is no longer Jew or Greek, there is no longer slave or free, there is no longer male and female; for all of you are one in Christ Jesus" (Gal 3:28).[3]

Paul voices his radical assertion of Christian equality in the context of a discussion about circumcision. In the Old Testament this ritual, which was a specifically male rite, marked the Israelites as the covenant people of God. In the New Testament era, however, circumcision has served its purpose. The older rite has been replaced by baptism, in which all believers—male or female—can participate. Paul indicates that the transition from circumcision to baptism has destroyed the significance of the distinctions between persons which formerly were used to establish social hierarchies. These include appeals not only to ethnic heritage (Jew and Gentile) and social status (free and slave) but also to gender differentiations (male and female). Therefore the hierarchy of male over female introduced by the Fall is now outmoded, even though the physical effects of sin, which are part of living in a fallen world, may remain.[4]

Complementarians remind us that Paul balances his egalitarian impulse with a heavy dose of reality. They rightly point out that the apostle cautions that those who were formerly in subordinate positions should not assert their new equality in Christ in ways that could work against the spread of the gospel (see 1 Cor 7:17-24).

At the same time, as we argued in chapter four, we should not read into Paul's words of caution a commitment to maintaining the status quo. Rather, like Peter (1 Pet 2:18-21), Paul encourages believing slaves to be willing to suffer social injustice in the short term for the sake of the gospel, knowing that their testimony will advance the cause of Christ (see Eph 6:5-8; 1 Tim 6:1; Tit 2:9-10). In the same manner he cautions believing women not to throw out social custom in the name of Christian liberty, lest the gospel be defamed.

The apostle is confident, however, that eventually the leaven of the gospel will destroy residual hierarchical structures, whether based on race, economic status or gender. Christ's church, therefore, is to be a foretaste of the egalitarian structure of God's reign. As an outworking of this new reality, Paul commands believers to live according to mutual submission, which is to be the overarching principle governing social relations within Christ's community: "Be subject to one another out of reverence for Christ" (Eph 5:21).

Unfortunately, the church has not always lived up to Paul's expectations. The people of God often fail to act on the egalitarian impulse derived from the vision of the new creation. Repeatedly Christians have appealed to the Bible to justify hierarchical structures based solely on human distinctions.[5] Nineteenth-century American Christians, for example, marshaled support from the Bible to maintain slavery in society and segregation in the church. Some today remain convinced that the Scriptures demand discrimination on the basis of sex, even when our society has become increasingly aware of the equality of the sexes.

As Stephen Barton notes, "In the sphere of gender relations . . . the great irony is that the Christian ideals of freedom, reconciliation and equality are being discovered and practiced outside the Church more than within it."[6]

The New Testament commands us to live according to the vision of the new creation. This vision looks forward to a day of complete reconciliation among people of all races, every social standing and both genders. The task of the church is to allow this vision to transform the present reality.

Willmore Eva sketches the implication of this mandate for gender relations: "It therefore becomes imperative that we, by acting in tune with Christ's redeeming act, do all that is possible for us to do as a believing community to remove the effects of the curse of Eve from our marriages, our communities, and our church."[7] Living in the light of the future consummation of Christ's redemption includes overturning structures and attitudes in the church which promote dominance and subordination.[8]

This vision of God's future community reveals what our corporate life now as God's people should look like. This means that the presence and participation of men and women is theologically vital for the church. Our task is to point toward the perfect fellowship of God with humankind that will characterize God's eschatological reign. This future reality will constitute a society of human beings enjoying community with each other (including fellowship between male and female). We must strive to reflect this vision in our present corporate life through structures that promote community and mutuality. In short, if we are to be the foretaste of God's eschatological community, we must welcome the contributions of both male and female in the church.

Our appeal to the eschatological vision does not mean that we set the new creation over against the old. On the contrary, what God inaugurated in Christ's coming and will bring to consummation at our Lord's return is of one piece with what he began at creation. The new creation vision consists of the renewal and completion of creation. The call for full participation of men and women in the church is the fulfillment of God's egalitarian intention from the beginning, as indicated in the Genesis creation narratives.

The Church and the Priesthood

The complementarian vision pictures the church as a hierarchy of men in authority over women: God calls men to provide leadership or headship, and he entrusts women with the role of assisting men. Some complementarians augment this picture with the concept of priesthood. They oppose the full participation of women in church leadership because they understand the ordained office as fundamentally priestly in nature. Their argument is simple: clergy constitute a priesthood, and women cannot serve as priests.

The appeal to the priestly character of the ordained office is succinctly articulated in C. S. Lewis's well-known essay "Priestesses in the Church?"[9] It has been reformulated by other writers, especially from more liturgical traditions, including the Roman Catholic[10] and Episcopalian.[11] And it has found supportive voices even in denominations with free church roots.[12]

We must now explore the concept of priesthood within the context of ecclesiology. In what sense should the concept of the Old Testament priesthood remain operative in the New Testament church? What is the nature of the New Testament priesthood? And what are the implications of our findings for women in ministry?

Clergy, Priesthood and the Old Testament. The case against the ordination of women rests in part on the assumption that Christ leads his followers to develop a hierarchical structure that endows a few of their number with certain priestly prerogatives and responsibilities. These prerogatives, complementarians add, can be exercised only by men. Let's take a closer look at this ecclesiological assumption.

Advocates of the idea that the ordained office in the church constitutes a priesthood that excludes women see this office as one example of a general biblical principle. The male priesthood is God's order throughout history, and it finds expression in various fundamental human structures. Hence Bernard Seton declares, "The Bible establishes an all-male priesthood or ministry, both within and outside the family."[13]

Proponents find evidence of this basic divine preference throughout salvation history. The male priesthood begins immediately after the Fall, for God appointed Adam and then his male descendants as priests for their families.[14] Later God established a specialized priesthood within larger societies. This order included the mysterious Melchizedek, "priest of God Most High," to whom Abraham paid tribute (Gen 14:17-24). After establishing Israel as his people, God selected the sons of Levi—specifically, Aaron and his male descendants—for this role.

Rather than overturning the Old Testament order, the complementarian argument contends, the New Testament reaffirms it. The foundation for this continuation lay in Jesus' selection of twelve male apostles. Although our Lord superseded the Levitical priesthood, he maintained the older principle of the male priestly ministry. As Seton notes, "The days of the Levitical priesthood had passed; the apostolic age was about to dawn. But in each age men filled the priestly roles."[15] The church followed the lead of our Lord by replacing Judas with a male successor and later by ordaining such outstanding men as Paul and Timothy.

Egalitarians admit that the Old Testament order allowed only men to serve in the priesthood. However, they are not convinced that this fact bars women from the ordained office in the church. Some proponents of women in ministry point out that the appeal to the male priesthood in Israel is too broad.[16] Maleness was not the sole prerequisite for service in this office. Rather, the instructions found in Leviticus and Numbers include additional and quite stringent requirements. Only middle-aged males from the tribe of Levi and the bloodline of Aaron who were perfect physical specimens and had married a virgin (or perhaps the widow of a priest) qualified as true priests of God, and then only when they were not ceremonially unclean.[17] On what basis, critics ask, can we conclude from the Old Testament priesthood that God establishes gender, but not the host of other restrictions set forth in the books of Moses, as the basis for restricting the ordained office in the church?

Eileen Vennum summarizes the implications of applying the Old Testament restriction of a male priesthood to the ordained office of the church:

To be consistent, handicapped men would also have to be excluded, as well as male dwarfs, young men and older men, men with skin diseases, single men, men married to a widow or men with a wife who had been raped. *All* Gentiles and *most* Jews would be disqualified! Even those who qualified would be considered much of the time to be physically unclean, and therefore unfit for communion with God.[18]

Other egalitarians have sought to determine why God would prohibit women from serving in the Old Testament priesthood. According to Pamela J. Scalise, the prohibition arose out of women's role in reproduction and the laws regarding ritual purity: "The childbearing function was a disability which exempted and disqualified Israelite women from certain cultic responsibilities, especially the priesthood (cf. the laws of impurity in Lev 11-17)." Scalise argues that this is not a theological reason: "The requirement of purity was a practical obstacle to the service of women as priests, but the Old Testament offers no theoretical or theological explanation of the all-male priesthood."[19] If her thesis is correct, Scalise's conclusion is unavoidable: "Since ritual purity is not a requirement for participation in Christian worship, Israel's practice in this matter should not be used to exclude women from Christian ministry."[20]

An alternative explanation argues that the male priesthood in the Old Testament was the product of cultural pressures.[21] Feminist scholars tend to see it as the religious outworking of a patriarchial society. Other interpreters look instead to Israel's struggles against the religious milieu of the ancient Near East. Because priestesses led the Canaanite peoples in the worship of fertility gods, the purity of Israel's worship of Yahweh was best expedited through male leadership.

Whatever the actual basis for the male priesthood in the Old Testament, the rebuttal continues, with the move from Israel to the church the social conditions of God's people changed. As a result, the exclusion of women from religious leadership is no longer culturally necessary.

The Church as a Corporate Priesthood. Although these considerations raise doubts about the appropriateness of the appeal to the male priesthood in Israel, the main difficulty lies deeper. The complementarian case begins with an erroneous understanding of the church and its connection to Israel. The argument assumes that Israel's religious structure exemplifies a divinely instituted pattern of order for God's people of all ages. Consequently, God intends that the church's pastoral office parallel the Old Testament priesthood. But is this connection valid? Are ordained church leaders the successors of the Levitical priests? The biblical principle of the priesthood of all believers suggests that the

New Testament parallel to the Levitical priesthood lies elsewhere: in the church as a whole rather than in the ordained office.

The great Reformation emphasis on the priesthood of all believers arose in the context of Luther's quest for a gracious God, which led to the theological question concerning access to divine grace. According to the theology of the Middle Ages, believers encounter grace through the sacraments of the church. Crucial to this process are the clergy, who as priests act as mediators between God and the people. The priests serve as God's instruments in dispensing divine grace and forgiveness and in bringing the offerings of the people to God.

Against this medieval understanding, Luther asserted that each believer enjoys direct access to God apart from any mere human mediator. Believers receive God's grace directly through faith and may bring their own spiritual offering to God (Rom 12:1; Heb 13:15) as well as intercede directly with God on behalf of others (2 Thess 3:1-5; 1 Tim 2:1-7; Jas 5:16).

The New Testament unveils a new priesthood, the universal priesthood of believers. The book of Hebrews notes that the Old Testament priesthood merely foreshadowed the great high priest, Jesus Christ himself (Heb 4:14—10:18). Because of Christ's work, all believers may now "approach the throne of grace with boldness" and receive mercy (Heb 4:15-16). All may enter the "Most Holy Place" (which in the temple had been the prerogative solely of the high priest) and "draw near to God" (Heb 10:19-22 NIV). Indeed, Christ has made all believers priests of God (Rev 1:6; 5:10; 20:6). Consequently, together we make up "a holy priesthood, offering spiritual sacrifices acceptable to God through Jesus Christ," that is, "the praises of him who called you out of darkness into his wonderful light" (1 Pet 2:5, 9 NIV). With a view toward this new status we all share, Jesus repeatedly warns his disciples against adopting the attitude of the Pharisees, who elevated themselves as teachers and masters over the people (Mt 23:8-12; see also Mk 10:42-45; 1 Tim 2:5).

We noted earlier that God intends the church to be the sign and foretaste of the eschatological community God is establishing. This eschatological community is a priesthood that all believers—and not merely the clergy—share. In short, the church is a fellowship of believer priests.

Believer Priesthood and Women's Ordination. Just as church structures should reflect the egalitarian dynamic that will characterize God's eschatological community, so also they should incorporate the priestly function all believers share. Within the church—the new priesthood—distinctions of race, economic status and gender are no longer valid considerations in ordering human relations. What are the implications of the universal priesthood of believers for the ordination of women? Specifically, does this Reformation principle require that the ordained office be open to both men and women?

While the principle of the priesthood of believers has gained nearly universal acknowledgment, complementarians question whether it is relevant to the debate about the ordination of women. Some believe that the universality of the New Testament priesthood does not necessarily entail that the ordained office is open to all believers regardless of gender.

It seems that even Luther himself did not draw this implication from his priesthood-of-believers theology. According to the Reformer, ordination bestows the authority to exercise a ministry on behalf of the whole body. He believed that women share equally in the royal priesthood that Christ inaugurated among his people, as indicated by the common practice of Lutheran midwives' baptizing newborns. Nevertheless, Luther denied that women could be called to the office of pastoral ministry, arguing that they were destined by God for the care of the home.

Paul Avis explains the dynamic within Luther's reasoning: "The logic of Luther's doctrine of the universal priesthood, as it arises out of the reality of justification in which there can be no distinction of persons, is that the question of the ordination of women should be answered purely in terms of social expediency."[22] Luther's argument, therefore, removes the question of women's role in the church from the realm of theology, making it solely a matter of practical utility. But this means that the Reformer provides as little support for the complementarian position as he does for the egalitarian. If the universal priesthood does not at least open the door to women in ministry, then the Reformation principle must be more radically separated from what appears to be its obvious implication.

At this point Susan T. Foh steps into the gap, providing a more radical appraisal of believer priesthood. She counters the egalitarian appeal to this principle by claiming that the universal priesthood concept is totally unrelated to women in ministry. Foh bases her conclusion on a clear separation of the Levitical priesthood and the ordained office: "There is no continuity between the office of priest, which ceased when Christ sacrificed himself once for all (Heb 7:11—10:25), and the office of elder or pastor-teacher."[23] According to Foh, the universal priesthood means that we must all offer ourselves as spiritual sacrifices to God and that we all have access to God through Christ. "Women are priests in these senses just as men," she affirms, yet "this status does not qualify anyone for any church office."[24]

Foh's statements constitute a marked departure from complementarians who appeal to male Levitical priesthood as a model for the church's ordained office. In fact, her disjoining of the Old Testament priest and the New Testament pastor—which when viewed from the perspective of actual mediatory function is technically correct—serves to knock a prop out from under the case for an all-male clergy.

Further, Foh correctly interprets the New Testament priesthood as universal. She rightly acknowledges that as priests all believers enjoy direct access to our heavenly Father and offer spiritual sacrifices to our God. Yet at one point she is quite mistaken. Rather than not qualifying anyone for any church office, as she concludes, the status of priest is exactly what forms the basic qualification for all church offices.[25] Because Christ has qualified us to stand in God's presence, regardless of race, social status or gender we are all ministers within his fellowship. As priests of God—and only because we are priests—the Spirit calls us to ministries, including positions of leadership, among Christ's people.

Recent attempts by complementarians to set aside the universal priesthood of believers as irrelevant to the question of the ordination of women have not been successful. It remains now to show that when placed within an evangelical understanding of the church this principle promotes the inclusion of both men and women in the ordained ministry.

Although the principle of believer priesthood has gained acceptance in nearly all Christian traditions, historically evangelicals have been at the forefront of emphasizing this concept. Our commitment to the principle is connected with the evangelical emphasis on the church as consisting ultimately in the people themselves and not in the ordained clergy. Hence we view the church less as a dispenser of divine grace than as a community of reconciled sinners.

Evangelicals have understood believer priesthood to mean that the task of the church belongs to the people of God as a whole. Consequently, it is the church, and not merely certain persons in the church, that is charged with the responsibility to represent God and Christ to the community of faith and to the world. The image of God is a social reality that is to be shared by all, for the entire church is the body of Christ.

This commitment has been the impetus behind the evangelical concern to include all believers in the life of the church and to recognize the importance of every believer's contribution to the ministry of the church. In short, the evangelical emphasis on the shared responsibility of all God's people for the work of the kingdom is closely linked to an egalitarian ecclesiology.

This ecclesiology leads to an egalitarian view of the ordained office. Egalitarians do not see the clergy as mediators between God and the people. Pastors are not a special class of Christians who mediate God's grace to the people. Nor do clergy mediate Christ's authority to the church. Rather, they assist the people in determining the will of the risen Lord for his church. Simply stated, ordained ministers are persons chosen by God and recognized by the church as having the responsibility to lead God's people in fulfilling the mandate Christ has given to the entire church.

The centrality of these themes means that the evangelical understanding of the church poses no inherent roadblocks to women's serving as clergy. This is not surprising, for it is in keeping with the manner in which Jesus related to women. As we noted in chapter three, our Lord elevated women, treating them as equally important as men. And he readily included women among his followers and disciples.

Not only does evangelical ecclesiology pose no roadblock to women, but we believe that its egalitarian impulse demands a partnership of male and female within the ordained office. Mary Evans summarizes the connection:

> In a very real sense, responsibility in the churches was corporate. In writing to the churches, Paul wrote to the whole congregation, not just to the leaders. . . . It was the responsibility of the whole con-

gregation to see that the instructions and exhortations given by Paul in this letter were followed. . . . The particular leadership of individuals must not be seen as taking away from this corporate responsibility. As far as this kind of corporate leadership was concerned, it was shared by men and women alike as equally members of the congregation.[26]

A church where all follow Christ's commands is one in which women and men work side by side in the varied ministries of the community. They learn from each other, uphold one another and contribute their personal strengths to the church's mission without being prejudiced by gender distinctions. In such a church how could the partnership suddenly dissolve and men serve alone in teaching and leadership? Why would this kind of church, with its commitment to inclusive corporate ministry, suddenly erect an ordained office characterized by a male-dominated hierarchy?

Believer Priesthood and the Ordained Office. Our quarrel with those who would deny ordination to a person solely on the grounds that the candidate is a woman rests not only on the theological and anthropological arguments outlined in chapter five. We also have grave reservations about the ecclesiological principles at work in the complementarian position. Our understanding of the universal priesthood results in an egalitarian view of the ordained office.

By extending the Old Testament structure of a male-only priesthood to the New Testament church, complementarians fail to understand the radical transformation that our Lord inaugurated. No longer do we look to a special God-ordained priestly class to carry out the religious vocation of his covenant people. Rather, we are all participants in the one mandate to be ministers of God, and to this end we all serve together.

Whatever may be the role of the ordained office, it arises solely out of the ministry of the entire fellowship of believers. Because the foundation of the ordained office rests within the people of God as a whole, the pastorate is an extension of the universal ministry of Christ's body. As such, it is best fulfilled by women and men working together.

Paul Jewett uncovers the implications within this ecclesiology for the ordination of women. Although we might quibble with his use of the term "individual priesthood," we cannot disagree with his conclusion:

If individual priesthood rests upon the general priesthood of the laity, then women, who, like men, are incorporated (symbolically) by baptism into the body of Christ and so made "to be priests unto his God and Father" (Rev 1:6), are equally qualified to become priests in the individualized meaning of the term. Whatever difference one may postulate between the priesthood in its general and in its individual form, this difference implies nothing for men that it does not imply for women.[27]

The sovereign Spirit calls different persons to various functions in the church, including oversight responsibilities. As the principle of the universal priesthood indicates, the Spirit may base the choice on certain considerations. But gender is not an overriding factor that either qualifies or disqualifies a believer-priest for selection to the ordained office. Rather than race, social status or gender, spiritual giftedness is of primary importance in the Spirit's sovereign choice. To this we now turn our attention.

The Church as a Priesthood of Gifted Persons

Marianne Meye Thompson offers this brief appraisal of the current discussion surrounding the ordination of women:

> Both those who favor women in ministry and those who oppose women in ministry can find suitable proof texts and suitable rationalizations to explain those texts. But if our discussion is ever to move beyond proof texting, we must integrate these texts into a theology of ministry. I suggest that the starting point for such a theology of ministry lies in the God who gives gifts for ministry and in the God who is no respecter of persons.[28]

Giftedness for church ministry plays a crucial role in any discussion outlining the ecclesiological implications of the ordination of women. The New Testament presents an egalitarian conception of spiritual gifts (or *charismata*). Paul unequivocally states that a common source lies behind all spiritual gifts (1 Cor 12:4-11). We do not receive spiritual gifts because of our own merit. Instead, gifts are distributed according to the sovereign will of the Holy Spirit (1 Cor 12:7-11) and the risen Christ (Eph 4:7-11). The Holy Spirit gives spiritual gifts to every believer, not merely a select few. And the Lord of the church bestows these gifts for the good of the church as a whole (1 Cor 12:7) and the completion of the common task of God's people (Eph 4:12-13).

In the context of our discussion of women in ministry, the New Testament teaching concerning spiritual gifts and gifted persons raises two crucial questions. What is the relationship between spiritual gifts and the ordained office? And what are the implications of spiritual gifts for women in ministry?

The Relationship of Gifts to the Ordained Office. Peter's apparent differentiation between speaking gifts and serving gifts (1 Pet 4:10-11) suggests two basic categories of *charismata*.[29] The first group of gifts emphasizes ministry in word: evangelistic proclamation, inspired utterance (prophecy, tongues, interpretation) and didactic speech (teaching, wisdom, knowledge, exhortation). The second group focuses on ministry in deed: gifts of supernatural power (miracles, healing) or practical assistance (helps, service, showing mercy, liberality). The *charismata* of oversight or leadership, however, are difficult to subsume under either category.

Our enumeration and classification of spiritual gifts leads us to ask about the relationship they bear to the church's ordained office. Some scholars find an irreconcilable conflict between the early church's focus on spiritual gifts as the foundation for ministry and the structured offices of the post-Pauline church.[30] Others, however, including many evangelicals, tend to see a continuity, or at least a natural development from unstructured to structured. This latter view suggests that the New Testament era was characterized by a fluidity of church ministry and structure.

The New Testament documents confirm the varied and developing structures of the early Christian communities along with a corresponding change in how spiritual gifts are linked to church offices. Hence the church did not exhibit a uniform connection between a certain kind of giftedness and the ordained office. As Ronald Fung notes, "While charismata can and do find expression in office, charisma cannot be subsumed under the rubric of ecclesiastical office."[31] At the same time, despite this fluidity of relationship, a certain stability also arose in the early church. We find what Fung calls an "interweaving of gift, task [function] and office."[32]

Gifts and office are interrelated in certain respects. First, although gifts should be exercised beyond the confines of the ordained office, the endowment of certain gifts is the prerequisite for ordination into pastoral ministry. Pastors engage in various aspects of church ministry, such as preaching, teaching and leading. Consequently, persons entrusted with *charismata* that facilitate these aspects of ministry are more likely to be candidates for ordination.

This observation leads to a second principle. The question of which gifts mark a person for possible ordination is answered in part by distinguishing between gifts used intermittently and in very specific contexts and gifts designed for regular, constant use within the ongoing life and structure of the church community. Persons gifted by the Spirit for ongoing public ministry in the community are more likely to function in the ordained office.

Third, the important connection between gifts and office is perhaps most evident in a third category of charismata—gifts of administration or leadership. Biblical texts pertaining to the ordained office contain a common theme: leaders must oversee the ministry of the corporate fellowship. Pastors facilitate the kingdom work which God's people carry out themselves. Hence, the church sets in office those whom the Spirit has endowed with the appropriate gifts for leading the whole people of God in "the work of ministry" (Eph 4:12).

Fourth, the work of ordained ministers and the ministry of the gifted people of God have the same goal. Both are designed to build up the whole body of Christ to the glory of God (1 Cor 12:4-31; Eph 4:11-16).

Finally, spiritual gifts always remain foundational to the ordained office. Pastors can only be those persons whom the Spirit has endowed with the appropriate *charismata*. For this reason, as Fung notes, "the charismata are the wherewithal, the tools, the means of the ministry. . . . It is by the endowment of charismata that its ministers are made sufficient."[33] Consequently, giftedness for the specific functions of the ordained office is an indispensable prerequisite for setting someone apart for such a ministry.

Women's Gifts for Ministry. The intimate relation between gifts and ministry has a crucial bearing on the issue of women in ministry. The fundamental conclusion resulting from our study is that the church must make room for all believers, whether male or female, to use their God-given gifts to build up the body of Christ. We must allow men and women to serve together with whatever gifts the Spirit bestows on them. But the question then becomes, does the Spirit endow women with the gifts essential for the ordained office?

On this point there seems to be little categorical disagreement. Alvera Mickelsen sums up what most scholars would admit: "In Paul's lengthy discussions about spiritual gifts, he never indicates that some gifts are for men and other gifts for women."[34] This is as we might expect, since the sovereign Holy Spirit endows people with gifts for ministry as he wills. Because the distribution of gifts is the prerogative of the Spirit, it is not our place to decide on whom he can and cannot bestow certain gifts. The Old Testament prophets anticipated a time when the Spirit would work through both women and men (for example, Joel 2:28-29); Luke announces that the promised era dawned at Pentecost (Acts 2:14-18). Consequently, the Spirit may freely endow whomever he chooses—whether male or female—with whatever gifts he wills.

The mandate Christ has given to the new community of faith includes worshiping God, building up the fellowship and reaching out to the wider world. To accomplish this task our Lord has poured out the Spirit, who endows each of us with spiritual gifts. These are distributed throughout the community according to the Spirit's will. The New Testament offers no hint that the Spirit restricts to men the gifts that equip a person to function in the ordained office (such as teaching, preaching, leadership), while distributing without distinction those necessary for other ministries. Margaret Howe raises the obvious question: If gifts equipping for pastoral ministry "are distributed by *God* to women, what higher authority does the Church have for denying the women their expression?"[35]

Complementarians are quick to respond. Important as the *charismata* are, they do not constitute the only factor in determining the role of women in the church. Rather, as Fung declares, "Paul's practice and his teaching with regard to women in ministry also need to be taken into account."[36] And complementarians are convinced that in this matter Paul follows the principle of male leadership and female subordination. Hence Fung concludes from his study of the New Testament, "A woman who has received the gift of teaching (or leadership, or any other charisma) may exercise it to the fullest extent possible—in any role which does not involve her in a position of doctrinal or ecclesiastical authority over men."[37]

As Fung's statements indicate, to skirt the ecclesiological implications of the New Testament teaching on spiritual gifts, complementarians must set forth a sharp distinction between *charismata* and the ordained office. Fung is a typical example. He finds no contradiction between "Paul's teaching concerning the indiscriminate distribution of spiritual gifts to men and women alike" and the restrictions he claims "Paul imposes on women's ministry by reason of woman's subordination to man." "What it does mean," he adds, "is that *gift* and *role* are to be distinguished."[38] In other words, to salvage the complementarian interpretation of Paul's attitude toward women in ministry, Fung, like others, imposes what we find to be an artificial dichotomy between the Spirit's gifting and the exercise of the ordained office.

Our problem with the complementarian argument, however, runs deeper. The limitation on a woman's use of the gift of teaching to those roles that do not place her in authority over men subsumes ecclesiology under anthropology. In this manner the argument simply reverts to the question of the relationship of the sexes, which complementarians find embedded in the creation order. This appeal, however, is biblically and theologically suspect. Even if God had built this principle into creation from the beginning (which he did not), it would not necessarily require that the church continue to practice male leadership and female subordination. Christ did not establish the church merely to be the mirror of original creation but to be the eschatological new community, living in accordance with the principles of God's new creation and thereby reflecting the character of the triune God.

The Ordained Office in the Church

We have argued that the sovereignty of the Spirit in bestowing *charismata* on God's people clearly shows that God welcomes the ministry of both men and women in all aspects of church life, including the ordained office. But such a position might lead us to question the practice of ordination itself. Should we not simply encourage God's people to function according to the gifts the Spirit has given them without regard to title or office?

Many voices today are calling the church to abolish the practice of ordination. As the Lutheran scholar Samuel Nafzger argues, "God did not institute an office but rather only a function. . . . In the beginning God did not say, 'let there be pastors,' but rather 'preach the Gospel.' "[39] Perhaps our Lord intended only to promote functions and not to establish offices among his people. Perhaps the Spirit endows every church member with spiritual gifts, and as a result all are called to service, but none to distinct offices in the church.[40]

In this manner some scholars not only question the ordination of women but reject ordination altogether. We must note, however, that terminating the contemporary practice of ordination would not end the discussion of women in ministry. It would simply recast the debate in the context of function rather than office. We would then need to ask the deeper question, Which tasks and responsibilities in the church are open to women? In which functions may women serve? In fact, function and office are similar if not equivalent.

Even though the question of women in ministry is not tied to the ordained office, we cannot skirt the matter of the propriety of ordination itself, especially given the recent voices who challenge the practice. We agree that in certain aspects our current ordination practices go beyond what may have been envisioned in the biblical era. Nevertheless, the act of commissioning persons to special ministries has been present with Christ's community since the first century, and the practice of ordination can claim a foundation in the Bible itself. Therefore we conclude our treatment of ecclesiology by looking more closely at the biblical basis for the ordained office.

The Pastoral Office Itself. In writing to the Ephesians, Paul suggests the presence of four offices within the early church: apostle, prophet, evangelist and pastor-teacher (Eph 4:11). Scholars have debated whether Christ intended that the first three continue throughout church history.[41] Less controversial is the ongoing validity of the pastoral function, regardless of how different ecclesiastical traditions choose to designate it. The basic ministry of a pastor is directed to a local congregation, but the ordained office also has ramifications for the wider fellowship.

Like Timothy, who sojourned in Ephesus for three years, most pastors serve local churches. In the local setting the pastor functions as part of the framework of congregational leaders (including laypersons who make up a church board) and perhaps a larger pastoral staff. Yet as Paul's injunctions to Timothy indicate, the pastoral ministry can have both greater depth and broader responsibility than that fulfilled by lay leaders.[42]

Included in the contemporary pastoral job description are administrative oversight, congregational leadership and caring for the members. These are augmented by such activities as leading worship, teaching, preaching and evangelism. According to Paul, however, all of these activities have one ultimate objective: "to equip the saints for the work of ministry, for building up the body of Christ" (Eph 4:12).

Above all, we believe that the pastor discharges the ordained office by functioning as visionary to the people of God. Pastors fulfill this role in various ways. They facilitate the well-being of God's people by constantly renewing their vision of the community ideal, the design of God toward which the local fellowship must direct its energies. This visionary role includes keeping alive the past by retelling the foundational community narrative—the story of Jesus. It also includes keeping the future always in view by embodying in word and symbol the glorious divine purpose that God will one day bring about in the renewed creation.

Generally a pastor's primary ministry occurs within the context of a specific congregation for an unspecified period of time. Yet the ordained office carries implications for ministry beyond the local fellowship. The wider ministry may be merely the informal authority of spiritual office within the local civil structure or the regional ecclesiastical network of sister churches. All pastors exercise an informal authority within associations simply because of their role as spiritual leader of a cooperating church.

Pastoral responsibility, however, may take the form of a more formal ministry, such as is fulfilled by association officials, area ministers, chaplains or teachers at theological colleges. These roles are extensions of the pastoral office, for such persons continue to provide pastoral ministry for the sake of the churches of the associations they serve.

Ordination to the Ministerial Office. Nearly all Christian traditions acknowledge the importance of setting apart leaders for service with the community of faith. Most Christian traditions incorporate into church life some specific pattern of designating community leaders. We generally speak of this process as *ordination.* Despite disagreements about the particulars and exact meaning of the rite, most Christian traditions agree that persons who enter pastoral ministry must be set apart for this task by Christ's church.

The practice of publicly setting apart persons for certain ministries has been a central feature of church life throughout the history of Christianity. Yet the New Testament provides no detailed account of how the early church selected its leaders. For this reason some scholars question whether ordination can claim New Testament precedence.[43]

Nevertheless, those who continue the practice are convinced that it has its roots in both ancient Israel and the New Testament. An important aspect of this rite includes the laying on of hands, which is widely practiced today in conjunction with ordination. H. E. Dana concludes from his study of the New Testament texts that mention a ceremonial laying on of hands, "We are convinced that ordination was a public and formal act employed for the setting apart of those whom God had called to tasks of Christian leadership. We may be perfectly sure that ordination as a ceremony of installation originated in apostolic times."[44]

Already in the Old Testament the act of laying on hands signified in certain cases the investment of a person with leadership responsibility and authority. Under the command of God, Moses laid hands on Joshua in the presence of the priest and the community (Num 27:18-23). A parallel act, anointing with oil, symbolized a person's entrance into a leadership role. Three offices were especially associated with the rite of anointing—prophet, priest and king.

Christian ordination was anticipated by Jesus' appointing twelve persons from among his disciples to play a special role in his mission (Mk 3:13-14). Later, the loss of Judas prompted the disciples in the upper room to add Matthias to the ranks of the Twelve (Acts 1:21-23).

In keeping with the precedent established in Jesus' calling of the twelve apostles, the early churches set apart persons to specific offices. The Jerusalem church commissioned the Seven through the act of laying on of hands (Acts 6:6). Later, the Antioch congregation used the same act to set apart Barnabas and Paul for missionary service (Acts 13:1-3).

Perhaps the model biblical example, however, is Timothy. His experience suggests that two elements—a divine personal call and confirmation by a local fellowship—work together in setting someone in pastoral ministry.[45] New Testament references indicate that the ordination of this young associate of Paul was precipitated by Timothy's own reception of a special divine call, mediated through a prophetic pronouncement about his future service (1 Tim 1:18; see also the similar case of Paul and Barnabas recounted in Acts 13:2-3). The subsequent public act confirming the call consisted in the laying on of hands by the leaders of a local congregation (1 Tim 4:14).

Taken together, the texts imply that New Testament ordination was related to the gift of the empowering Holy Spirit (1 Tim 4:14; 2 Tim 1:6-7), and it was marked by a public commissioning (Acts 13:3; see also Num 27:18-23). Hence through a public act of acknowledgment, the early church set apart persons whom they sensed the sovereign Spirit had selected and endowed for the fulfillment of certain special tasks in service to the people of God.

The biblical documents provide historical precedents for ordination. We continue the practice because we are convinced that this act serves an important function within God's program in history. As in the first century, the Holy Spirit still sovereignly calls persons to places of service in behalf of Christ and endows them for ministry within God's plan for human history. Ordination is the act by which the community recognizes and confirms the presence of the Spirit's call and endowment in a particular individual.[46] Hence ordination serves the Spirit's intent to provide gifted persons for the ongoing work of Christ's disciples in service to God's purposes in the world.

The focal point of God's action in the present age lies with the church. We are to be the eschatological covenant community, the sign to the world of the coming consummation of God's program for creation, and the image of the triune God. The entire community of God's people is responsible to obey this mandate. However, as a community we are dependent on certain persons to facilitate, expedite and coordinate our individual contributions for the sake of our common task.

Ordination finds its significance in this context. It is the act by which the community sets apart gifted persons for the effective working of the whole community toward the completion of their common purpose.

From its beginning, the community has set apart by a public act persons whom the Lord of the church through his Spirit has called to pastoral ministry. The foundation of the act within its ecclesiological context means that the function of pastoral leadership is itself tied to the community. As the recent consensus statement *Baptism, Eucharist and*

Ministry declares, "Ordained ministry has no existence apart from the community."[47] Hence the central task of the ordained person is directed to the people who constitute the church.

Again to cite the words of *Baptism, Eucharist and Ministry,* "The chief responsibility of the ordained ministry is to assemble and build up the body of Christ by proclaiming and teaching the Word of God, by celebrating the sacraments, and by guiding the life of the community in its worship, its mission and its caring ministry."[48]

Because it is grounded in the life of the community, ordination to pastoral ministry arises out of the universal priesthood of believers. All members share the ministry Christ entrusted to his people. To this end, all are called by the Holy Spirit to ministry. Baptism is the sign of our universal call, for baptism signifies our new birth by the Spirit, our new identity as disciples of Jesus and our new relationship to one another as participants in the one fellowship of Christ. Ordination to pastoral ministry, therefore, is embedded in the Spirit's universal calling of all to the ministry of the church and his universal endowment of all for this task.

From within this context of universal ministry, the Spirit calls certain persons to pastoral leadership. Thereby he provides overseers for the work of the "royal priesthood" (1 Pet 2:9), which is the whole church community. As Daniel Migliore has noted, "Ordination is properly understood *missiologically rather than ontologically.*"[49] Ordination does not facilitate an ontological change in the clergy, elevating them above other Christians. Instead the act commissions a person into a special ministry for the sake of the mission of the entire people of God. In short, we ordain persons to pastoral office in order that they may serve in this manner on behalf of the entire people.

Personal Call and the Ordination of Women. Our focus on ordination as a corporate confirmation of a personal call admittedly adds a certain credence to complementarians who do not find convincing the testimonies of women who have sensed a call to ministry. Piper and Grudem, for example, bluntly state,

> We do not believe God genuinely calls women to be pastors. We say this not because we can read the private experience of anyone, but because we believe private experience must always be assessed by the public criterion of God's Word, the Bible. If the Bible teaches that

God wills for men alone to bear the primary teaching and governing responsibilities of the pastorate, then by implication the Bible also teaches that God does not call women to be pastors. The church has known from its earliest days that a person's personal *sense* of divine leading is not *by itself* an adequate criterion for discerning God's call.[50] Piper and Grudem are correct in refusing to place a personal sense of call on the same level as scriptural teaching. Nevertheless, they fail to see that repeated testimonies to an experience of call ought at least to alert us that our understanding of the Scriptures may need a thorough reevaluation.

Our chief quarrel with Piper and Grudem, however, lies elsewhere. We simply are not convinced that God wills that the pastorate be limited to men. Nor are we sympathetic to the authoritarian understanding of the ordained office suggested by their statement.

In this chapter we have presented our case for the partnership of women and men in all aspects of the fellowship of believer priests, including in the exercise of gifts that endow God's people for various ministries. Now we turn our attention to the nature of the authority inherent in the ordained office itself.

SEVEN

WOMEN IN
THE ORDAINED
MINISTRY

◆

O PPONENTS OF THE ORDINATION OF WOMEN appeal to the nature of
the ministerial office for the basis of their position. Ordained ministers,
they claim, function in capacities that only men can fulfill. Because only
men can exercise the spiritual prerogatives demanded by the ordained
office, the people of God cannot set apart women for ministry. Women
do have a place in the church, of course, but their activities are limited
to supportive roles.

With the findings of the previous chapters in view, we now tackle
this argument head-on. Is the complementarian understanding of the
ordained ministry correct? Does Christ intend that only men be set
apart for ordained positions among his people?

If ordained ministers fulfill roles that God designed for men only, the
Holy Spirit cannot call women to such positions in the church. However, if through the act of ordination the community sets persons apart
for ministries that believers can pursue regardless of gender, we would
expect the Spirit to call both men and women to ordained roles.

At the heart of the debate is the question, Are certain dimensions of the ordained ministry inappropriate for women? To answer this question we must explore the primary elements of the ordained office. Here we focus our attention on the theological aspects of the ordained office. Specifically we ask, Do clergy carry a representative significance that is inappropriate to women? And does the ministry entail an authoritative role that women cannot exercise? Our thesis is that rather than eliminating women from serving, the representative and authoritative dimensions of the ordained office demand the full participation of men and women.

Woman and the Representative Office

The ordained ministry today entails a wide variety of roles. In many ecclesiastical traditions, none is more significant—and for women in ministry more problematic—than the representative role. Many people view ordained persons as in some sense representative. Clergy represent Christ to the congregation; they represent the local church to the broader fellowship; they represent the church to the world.

This representative function may be quite formal. Pastors (or priests) may minister on the basis of a well-defined theological understanding of the nature of the ordained office within the church structure. The representative function may also operate quite informally, as the people simply view pastors as symbols of certain spiritual realities. In either case, the ordained office carries an explicit or implicit ontological dimension.

Complementarians assert that the representative role (with the resultant ontological associations) bars women from the ordained office. Women simply cannot represent the realities connected with pastoral ministry. We must look more closely at this argument.

The Representative Function of the Ordained Office. The representative role of the ordained office arises in several ways. For example, an ordained minister may represent the local congregation within the wider Christian fellowship. This function is formally present in ecclesiastical traditions that emphasize the foundational role of clergy for the continuance of the church (such as through adherence to apostolic succession). Because of the close connection of pastors to the congregations they serve, the representative function is informally evident in most other traditions as well.

The roots of the representative role of clergy may lie in the New Testament itself. The book of Revelation provides one possible example. The opening chapters contain seven letters from the risen Lord to the churches in Asia. Each epistle is addressed to "the angel" of the respective church. Some commentators see in this form of address a reference to the pastor, whom the Lord designates as the representative of the church.[1]

In addition to representing the local church within the wider fellowship, clergy represent the church in the world. Like the former, this representation may be either formal or informal. Formal representation occurs in traditions that view the ordained office as in some sense constituting the church. Clergy therefore act on behalf of the church, even offering official public pronouncements in its name. Even when such formal structures are lacking, people readily associate an ordained person with a local congregation, a specific denomination or the Christian church in general.

Neither of these two aspects of representation is inherently incompatible with the ordination of women. There is no obvious reason that gender should disqualify a person from representing a local congregation within the wider fellowship or representing the church in society. In fact, insofar as the church is the bride of Christ we could conclude that these tasks are better served by women ministers, for only women can be brides.[2]

Difficulties arise, however, with a third aspect which many traditions associate with the ordained office. Clergy represent the divine reality to the people. In chapter five we explored one dimension of this—pastors (or priests) as representatives of God. Now we must look at the other aspect. Do ordained ministers represent Christ? And if so, does this bar women from ordination?

The Ordained Minister as Christ's Representative. Complementarians argue against the ordination of women on the basis of the representative function of the ordained office. Because Jesus was male, the ordained person—as Christ's representative—must also be male; a woman cannot be an "image" (eikon) of Christ.[3]

Many complementarians conceive of the representative nature of the ordained office in somewhat static terms. Michael Novak speaks for many:

That the priest be male is fitting to the essence of Jesus, a divine Person embodied as a male, a fully human male. One can "see Christ" in every human being, male or female, but a female cannot represent the male Christ before the community. Not, at least, without jangling symbols beyond their meaning, without communicating something essentially different.[4]

The evangelical Anglican James I. Packer presents the same position in more active categories: "Since the Son of God was incarnate as a male, it will always be easier, other things being equal, to realize and remember that Christ is ministering in person if his human agent and representative is also male."[5] But in what sense do ordained ministers represent Christ?

Eucharistic Representation. Some Christian traditions view the celebration of the Lord's Supper (the Eucharist) as the central event of community life. Consequently they teach that ordained ministers represent Christ primarily as they preside at the Lord's table. According to opponents of the ordination of women, the ordained person must be a biological resemblance of Jesus, because the officiator at the Eucharist is the representative—perhaps even the representation—of Christ.

This argument has gained proponents within both Roman Catholic and Protestant ranks. The contemporary Catholic appeal to eucharistic representation as barring women from the priesthood arose as the result of an important theological development within the church, namely, the commonplace designation of the ordained priest as acting "in the person of Christ" *(in persona Christi).*

Some historians credit Thomas Aquinas with the first significant theological use of this phrase in the context of the ordained priesthood.[6] The great scholastic theologian argued that because the priest speaks the words of consecration "in the person of Christ, it is from His command that they receive their instrumental power from Him."[7]

The designation stems from developments in eucharistic doctrine stemming from the Middle Ages. The Roman Catholic Church teaches that the elements of bread and wine truly become the body and blood of Christ. This occurs as the priest, on behalf of the entire congregation and on the basis of Jesus' words at the Last Supper, petitions God the Father that the elements on the altar may become for them Christ's body and blood. Because Christ is thus made truly present, his sacrifice on Calvary is realized again in the mass and its power invoked for the salvation of the communicants.

Popular piety, however, has circumvented whatever precision theologians used to nuance church teaching. Many Catholics believe that the priest offers Christ's sacrifice to the Father at the moment when the officiant says the words of Christ and raises the host to be adored.[8] Because no mere human can present Christ's offering to God, Christ must be present not only in the elements but also in the priest. The officiator, therefore, becomes a "second Christ."

Despite Aquinas's legacy, only since the Second Vatican Council has *in persona Christi* gained widespread use. It describes the priest as impersonating our Lord. As official church teaching declares, the priest "acts not only through the effective power conferred on him by Christ, but *in persona Christi,* taking the role of Christ, to the point of being His very image, when he pronounces the words of consecration."

Official church teaching draws from the contemporary understanding of *in persona Christi* a powerful argument for the exclusion of women from the priesthood. Those who take Christ's role must have a natural resemblance to him. Hence as the members of the Congregation for the Doctrine of the Faith concluded, "His role must be taken by a man."[9]

While Protestants generally reject the Roman Catholic theology of the mass, the idea of eucharistic representation remains embedded in the widely held perception that the Communion service is a reenactment of the Last Supper. In this drama the officiating pastor plays the part of Jesus, speaking our Lord's words and tracing our Lord's actions when he instituted the memorial meal. As a consequence, in the eyes of many only a man can officiate at the Communion observance, because a man best represents the male Jesus in the reenactment of that first-century event.

How should we evaluate these appeals to the eucharistic representation of the ordained office? First, we acknowledge that the officiant at the Lord's Supper does fulfill a certain representational function. But this representation is fundamentally vocal rather than actual. Appealing to Lutheran perspectives on the Lord's Supper, Mark E. Chapman provides a helpful perspective. He argues that the minister of the sacrament represents Christ orally, not bodily. In defending this suggestion, he draws from the tradition that the Word the minister speaks, and not the minister's person, determines the validity of the sacrament: "And so, a fit minister of the sacrament, one whose ministry makes the sacrament valid and efficacious, is not one whose person represents Christ but one whose Word, whose proclamation, speaks the Word of Christ."[10]

In the eucharistic celebration, the one who presides announces Christ's words of invitation and Christ's declaration that the physical elements in some sense are his own body and blood. In so doing the one who officiates serves as the mouthpiece for the risen Lord, who is the true host inviting communicants to enjoy table fellowship. Nothing inherent in this representational function would bar a believer from officiating at the table on the basis of gender. (Not even ordination is inherently a prerequisite for presiding at the Lord's Supper celebration, for the community could conceivably designate any member to voice Christ's words of invitation at the celebration.)

Second, we conclude that rather than eliminating women from the ordained office, the church's eucharistic doctrine may be enhanced by women representing Christ at the Lord's table. As we noted above, many communicants view the event either as a mass in which the priest acts as Christ, offering our Lord's body and blood to God, or simply as a reenactment of the Last Supper in which the pastor acts the part of Jesus. A number of theologians from various denominations conclude that an all-male clergy perpetuates these theological misconceptions about the Eucharist. The British Anglican John Austin Baker sets forth a lucid summary of current thinking:

> An iconic theory of the eucharistic presidency, confining that role to someone of the same gender as the incarnate Lord, runs the risk of suggesting that Christ is present and active in the eucharistic minister in a unique mode and degree, an idea for which there is no basis in the general doctrine of grace or in specific authoritative teaching. By so doing it obscures the central affirmation of Catholic eucharistic theology, that Christ and his sacrifice are contained and communicated within the consecrated elements, and that is where his people are to find, adore and receive him. Furthermore, it blurs the nature of the Eucharist by presenting it as a re-enactment of the Last Supper, rather than a fulfillment of the command there given to plead the sacrifice of the cross before God by the sacramental means proleptically provided.[11]

The Lord's Supper is not a reinstitution of Calvary. Although it is in a sense a reenactment of the upper room, it is more than an artistic drama. Limiting the privilege of officiating at the Eucharist to males fosters insufficient and incorrect understandings of the event. For this reason the use of women *and* men as officiators could enhance the church's experience of this significant ordinance.[12]

Ontological Representation. Officiating at the Eucharist provides perhaps the most obvious expression of the representative function of the ordained ministry. Yet this visible dimension points toward another aspect which is both deeper (for it lies behind the eucharistic representation) and broader (in that it encompasses all aspects of the clergy task). Several ecclesiastical traditions teach that the ordained person functions as an *ontological* representation of Christ: the minister embodies in some symbolic manner the actual nature of our Lord.

To many complementarians, ontological representation provides an unassailable rationale for the exclusion of women from the ordained office. They point out that in the incarnation our Lord became a male, and he retains his maleness even in his exalted state.[13] Rather than being inconsequential, Jesus' maleness has timeless, cosmic significance.[14] Consequently those who represent Christ to the community must likewise be male.

Egalitarians have been quick to dismiss the force of this argument. Constance Parvey notes the pervasiveness of the negative response, claiming that the traditional position "has been criticized by almost all prominent Roman Catholic scholars as well as scholars in other churches."[15] Critics of the complementarian position do not necessarily reject the representative function of the ordained office. They may agree that the pastor or priest directly represents Christ. Rather, their disagreement lies in the specific aspect of Christ's nature which is thus represented. Egalitarians assert that clergy symbolize Christ in his humanness, not in his maleness. Stephen Barton summarizes this thinking:

The Christian doctrine of Christ as Savior and leader . . . has nothing to do with his coming as a man. What is important is his being fully human. For it is his being fully human which enables him to represent all humanity, both male and female, before God. Therefore, when the Christian priest ministers to God's people, what is important is being the representative of Christ, the truly human One.[16] In support of their position, egalitarians appeal to the Bible and the church fathers. The great declarations of the incarnation in the New Testament emphasize that Christ became human, not that he became male. John announces that "the Word became flesh" (Jn 1:14). And in speaking of Jesus Christ as "being born in human likeness" (Phil 2:7), Paul uses the general Greek word *anthrōpos* (human) rather than the gender-specific *anēr* (man).

The patristic writers and church councils followed the lead of the New Testament in emphasizing Jesus' humanity rather than his maleness. The Nicene Creed, for example, clearly declared that our Lord became a human being (from *enanthrōpeō*), thereby taking to himself the likeness of all who are included within the scope of his saving work. For the church fathers, the focus on the inclusiveness of Jesus' humanity was a theological necessity based on an important theological principle: what the Son did not assume in the incarnation he could not redeem.[17]

Egalitarians find in Jesus' inclusive humanness important implications for the ordination of women. Maleness, they assert, cannot be elevated to an essential requirement for ministry. To do so would stand in opposition to the inclusive significance of Christ's saving work. As Stephen Barton observes, "The restriction of the representative, priestly role to men alone is indefensible theologically. It is a denial of the universality of the salvation which is God's gift through Christ to all."[18]

Rather than barring women from ordination, egalitarians argue, classical christology demands the inclusion of women in the ordained office. As Madeleine Boucher states: "It may be argued that a priestly ministry of women and men would better image and represent the universality of Christ and redemption."[19]

Of course, not all scholars find the egalitarian case convincing. The Roman Catholic feminist-turned-complementarian Sara Butler admits that viewed in isolation, the individual arguments against women's serving in the priesthood are open to criticism. Yet she finds an integral relationship among the insights complementarians offer, which results in a comprehensive logic that egalitarians have yet to examine.[20]

The most pressing problem complementarians find in the egalitarian position is its inability to deal satisfactorily with the undeniable maleness of Jesus. For their part, egalitarians do not wish to discount Jesus' gender any more than his Jewishness or his socioeconomic status. As Boucher notes, "To speak of Christ as male, Jewish, poor, and so on is to speak of him as a historical person, Jesus of Nazareth. The theological importance of affirming Jesus as a historical person is that we thereby also affirm that the earthly is the sphere of revelation."[21]

The question egalitarians raise is whether these aspects of our Lord's earthly existence carry *soteriological* significance. Is Jesus' maleness essential for God's redemptive work in him? Or is merely his humanness crucial? Boucher again explains:

> We affirm—and affirm properly—that Christ redeems us *as* a man, as a Jew, as a poor person, and so on. The difficulty arises when it is implied that Christ redeems us *by virtue of the fact* that he is a man, as though his maleness were a necessary condition for God's saving work in him. The problem lies in the attempt to attach soteriological significance to the maleness of Jesus Christ.[22]

Hence although egalitarians acknowledge that the incarnation in the form of a male may have been historically and culturally necessary, they deny its soteriological necessity. To suggest otherwise would undercut Christ's status as representing all humans—male and female—in salvation. As Parvey asserts, "The Risen Christ of the Eucharist is the representative for the whole community, not only for that of male human beings. The reconciling and atoning Christ is the human one for all humanity (Galatians 3:27-28)."[23]

What are we to conclude from the contemporary discussion of ontological representation? In two respects the egalitarians are correct. If clergy do function as the representatives of our Lord, then restricting the ordained office to males can readily cloud the symbolism of Christ's inclusive humanity. Ontological representation demands that women and men serve together within the ordained office. Further, as the ecclesiological considerations of chapter six suggest, whatever representative function ordained ministers fulfill is indirect, arising from their role within the church. Pastors do not represent Christ directly. Rather, ordained ministers function as ontological representatives of our Lord only indirectly, in that they represent the church which is the body of Christ.

Writing from a Roman Catholic perspective, Edward Kilmartin draws out the implication of this conclusion for the question of women and the priesthood:

> Since the priest directly represents the Church united in faith and love, the old argument against the ordination of women to the priesthood, based on the presupposition that the priest directly represents Christ and so should be male, becomes untenable. Logically the representative role of the priest seems to demand both male and female office bearers in the proper cultural context; for the priest represents the one church, in which distinctions of race, class, and sex have been transcended, where all are measured by the one norm: faith in Christ.[24]

Kilmartin's thesis is equally appropriate to Protestant understandings of the ordained office. Ultimately, the image of God—of which Christ is the perfect exemplar—is a social reality. We do not reflect the divine image primarily as isolated individuals but as a corporate whole, the fellowship of Christ's disciples who make up his body. Therefore the church, the community of believers of every race, class and sex, is the ontological representation of Christ.

The ordained ministry does fulfill a representative function. Pastors embody the church, whether formally or merely informally. As the representation of the body of Christ, clergy likewise become the ontological representation of our Lord. Because Christ is creating one new human reality (Eph 2:15) in which distinctions of race, class and gender are overcome (Gal 3:28), the church—and consequently Christ—is best represented by an ordained ministry consisting of persons from various races, from all social classes and from both genders.

Representation and Jesus' Maleness. Despite our fundamental agreement with the egalitarian position, however, we cannot follow those who deny all soteriological significance to Jesus' maleness. To do so would lead us to a grave anthropological difficulty, the reduction of the importance of our sexuality. This is the valid caution embedded in the complementarian critique of egalitarianism as articulated, for example, by Butler: "We need to come to grips with the significance of sexuality in the constitution of the human person. The claim, for example, that Jesus' sex should be accorded no more weight than his Jewishness or his blood type simply is not convincing."[25]

Sexuality—our fundamental maleness and femaleness—is an indispensable dimension of our existence as embodied human creatures. Because Jesus was a particular historical person, his maleness was integral to the completion of his task. This is not to say that the incarnation of our Lord as a male means that maleness constitutes essential humanness or that women are in any sense deficient humans. Rather than enthroning the male as God's ideal for humankind, the maleness of Jesus provided the vehicle whereby his earthly life could reveal the radical difference between God's ideal and the structures that characterize human social interaction. In the context in which he lived, Jesus' maleness was an indispensable dimension of his vocation. Only a male could have offered the radical critique of the power systems of his day, which is so prevalent in Jesus' message.

To see this, we need only look at the alternative. Had the Savior of humankind come as a woman, she would have been immediately dismissed solely on the basis of her sex. Nor could her actions have been interpreted as defying and correcting the social norms of the day, for her self-sacrificial ministry would have been interpreted as merely the outworking of her socialized ideal role as a woman.[26] Thus to be the liberator of both male and female, Jesus needed to be male.

The liberating work of the male Jesus occurred in the context of the male-female roles within the orders of human society. The Genesis creation narratives teach that in the beginning God created male and female to live in egalitarian mutuality. Thereby humans could reflect the image of the triune God. In the Fall, mutuality was replaced by hierarchy (see Gen 3:16). Into this situation Jesus brought a new paradigm. Our Lord liberated men and women from their bondage to the social orders that violate God's intention for human life-in-community. Jesus freed males from the role of domination that belongs to the fallen world, in order that they can be truly male. On behalf of women Jesus acted as the model human standing against the patriarchal system, bringing women into the new order where sex distinctions no longer determine rank and worth.

These christological observations lead to a crucial conclusion: *in the church we can best reflect the liberating significance of Jesus' incarnation as a male by following the principle of egalitarian mutuality that he pioneered.* Mutuality occurs as women and men work together in all dimensions of church life, including the ordained ministry. In this way we begin to model the new order Jesus came to establish.

Woman and the Authoritative Office

The discussion of women's ordination in liturgical traditions, where the sacraments are central, often focuses on the implications of the minister's role as officiator at the Lord's Supper celebration. This, however, is only one dimension of pastoral ministry. Not only do ordained ministers fulfill a representative role, but they also exercise authority. Like the representative dimension, the authoritative dimension of the ordained office may be either formal or informal, and it may be sensed both within the church and in the wider society.

Among evangelicals, discussions of the role of women in the church often focus on authority. Complementarians argue that the authoritative aspect of the ordained office is an impediment for the ordination of women. Only men can rightly exercise the authority integral to this ministry. Specifically, they find in the ordained office two types of authority which are inappropriate to women: leadership authority and teaching authority. We must explore these two dimensions and then examine the nature of pastoral authority itself.

Women and Leadership Authority. In an article written for the massive volume *Rediscovering Biblical Manhood and Womanhood,* Thomas Schreiner sets forth the complementarian view of women and church leadership:

I propose to prove below that women participated in ministry in the Scriptures, but their ministry was a complementary and supportive ministry, a ministry that fostered and preserved male leadership in the church. Thus, the ministry of women in the church was notable and significant, but it never supplanted male leadership; instead it functioned as a support to male leadership. This view does not rule out all ministry for women. Instead, it sees the ministry of women as complementary and supportive.[27]

Because women's responsibility is to support male leadership, some complementarians infer that it is sinful for women to exercise leadership over men. For example, a report to the Free Church of Scotland on the role of women concludes,

By basing its argument upon authority-relations within the prelapsarian family, Paul explains why women would wish to lead in the churches. It is an expression of the curse which has made a woman insubordinate to her husband. By the grace of God, women should try to overcome such sinful desires for leadership over men in the churches.[28]

Indeed, it is a short, seemingly logical step from asserting that God designed women to fulfill only supportive roles to the conclusion that for a woman to seek a leadership position entails a grievous sin.

This way of framing the complementarian position returns us to the issue of gender role distinctions. In chapter five we explored this topic in the context of creation. Now we must pursue it in the context of the church, asking whether men and women are to fulfill different roles in Christ's fellowship. Did Christ intend that only men exercise the authority associated with leadeship?

Gender Distinctions and the Apostolate. Complementarians believe that Christ's establishment of an all-male apostolate indicates his intention for the church to observe role distinctions based on gender. Jesus chose only men to be the original apostles, and he gave them the prerogatives of leadership, rulership and reception of divine revelation.[29] James Borland provides the clinching biblical case: "As a testimony of the fact that male leadership in the church has been permanently established by Christ, the names of the twelve apostles are forever inscribed on the very foundations of heaven itself" (see Rev 21:14).[30]

Although some scholars believe that women did later carry the title *apostle* (as in Rom 16:7), that the original Twelve were all men is uncontestable. However, the maleness of the twelve apostles does not provide sufficient grounds from which to conclude that all ordained persons must be male. Such a conclusion fails to understand the foundational, unique and temporary role played by the Twelve, one that in the strict sense cannot be passed on to subsequent believers.[31]

Further, even if our Lord's selection indicated that only men were to play a foundational role in establishing the church, there is nothing in this choice that suggests that Christ wills that male leadership continue to be the norm. In fact, Jesus' own demeanor, which we outlined in chapter three, suggests the contrary. The early believers followed our Lord's egalitarian attitude toward women, for they served side by side with men in the New Testament communities. The practice of the New Testament church, therefore, points beyond the limitations complementarians draw from the maleness of the original Twelve.

In addition, the complementarian argument fails to understand the actual significance of Christ's choice of twelve men. The importance of this act does not lie in a permanent distinction of roles among his followers based on gender. Our Lord's selection was a symbolic act, understandable only in the context of Israel's history. His selection of twelve male apostles, reminiscent of the original patriarchs, was an eschatological sign[32] denoting that Jesus was reconstituting the ancient people of God.[33]

Considerations such as these lead many egalitarians to place the maleness of the original Twelve on the same level as their Jewishness. Paul Jewett, for example, cautions that we can no more conclude from the maleness of the Twelve "that the Christian ministry must remain masculine to perpetuity" than we can "infer from the fact that the apostles were all Jews that the ministry must remain Jewish to perpetuity."[34]

Although Jewett may be criticized for overstating the case,[35] his argument does have merit. Even more than the maleness of the Twelve, their Jewishness forges a link between Christ's new community and the Old Testament covenant nation. Hence the ethnic heritage and, to a lesser extent, the gender of the original apostles are theologically significant. But once the foundational connection between Israel and the church was established, the New Testament communities were free to broaden the ranks of their leaders to include gifted people of all nations and both genders.

The Representative Role of Leaders. In addition to the male apostolate, complementarians appeal to the representative function of the ordained office, which they extend to the leadership aspect. Because it is Christ himself who leads his people through his representatives, in their leadership role pastors act as representatives of the Lord. Women, however, simply cannot represent Christ, and as a consequence they cannot represent his leadership in the church.

But the complementarian argument proves too much. Carried to its logical conclusion, it would preclude women from involvement in *any* form of ministry. Ultimately all ministry is representative; Christ is the ultimate agent at work—through his Spirit—in all the activities of his community. If women cannot represent our Lord as the one who leads his people, they also are unable to represent him as acting in other dimensions of church life.

More crucial, however, is another flaw in the complementarian appeal to the representative view of leadership. The joyous responsibility of representing Christ does not belong to leaders alone but is the work of the whole people of God. As Christ's body, the church in its entirety is our Lord's representative. The task of leaders, in turn, is related to the representative character of the church.

The Nature of Leadership

But if the primary task of leaders is not to represent Christ to the church or to be the mediators of his leadership to his people, wherein does their role lie? To find an answer, we must look at the nature of leadership itself.

In recent years leadership theory has become an important academic pursuit. Thinkers have proposed a wide variety of definitions.[36] Although these vary greatly, Gary A. Yukl finds that most definitions reflect the assumption that leadership involves a process "whereby intentional influence is exerted by the leader over followers."[37] This dimension is evident in John W. Gardner's useful statement, "Leadership is the process of persuasion or example by which an individual (or leadership team) induces a group to pursue objectives held by the leader or shared by the leader and his or her followers."[38]

On the basis of the ecclesiological considerations set forth in chapter six, we would amend Gardner's definition. Leadership, we assert, is the art of facilitating a community in the process of embodying corporately and individually the vision and values they all share. Leaders assist a group in tapping their resources in order to accomplish a common mandate.

Although the role of leaders may vary from group to group, persons in leadership fulfill certain general tasks.[39] First, leaders envision goals. This may occur as they constantly remind the group of what it should become, or as leaders articulate the vision which the group, despite its diversity, shares. Second, leadership includes the task of affirming values. Leaders help the group to examine the values that have given it identity, both by eliminating those that they no longer find meaningful and by reaffirming and reappropriating values that remain central to the community.

Third, leaders are motivators. According to Gardner they tap into the motives within the group which "serve the purposes of collective action in pursuit of shared goals."[40] And they foster the alignment of individual and group goals. Fourth, leadership includes certain aspects of managing. Leaders facilitate planning, organizing, maintaining and decision-making. Not to be overlooked is a fifth task, explaining. Leaders seek to communicate to the group a plausible explanation of current situations in the light of underlying realities.

Sixth, leaders both are symbols of the ideals shared by the community and act as representatives of the group. For the members of a community, leaders embody the group's collective identity and continuity. As an extension of this aspect, within the group itself leaders represent the shared values, vision and mandate. In short, leaders embody the group ideal. At the same time leaders represent the group and its ideal in the wider society.

Finally, leadership entails fostering renewal within the group. Gardner ably summarizes the internal problems communities eventually encounter: "Motivation tends to run down. Values decay. The problems of today go unsolved while people mumble the slogans of yesterday." And they maintain an organizational structure "designed to solve problems that no longer exist."[41] As a consequence, effective leaders set in motion processes that revitalize the community. Renewal includes releasing the potentials with the group which have remained untapped or which have been stymied by outmoded aspects of community life.

Taken together, these interconnected elements suggest that fundamentally leadership is empowerment. Gardner notes the centrality of this concept in contemporary secular leadership theory: "Reference to *enabling* or *empowering* has become the preferred method of condensing into a single word the widely held conviction that the purpose of leaders is not to dominate or diminish followers but to strengthen and help them to develop."[42] The popularity of the designation is illustrated in the title of W. Warner Burke's article "Leadership as Empowering Others," in which he argues that "leaders empower via direction and inspiration and managers via action and participation."[43]

Interestingly, what has become common parlance in academic circles lies at the heart of the understanding of church leadership in the New Testament. Christ places leaders within his fellowship so that they might facilitate the people themselves in fulfilling their mandate. Perhaps Paul set forth the blueprint for this understanding when he declared, "The gifts [Christ] gave were that some would be apostles, some prophets, some evangelists, some pastors and teachers, to equip the saints for the work of ministry" (Eph 4:11-12). Here Paul recites a facilitative goal; these persons *facilitate* the ministry of the entire community.

The New Testament writers suggest a similar purpose for the leaders of local congregations known alternatively as elders and bishops.[44] Both terms give some indication as to the functions these first-century persons fulfilled. The designation *bishop (episkopos)* means "one who supervises" (see Acts 20:28; 1 Tim 3:1-7; Tit 1:5-9). Hence this office is "almost always related to oversight or administration."[45] Bishops directed the ongoing functioning of the congregation in the various aspects of its corporate ministry. They were to "shepherd" or guide the people of God (Acts 20:28; 1 Pet 5:1-4). And by providing administrative leadership, they coordinated congregational ministry (1 Tim 3:5; 5:17).

The term *presbyter (presbyteros)* or *elder* (Acts 20:17; 1 Tim 5:17-18; Tit 1:5; Jas 5:14; 1 Pet 5:1-4) could refer either to chronological age or to special status within the community.[46] The name suggests spiritual oversight, for elders fulfilled certain ministries such as anointing the sick (Jas 5:14) as well as preaching, teaching, admonishing and guarding against heresy (Tit 1:9).

Whatever the word used, the New Testament writers clearly indicate that church structure is always subservient to mission. Central to the task of completing the work of the church is the giftedness of God's people. Ministry occurs as all persons use their Spirit-endowed gifts to carry out the mandate Christ has entrusted to the entire fellowship (Rom 12:3-8; 1 Cor 12:4-31; 1 Pet 4:10-11).

This truth leads to far-reaching consequences for the ministry of women. It means that women must use whatever gifts the Spirit bestows on them. And there is no evidence in these texts that the Spirit applies gender considerations in apportioning any of the gifts, including the gift of leadership.

Further, the New Testament emphasis on facilitative leadership means that leaders of both genders best serve the church. Complementarians claim that Christ calls only men to leadership in the church, which according to Piper and Grudem means that men alone "bear the responsibility for the overall pattern of life."[47] Limiting leadership to men results in a truncated understanding of the church's mandate, for male voices easily elevate and articulate a solely male-oriented "pattern of life." Consequently, the church's task of being the image of God can truly occur only when men and women contribute their unique perspectives to the whole.

Servant Leadership. Leadership primarily involves empowerment; above all leaders serve God's people as facilitators of the kingdom work. The church best reflects its true nature as the body of Christ when all its members—men and women—use their God-given gifts in obedience to Christ. But one topic still remains, that of leadership style. Does not the male-oriented, aggressive style of church leadership eliminate women from the ordained office?

Male dominance in the church coincides with what we may term a distinctively male conception of leadership style. In the Middle Ages the priest was primarily viewed as a mediator of divine grace, the representative of Christ in the struggle against human sin. Many participants in the contemporary debate over women in ministry understand leadership as the exercise of power over others: the leader must use the power inherent in the office to carry out his views, program or agenda. Adopting this perspective of leadership raises the question whether women can properly exercise power, especially over men.

The chief flaw in this understanding of leadership, however, is that it sets aside our Lord's teaching. Jesus reveals in both word and deed that the divine way of life lies in humble servanthood. Consequently our Lord overturned accepted norms, teaching that to be a leader means above all to be a servant to others:

> You know that among the Gentiles those whom they recognize as their rulers lord it over them, and their great ones are tyrants over them. But it is not so among you; but whoever wishes to become great among you must be your servant, and whoever wishes to be first among you must be slave of all. For the Son of Man came not to be served but to serve, and to give his life a ransom for many. (Mk

10:42-45)

The concept of servant leadership is gaining adherents in society today. For example, management consultant Robert Greenleaf writes,

A new moral principle is emerging which holds that the only authority deserving one's allegiance is that which is freely and knowingly granted by the led to the leader in response to, and in proportion to, the clearly evident servant stature of the leader. . . . To the extent that this principle prevails in the future, the only viable institutions will be those that are predominantly servant led.[48]

This principle directly applies to the ordained office. It means that ordination sets a person apart to be a servant leader. In fulfilling a leadership role in the church, the ordained person seeks to be a servant to the people. Indeed, the pastor's fundamental task consists of leading the whole people of God in service (Eph 4:11-13). Consequently, rather than being placed in a position of dominance over the people, the ordained person stands with them, as together they seek to obey the Lord of the church. The consensus document *Baptism, Eucharist and Ministry* articulates the point well: "Ordained ministers must not be autocrats or impersonal functionaries." Rather they should "manifest and exercise the authority of Christ in the way Christ himself revealed God's authority to the world, by committing their life to the community."[49]

Our Lord intends that humble servanthood characterize each of his followers. But in this, pastors must lead the way. They should be "examples to the flock" (1 Pet 5:3) "in speech and conduct, in love, in faith, in purity" (1 Tim 4:12). In short, they must be models to the congregation of Christlike character and servanthood. As those chosen by the Spirit and endowed with special responsibilities, these persons have been entrusted with positions of leadership. Their positions, however, do not entail license to promote selfish or even personal goals. Rather they should enter into office with all humility and with the intent of seeking the good of the whole community.

Ordained persons can find encouragement in the New Testament for their task of acting as servant leaders. Peter, for example, exhorts elders to serve willingly and eagerly, not out of greed or a desire to "lord it over" those entrusted to them (1 Pet 5:1-3). Above all, the New Testament sets before us the example of Christ. Our Lord declared that those who would lead his people must be humble servants (Mk 10:42-

44). And he illustrated his teaching with his own example of humble service on our behalf (2 Cor 8:9; Phil 2:5-8).

Most Christian traditions today acknowledge servant leadership as the ordained person's primary function.[50] Not even contemporary complementarians intend to deny the servant nature of the ordained office. Piper and Grudem, for example, claim that they attempt to hold leadership and servanthood in a proper biblical balance.[51] We applaud their efforts to do so. Nevertheless, the complementarians' more hierarchical understanding of church structure tends to undermine their good intention to maintain a servant focus. It is difficult to see pastors primarily as servants of God's people when ordination appears to endow a privileged few with power and status. This problem is compounded when over half of the membership of the church find the door to ordination barred by restrictions based solely on gender.

We must acknowledge that women have often displayed a more perceptive understanding of the significance of servant leadership than men have. In addition, in our culture women form a more effective symbol of servanthood than do men. Yet many Christians who quite willingly encourage women to be servants in the church deny them the ordained office as an avenue of service. Biblical, servant-oriented leadership, however, is best symbolized by men and women ministering together in this crucial dimension of church life. These considerations should dispose us toward anticipating that the Spirit will call women, as well as men, to servant leadership positions in Christ's church.

Women and Teaching Authority

Complementarians argue that women cannot serve in the ordained office because the pastorate entails a leadership function that is appropriate only to men. In addition, they oppose the ordination of women on the basis of the teaching authority bound up with the pastoral office. Their difficulty here is not that teaching itself is inappropriate for women. Indeed, complementarians know that the Bible encourages women to teach in certain circumstances (see, for example, Tit 2:3-5), and some acknowledge that women can even teach men.[52] Rather, they do not allow women to teach when it violates the so-called biblical principle of male leadership and female subordination. Hence complementarians conclude that the Bible prohibits a woman from "publicly teaching men in the religious realm and exercising authority over men in the Christian community."[53] Piper and Grudem write,

We would say that the teaching inappropriate for a woman is the teaching of men in settings or ways that dishonor the calling of men to bear the primary responsibility for teaching and leadership. This primary responsibility is to be carried by the pastors or elders. Therefore we think it is God's will that only men bear the responsibility for this office.[54]

Susan Foh articulates the rationale for the complementarian position: "In 1 Corinthians 12:28 Paul lists several gifts given to Christians in hierarchical order: apostles, prophets, teachers, workers of miracles, healers, helpers, administrators, speakers in tongues." Of these, Foh asserts,

only two are not given to women. Historically, there were no female apostles. And since in this context *teacher* refers to the official teachers of the church, women were excluded from this position. All other offices are open to women. Ephesians 4:11 has a slightly different listing: apostles, prophets, evangelists and pastor-teachers. . . . It is evident that women should not be pastor-teachers, the biblical designation closest to the modern concept of minister.[55]

Complementarians bar women from the ordained office in the church because it encompasses the authority to teach men. Proponents of women's ordination, in contrast, find nothing in the Bible which prohibits women from exercising this prerogative. As we noted in the biblical section, egalitarians appeal to situations in the early church where women did in fact teach men, such as the instruction Priscilla and Aquila administered to Apollos. They also point out the absurdity of permitting women to teach impressionable children but not men who should possess the spiritual acumen to discern heretical statements.

Teaching and Prophecy. Questions more at the heart of theological concerns include the relationship of teaching to prophecy and the relationship of women teachers to ecclesiastical authority. The theological question moves from the practices of early Christians to the general order of offices in Christ's church. As noted in chapter three, many egalitarians dispute the complementarians' claim that no women served as apostles. They appeal to Paul's important but exegetically problematic commendation of Junia(s) as "prominent among the apostles" (Rom 16:7).

More important, however, are certain facts that all parties in the debate acknowledge. Women did engage in prophecy. The ancient communities considered women prophets authoritative, including Old Testament figures such as Miriam (Ex 15:20), Deborah (Judg 4:4) and Huldah (2 Kings 22:14-20).[56] In enumerating the gifts and offices in the church Paul lists prophecy ahead of teaching (1 Cor 12:28; Eph 4:11). From considerations such as these, egalitarians conclude that the prophetic office encompasses authoritative teaching and that it may even surpass the teaching office, at least within the early church. If this is so, they wonder, how is it that women can serve as prophets but not as teachers?

Complementarians, of course, do not agree with the egalitarian understanding of the relationship between these two functions.[57] Central to their position is a distinction between authoritative teaching (including preaching) and prophecy. The case against ordaining women depends on the conclusion that of the two distinct functions, teaching carries more authority and consequently must remain solely the prerogative of men.

Foh offers one example of how the two activities differ: "With prophecy, God puts the very words into the mouth of the prophet (Deut 18:18-19); they are not the result of the prophet's reasoning. Preaching is the result of the speaker's preparation and study. Its source is Scripture, not the mouth of God."[58] Foh's distinction suggests that prophecy, being the very words of God, is more foundational than teaching, which is in the end merely human reflection on God's Word. Contrary to Foh's intention, however, this conclusion suggests that the prophetic office has preeminence over that of teaching.

Perhaps in part to counter this possibility, other complementarians find the crucial differentiation within prophecy itself. They distinguish between the unquestionable and authoritative prophecy in ancient Israel and the type exercised in the New Testament (and hence in the church), which demanded corporate discernment. Schreiner, drawing from the work of Wayne Grudem, explains:

> Old Testament prophets spoke the word of the Lord, and what they said was absolutely authoritative—no part of it could be questioned or challenged. Every word was to be received as God's very word.

But the words of the New Testament prophets do not have this kind of absolute authority. . . . Instead, New Testament prophecies are handled not as authoritative words from God but as spontaneous impressions or insights that may or may not be, either in whole or in part, from God. Thus, the church must judge and evaluate prophecies in order to determine whether they, either in whole or in part, are sound.[59]

Schreiner simply makes too rigid a distinction. It is hardly conceivable that Old Testament prophets such as Joel anticipated an experience categorically inferior to their own when they announced a coming day when God would pour out his Spirit on all people so that "your sons and your daughters shall prophesy" (Joel 2:28). Further, Paul's instructions to the early church to evaluate prophetic statements finds its Old Testament counterpart in the commands given to the ancient Hebrew community to discern whether prophetic utterances were from the Lord (such as Deut 18:21-22). In fact, as prophets such as Jeremiah indicate, many voices competed for the ear of the Old Testament people.

If the complementarian distinction between two types of prophecy is unwarranted, what about the more obvious differentiation between prophecy and teaching? We must acknowledge that complementarians point out an important distinction. But again they go too far in positing a strict delineation between the two functions. Egalitarians correctly remind us that despite their differences, prophecy and teaching are interconnected, and the relationship between them is fluid rather than rigid. Like prophecy, teaching is subject to community evaluation (hence the commendation of the Bereans in Acts 17:11). And like teaching, prophecy should strengthen and edify the hearer (1 Cor 14:3-4).

New Testament scholar David Scholer rightly concludes:

Defining *prophecy* is difficult, but recent major studies of prophecy in the early church . . . clearly indicate that prophetic utterances and prophecy did function as authoritative teaching within Paul's churches. . . . Paul's definition of prophecy in 1 Corinthians 14:3 makes it, along with the whole argument of 1 Corinthians 14:1-25, a functional equivalent of authoritative teaching.[60]

In the early church the Holy Spirit gifted women for the task of prophecy. Implicit in the exercise of this function is authoritative teaching, including the teaching of men. Consequently this dimension of the ordained office ought not to bar women from ordination.

Women Teachers and Ecclesiastical Authority

Some contemporary complementarians have given consideration to how women might serve in church staff positions,[61] including teaching both women and men, and still remain within the boundaries of the principle of subordination.[62] Perhaps the most widely held position, albeit one that has not won the support of all,[63] declares that women can minister insofar as they do so under male authority.

Complementarians opposed to this compromise position mainly object to its lack of explicit biblical foundation. Where does the Bible teach this idea? Indeed, the position is not the product of explicit biblical teaching but a conclusion that its proponents draw from other principles. So long as male leadership and female subordination are honored, they argue, women ought to be encouraged to engage in any and all functions in the church.

Although this position may appear to be a useful step in the right direction, it suffers from a quite different theological flaw beyond the lack of direct biblical support. The suggestion that women ministers function under the umbrella of male authority maintains an illegitimate view of the ordained office. Contrary to the spirit of the New Testament, it views clergy as endowed with a special status above the people they serve.

We believe that rather than endowing ordained persons with authority above the church, Christ entrusted final authority to the entire people of God. Under the guidance of their leaders, all Christ's disciples—not merely the ordained members of the church—must together take responsibility for determining the will of our Lord and seek to obey that will. This ecclesiological understanding means that all ordained persons minister under the authority of others. Specifically, they function under the authority of the entire congregation they serve.

The emphasis on the authority of the congregation is no longer limited to those denominations (like the Baptists) that practice congregational polity. Rather, in recent years it has come to enjoy widespread acceptance even in more hierarchical bodies, such as the Roman Catholic Church. Hence the ecumenical document *Baptism, Eucharist and Ministry* acknowledges that the foundation for the pastoral office lies within the church as a whole: "The ordained ministry has no existence apart from the community."[64]

But we ought not to forget that the people of God under whose authority clergy serve consists of male and female. Consequently we might say that the biblical principle of the mutual submission of the sexes is implicitly present in all church structures. Male members of the clergy always serve under the authority of a body that includes females. And female leaders always minister under the authority of a congregation that includes male members.

David A. Yukl maintains that "the essence of leadership is influence over followers."[65] Such influence assumes a certain kind of authority and power, which in the church is associated with the ordained office. The influential nature of the pastorate remains at the heart of the complementarian objection to the ordination of women.

We have viewed the question of women's ordination in the context of the authoritative dimensions of the ordained office. The pastoral charge encompasses both leadership authority and teaching authority. But now we must look behind both aspects and explore the idea of authority itself, further clarifying the issues we have been considering in this section. Hence, we now ask, In what sense does the ordained office carry authority in the church? What kind of authority do clergy exercise? What can we conclude from these findings about the question of woman's role within Christ's community?

The Nature of Authority. Foundational to our discussion is the question of the nature of authority. What do we mean when we speak of a person's possessing or exercising authority? And what is the relationship between authority and power? We may define authority as "the right to command, enforce obedience, make decisions"[66] or "the right to act by virtue of office, station or relation."[67] In contrast, we may define power as the "ability to act so as to produce some change or bring about some event"[68] or the "capacity to exercise control."[69] Although power is a broad concept, it carries significant weight when one is speaking about interpersonal relations. Hence, more narrowly understood, power may be defined as "an agent's potential influence over the attitudes and behavior of one or more designated target persons."[70] In this context, control over things becomes one source of power.

Power, then, focuses on ability, whereas authority has to do with the right to exercise power.[71] This means that ideally authority precedes power.

The exercise of power in human relationships may take several forms. In his monumental study *The Anatomy of Power,* John Kenneth Galbraith describes three varieties: condign, compensatory and conditioned power.[72] Condign power is the process of influencing others by threatening adverse consequences. In Galbraith's words, it "wins submission by the ability to impose an alternative to the preferences of the individual or group that is sufficiently unpleasant or painful so that these preferences are abandoned."[73] Compensatory power moves in the opposite direction. It is the process of influencing others by offering affirmative reward, something the individual or group values. Conditioned power, in contrast to the others, operates through the belief structures of its targets: "Persuasion, education, or the social commitment to what seems natural, proper, or right causes the individual to submit to the will of another or of others."[74]

In addition, the source of power stands as a crucial element in this discussion. Yukl summarizes organizational power:

Power is derived in part from the opportunities inherent in a person's position in the organization; this "position power" includes legitimate authority, control over resources, control over information, control over punishments, and ecological control [i.e., control over the physical environment, technology, and organization of the work of subordinates]. Power also depends on attributes of the interpersonal relationship between agent and target person; this "personal power" includes relative task expertise, friendship and loyalty, and a leader's charismatic qualities. Finally, power depends upon some political processes ("political power") such as controlling key decisions, forming coalitions, and co-opting opponents.[75]

Aspects such as these have led many people to conclude that the exercise of power always favors the agent of power at the expense of the target person. Max Weber reflects this perception when he speaks of domination and power as "the possibility of imposing one's will upon the behavior of other persons"[76] or "the probability that one actor in a social relationship will be in a position to carry out his own will despite resistance, regardless of the basis on which this probability rests."[77] In his essay "Theology of Power," the Roman Catholic theologian Karl Rahner suggests an equally negative understanding, defining power as "a certain self-assertion of acting spontaneously without the previous consent of another, to interfere with and change the actual constitution of that other."[78] Some scholars likewise imply that inequality or hierarchy remains inherent in all structures of authority. Hence in his Sigmund Freud Memorial Lectures at the University of London, Richard Sennett declared, "Authority is a bond between people who are unequal."[79]

But we need not take such a pessimistic view. Understood more simply as the ability to cause or prevent change,[80] power is an intrinsic element in all human relationships. The presence of power promotes personhood, for it enables independent choice and action. And lying behind power is the question of the right or authority to use it. More important than the use of power in general, therefore, is the type of power used. Rollo May notes that power may be exploitative, manipulative, competitive, nutrient or integrative.[81] Exploitative power consists in subjecting others to whatever use they may have to the one with the power. Manipulative power uses others' desperation or anxiety to gain an advantage over them. Competitive power consists in one person "going up" merely because another has "gone down." May defines nutrient power as "power *for* the other person," best illustrated by parents' care for their children. Finally, integrative power is "power *with* the other person." This power recognizes and encourages the power of the other.

Properly executed in a proper context with a proper motive and for a proper goal, the exercise of power is a positive good. The use of power can be a legitimate component of true leadership, when it is the outworking of properly constituted authority. Ideally leaders exercise nutrient and integrative power for the benefit of the community they serve. And they exercise this power based on the authority derived from their position in a community, which members have granted to them because of their personal qualities. In the case of church leaders, their installation in positions of authority ought to come by the Holy Spirit's choosing and gifting for leadership as acknowledged by the community. In this context, the question of ordaining women raises the issue of whether women can properly be invested with authority and can properly exercise power.

A grave impediment to the prospect of women clergy lies in the popular understanding that sees authority and power—which are inherent in the ordained office—as masculine traits, whereas submission and powerlessness are feminine traits. Madeleine Boucher explains: "On the one side we have authority, power, the male: God as Father, Jesus Christ as Lord, and the pastor and father as representative of God and Christ. On the other side we have submission, powerlessness, the female—and no corresponding connection between God, Christ, and woman."[82]

But this is not the New Testament picture. The foundation for our conclusion lies in the distinction between two related Greek terms, *exousia* (the "ability to perform an action to the extent that there are no hindrances in the way") and *dynamis* ("intrinsic ability").[83] Despite their close connection, *exousia*, more than *dynamis*, came to be associated with the concept of right or authority, referring to "the right to do something" or "the right over something."[84]

The translators of the Hebrew Scriptures into Greek (the Septuagint) used *exousia* to denote "right, authority, permission or freedom in the legal or political sense"[85] and to express "the unrestricted sovereignty of God as the One who has the say, whose word is power."[86] This provided the foundation for the specifically theological use of *exousia* in the New Testament. In the New Testament documents, the word signifies "the absolute possibility of action which is proper to God, who cannot be asked concerning the relationship of power and legality in this *exousia*, since He is the source of both."[87] The term also denotes Christ's "divinely given power and authority to act,"[88] which comprises both right and power. Finally, *exousia* refers to the authority Christ imparts to his community.[89]

Whereas *exousia* carries the idea of power based on right, *dynamis* means "being able" or having a " 'capacity' in virtue of an ability."[90] According to the Gospels, in Jesus *exousia* and *dynamis* converge. Jesus' connection with God through the endowment of the Spirit gave him a definite personal authority *(exousia)*, which he had the actual power *(dynamis)* to exercise.[91] In turn, when Christ commissioned his disciples, he granted them authority by virtue of his authority and equipped them with his power.

But the authority and power that Jesus demonstrated radically differ from the understanding prevalent in the world. Both our Lord and the New Testament authors teach that divine power is made evident in human weakness.[92] Christ declared that God's reign often comes through what seems insignificant to us. In fact, he finds even the mundane work of a woman to be a worthy metaphor for the saving power of God (Lk 13:20-21). What our Lord preached he also modeled. Jesus repudiated the royal ideal of the Messiah[93] and with it the authoritarian roles that the Jews expected Messiah to fulfill. He came as a prophet endowed with power,[94] but above all he was endowed with the power of a servant.

This does not mean that Jesus was devoid of authority and power. On the contrary, he possessed the authority of the Son sent by the Father with a mission, namely, to inaugurate God's reign on earth for the sake of needy people. Jesus had the authority to forgive sins (Mk 2:10), to cast out unclean spirits (Mk 1:27) and to preach the good news (Mk 1:22). Hence Jesus never exercised authority through the display of power with the purpose of dominating, but rather always to minister to human need—to serve others as God's servant. The New Testament understands the authority and power that Jesus gives to his disciples in exactly the same way (see, for example, Mk 3:15; 6:7; Lk 9:1; 10:19).[95] Thus the New Testament portrayal of Jesus provides the basis for a proper understanding of authority and power in connection with the ordained office.

Ordination and Authority. Complementarians, of course, are keen to connect authority and power—understood as dominance—with church structures. According to Piper and Grudem, "the New Testament shows that the basic relationships of life fit together in terms of authority and compliance. . . . Most social institutions have structures that give to some members the right to direct the actions of others."[96] Consequently these authors define authority as "the right, power, and responsibility to direct others."[97] Although Piper and Grudem note that "for Christians, *right* and *power* recede and *responsibility* predominates," they conclude that "none of this is the abolition of authority structures, only their transformation as loving responsibility seeks to outrun rights and power."[98] Therefore, while acknowledging such principles as the priesthood of believers and the servant nature of leadership, they adamantly assert that the New Testament writers instruct the people to follow their leaders.[99]

Statements such as these indicate that complementarians maintain a basically authoritarian conception of the ordained ministry. And this authoritarian model provides the strongest impediment to women's being ordained to the pastorate. Traditionally, inducement with this kind of authority and the exercise of authoritarian power have been seen as the sole prerogative of men.

From the New Testament perspective we can speak of the authority inherent in the ordained office, an authority that confers the right to exercise power. But this authority and this power are of a different kind from the authoritarian model. The authority Jesus wills for his disciples is a derived authority, not an intrinsic one. It flows from the whole people of God upon whom Christ bestows his own authority. Likewise, it is directed back toward the community of faith. And Christ's disciples exercise the kind of power limited to its nutrient and integrative forms. In short, leaders exercise authority and use power for the benefit of the mandate that all share.

Several implications follow from this principle. It means that the authority of the ordained office is ultimately an authority to serve and facilitate. The model for the pastorate is not the ruler but the shepherd. As a result, leaders in the church possess authority to care for others by acting as servants and examples (Mk 10:41-44; 1 Pet 5:1-3). Leaders use the authority delegated to them by the people to facilitate the ministries of those under their care. Each member of Christ's body should serve others with the gifts and strength God provides. Walter Liefeld offers this keen observation: "It is striking that when Paul lists the qualifications for elders, his reason for mentioning the importance of ruling one's family well is not so the elder can 'rule' the church, but rather so he can 'care' (epimeleomai) for it (1 Tim 3:4-5)."[100] In fact, translated correctly, the New Testament never calls church leaders "rulers."[101]

As Jesus' own example indicates, true servant leadership carries its own profoundly powerful authority. Yet how are we to understand this apparent paradox between the New Testament emphasis on servant leadership and exhortations for the church to "obey" its leaders (as in

Heb 13:17)? How can a person who assumes the role of a servant command authority? E. Margaret Howe offers this insight: "When a congregation perceives in its minister a life of humble devotion to God and selfless commitment to people, then it will be ready to respond with respect and an attitude of obedience."[102]

The derived nature of clerical authority also means that in the church, hierarchical models must give way to more egalitarian ways of relating to each other. Jesus did not come merely to reverse the location of people in the old social structures. He did not intend to install underlings in dominant positions and reduce the upper classes to subordinate status. Rather, he called into question the very idea of society based on dominant-subordinate relationships. Consequently, in the church any dominance of clergy over laity must give way to the mutual submission of all.

The promotion of mutuality is one of the central challenges the contemporary situation sets before the church. John W. Gardner indicates, however, that this challenge is wholly in keeping with trends in current leadership theory: "Leaders today are going to have to help people recover an understanding of the mutual dependence of individual and group that have existed in all healthy communities from the beginning of time."[103]

Church leaders can take a giant step in this direction by modeling mutuality. This includes widening the circle of those who contribute to the leadership process. The various dimensions of leading need not be vested in those with formal authority, but can be distributed among the members of a group. Writing about leadership in organizations, Edgar H. Schein declares,

Leadership is a function in the organization, rather than the trait of an individual. It is distributed among the members of a group or organization, and is not automatically vested in the chairman or the person with the formal authority. . . . Good leadership and good membership . . . blend into each other in an effective organization.[104]

The authors of Baptism, Eucharist and Ministry echo this insight, calling for a shared leadership among Christ's people: "Strong emphasis should be placed on the active participation of all members in the life and the decision-making of the community."[105] As the division between "leader" and "follower" loses its rigidity, we will begin to see that leadership is never the prerogative of one designated person working in isolation. Indeed the concept of the leadership *team* is gaining momentum today.[106] Shared leadership benefits the community by fostering the use of a variety of differing leadership gifts. In the single-leader model (one leader and many followers), one person attempts to fulfill all the tasks demanded by the leadership role—with varying success based on that person's own strengths, gifts and abilities. The shared-leadership model, in contrast, promotes the contribution of many persons on the basis of their differing perspectives. As Gardner notes, "The best leader is one who ensures that the appropriate talent and skill are built into the team."[107]

This model lies at the heart of the plea for women's ordination. Egalitarians want the church to avail itself of the particular contributions of men *and* women in every aspect of its life. The egalitarian case is not built on the myth of androgyny, the claim that men and women are essentially the same. Rather, the differences between the sexes demand the inclusion of both in leadership. Because men and women view the world in different ways,[108] the church leadership team is enhanced by the presence of both.[109]

In these pages we are advocating a revised understanding of the pastoral office. The Van Leeuwen study group put it well:

Simply letting women "join the old boys' club" solves very little, for it assumes that the competence of women pastors and elders will be measured by their success in thinking and acting just like men. If male-dominated, overly hierarchical modes of church management remain in place . . . then the ordination of women turns out to be a questionable victory.[110]

Indeed, we have done the entire people of God a disservice if we merely give women access to the power structures of the church while maintaining unbiblical hierarchical organizational patterns.[111]

EPILOGUE

◆

Sally continued to wait for an opportunity to serve the local church. But following her graduation from seminary, no opportunities came her way. Because she needed to supplement her income once her student loans began to come due, she took a secretarial job in an office. At the same time Sally served in several voluntary roles in her church. Many recipients of her volunteer work spoke highly of her as a person gifted and called to ministry. The church experience was, however, bittersweet. The congregation that supported her volunteer service was affiliated with a denomination that continued to struggle over the role of women in vocational Christian ministry.

After two years of waiting, Sally learned about a part-time position on the staff of a nearby congregation. Because she had met the senior pastor and believed they could work well together, Sally submitted her name for consideration, even though the position would not allow her to express her gifts and training fully. Fortunately, she had several advocates in positions of power, and because they were willing to speak in favor of hiring her, Sally was offered the position. She thanked God for finally opening the door for her in vocational ministry. Her faithful, diligent work won the appreciation of staff and people alike.

Concerns about how she would make ends meet led Sally to keep her secretarial job. Being torn between two worlds is often frustrating for Sally. Because the pull toward the ministry is definitely the stronger of the two, Sally would gladly give up her secular employment. But financial restraints necessitate that she continue to supplement her church income. She longs for the day when she might minister in a full-time church position.

Sally occasionally experiences opposition to her role in the church. But she finds strength through her involvement in a support group consisting of several women and men within the congregation and in the city who share her convictions regarding women in ministry. At times Sally finds that she must vent her frustrations, and at other times she longs to celebrate the victories she experiences. This group of people offers her the opportunity to do both within a community of care and support.

Sally keenly follows the ongoing discussions regarding women in ministry within her denomination. She remains hopeful that someday the doors will swing open for all whom God has gifted and called to church leadership, regardless of gender. She keeps posted on the developments in other church bodies as well.

At times Sally wonders if she should remain with her denomination. On one occasion she raised the subject with a trusted mentor. His advice was poignant: "Sally, you can either be a pioneer in familiar territory or become a pilgrim in a foreign land. Both options have advantages and disadvantages. Your task is to discern which the Lord is calling you to at this time."

Today Sally believes that God is calling her to stay and serve within the familiar terrain of her denomination of origin. However, she also realizes that the time may come when she can no longer bear the pressures of being a pioneer. Should that occur, she may need to leave "home"—forsake the church fellowship in which she was raised—and continue to serve God and answer her call in a "foreign land"—within a denomination more accepting of women in ministry.

Sally is not angry, despite what she sees as the injustice of her situation. At times she does feel the acute pain of the restrictions placed on her because she is a woman. But overall, she is simply tired of the whole discussion. Sally has settled the biblical and theological issues for herself and now wishes to move on. She wearies of being embroiled in the heat of controversy. She tires of being the "token" female minister at ministerial gatherings for pastors and their wives. Sally longs for the day when she can merely serve God and minister to people, allowing her gender to be a gift that is treasured in church ministry rather than a liability to be overcome.

Notes

Introduction

[1]See, for example, the discussion in the *Mennonite Brethren Herald* 31, no. 22 (November 20, 1992): 4-14.

[2]For a closer look at recent developments in the CRC, see chapter one.

[3]These discussions have even been waged in publications by groups on the periphery of evangelicalism, such as the Church of the Brethren (see Nadine Pence Frantz and Deborah L. Silver, "Women in Leadership: A Theological Perspective," *Brethren Life and Thought* 30 [Winter 1985]: 37-40) and the Seventh-day Adventists (see Willmore Eva, "Should Our Church Ordain Women? Yes," and Bernard E. Seton, "Should Our Church Ordain Women? No," *Ministry* 58, no. 3 (March 1985): 14-22.

[4]Paul K. Jewett, "Why I Favor the Ordination of Women," and Elisabeth Elliot, "Why I Oppose the Ordination of Women," *Christianity Today* 19, no. 18 (June 6, 1975): 7-16. Six years later another pairing of articles occurred: Austin H. Stouffer, "The Ordination of Women: Yes," and George W. Knight III, "The Ordination of Women: No," *Christianity Today* 25, no. 4 (February 20, 1981): 12-19.

[5]John G. Stackhouse Jr. breaks these two basic positions into five in "Women in Public Ministry in Twentieth Century Canadian and American Evangelicalism: Five Models," *Studies in Religion* 17, no. 4 (1988): 471-85.

[6]Stephen C. Barton, "Impatient for Justice: Five Reasons Why the Church of England Should Ordain Women to the Priesthood," *Theology* 92, no. 749 (September 1989): 405. See also Klyne R. Snodgrass, "The Ordination of Women—Thirteen Years Later: Do We Really Value the Ministry of Women?" *Covenant Quarterly* 48, no. 3 (August 1990): 30-33.

[7]Gretchen Gaebelein Hull, *Equal to Serve* (Old Tappan, N.J.: Revell, 1987), p. 230.

[8]Mark E. Chapman, "The Ordination of Women: Evangelical and Catholic," *Dialog* 28, no. 2 (Spring 1989): 134.

[9]Ibid.

[10]For the importance of developing a creation-affirming rather than a creation-denying apologetic, see John Bolt, "Eschatological Hermeneutics, Women's Ordination and the Reformed Tradition," *Calvin Theological Journal* 26, no. 2 (1991): 370-88.

[11]John Piper and Wayne Grudem, introduction to *Recovering Biblical Manhood and Womanhood: A Response to Evangelical Feminism*, eds. John Piper and Wayne Grudem (Wheaton, Ill.: Crossway, 1991), p. xiv.

[12]Ronald W. Pierce, "Evangelicals and Gender Roles in the 1990s: 1 Tim 2:8-15, a Test Case," *Journal of the Evangelical Theological Society* 36, no. 3 (September 1993): 343, n. 4.

Chapter 1: Women in the Churches

[1]John Piper and Wayne Grudem, eds., *Recovering Biblical Manhood and Womanhood: A Response to Evangelical Feminism* (Wheaton, Ill.: Crossway, 1991).

[2]Susan McCoubrie, "Happy Birthday—Now We Are Four! A Brief History of Christians for Biblical Equality," *Priscilla Papers* 5, no. 3 (Summer 1991): 14.

[3]Christians for Biblical Equality brochure.

[4]Pamela Salazar, "Theological Education of Women for Ordination," *Religious Education* 82, no. 1 (Winter 1987): 71.

[5]D. B. Fraser, "Women with a Past: A New Look at the History of Theological Education," *Theological Education* 8, no. 4 (Summer 1972): 220.

[6]Nancy Hardesty, "Women and the Seminaries," *Christian Century* 96, no. 5 (February 7-14, 1979): 122-23.

[7]Salazar, "Theological Education of Women," p. 74.

[8]A. Gordon Wetmore, "God-Called Women," *The Seminary Tower* 49, no. 1 (Fall 1993): 1.

[9]Beth Spring and Kelsey Menehan, "Women in Seminary: Preparing for What?" *Christianity Today* 30, no. 12 (September 5, 1986): 18.

[10]Ibid., p. 21.

[11]Barbara Brown Zikmund, "Women in Theological Education," *Ministerial Formation* 38 (June 1987): 7-8.

[12]Mark Wingfield, "Women Gaining Ground in Baptist Ministry Roles," *Religious Herald* 71, no. 1 (February 11, 1993): 5.

[13]Ibid.

[14]"Ordination Guidelines and Study Documents," drafted by the Task Force on Ordination and adopted by the General Council of the North American Baptist Conference on June 6-7, 1985, p. 39.

[15]Ibid., p. 33.

[16]Ibid., p. 34.

[17]For the situation in Methodist, Anglican and Roman Catholic communions, see Jacqueline Field-Bibb, *Women Towards Priesthood: Ministerial Politics and Feminist Praxis* (Cambridge: Cambridge University Press, 1991).

[18]Synod Report, 1992.

[19]Randy Frame, "Vote Overturns Women's Ordination," *Christianity Today* 38, no. 9 (August 15, 1994): 52.

[20]Subsequent to the synod meeting in June 1994, one influential regional body of the CRC, Classis Grand Rapids East, defied the decision of the national synod, stating that in principle it is acceptable for its churches to ordain women. Joe Maxwell, "Churches Challenge Synod Ruling," *Christianity Today* 38, no. 11 (September 12, 1994): 70.

[21]As quoted in "Female Ordination Gains Local Option," *Christianity Today*, August 14, 1955, p. 60.

[22]J. I. Packer, "Let's Stop Making Women Presbyters," *Christianity Today* 35, no. 2 (February 11, 1991): 19.

[23]Patricia Gundry, *Neither Slave Nor Free* (San Francisco: Harper & Row, 1987), p. vi.

[24]Ibid., pp. vi-vii.

[25]Susan Lockwood Wright, "SBC Women Ministers Break Their Silence," *Christian Century*

103, no. 34 (November 12, 1986): 998.

Chapter 2: Women in Church History

[1]Robert P. Meye, "Women and the Evangelical Movement," in *Women and the Ministries of Christ*, ed. Roberta Hestenes and Lois Curley (Pasadena, Calif.: Fuller Theological Seminary, 1979), pp. 157-58.

[2]Maria L. Boccia, "Hidden History of Women Leaders of the Church," *Journal of Biblical Equality*, September 1990, p. 58.

[3]Roberta Hestenes, "An Historical Perspective of Women in Christian Leadership," paper presented at the North American Professors of Christian Education Annual Conference, October 21-24, 1993.

[4]Janette Hassey, *No Time for Silence* (Grand Rapids, Mich.: Zondervan/Academie Books, 1986), p. 45.

[5]For a detailed examination of women leaders in the early church, see Catherine Clark Kroeger and Richard C. Kroeger, *I Suffer Not a Woman* (Grand Rapids, Mich.: Baker, 1992).

[6]Boccia states that both Ignatius and Tertullian list the order of widows as clergy rather than as a domestic order ("Hidden History of Women Leaders," p. 59).

[7]Constance J. Tarasar, "Women in the Mission of the Church: Theological and Historical Reflections," *International Review of Mission* 81, no. 322 (April 1992): 195.

[8]Boccia, "Hidden History of Women Leaders," pp. 59-60.

[9]See, for example, the discussion in Tarasar, "Women in the Mission of the Church," pp. 196-98.

[10]Jerome *Epistle* 108.5-6, 26, quoted in Ruth A. Tucker and Walter L. Liefeld, *Daughters of the Church* (Grand Rapids, Mich.: Zondervan, 1987), pp. 118-19.

[11]Boccia, "Hidden History of Women Leaders," pp. 58, 67.

[12]Ibid., pp. 64-65.

[13]Ibid., p. 66.

[14]Ibid.

[15]Tucker and Liefeld, *Daughters of the Church*, p. 245.

[16]Donald W. Dayton and Lucille Sider Dayton, "Recovering a Heritage, Part 2: Evangelical Feminism," in *Women and the Ministries of Christ*, ed. Roberta Hestenes and Lois Curley (Pasadena, Calif.: Fuller Theological Seminary, 1979).

[17]Tucker and Liefeld, *Daughters of the Church*, p. 237.

[18]Hassey, *No Time for Silence*, p. 8.

[19]Tucker and Liefeld, *Daughters of the Church*, p. 242.

[20]Martin E. Marty, *The Pro and Con Book of Religious America* (Waco, Tex.: Word, 1975), p. 98.

[21]Tucker and Liefeld, *Daughters of the Church*, p. 250.

[22]Donald Dayton, *Discovering an Evangelical Heritage* (New York: Harper & Row, 1976); Nancy Hardesty, *Women Called to Witness: Evangelical Feminism in the Nineteenth Century* (Nashville: Abingdon, 1984).

[23]Tucker and Liefeld, *Daughters of the Church*, pp. 252-53.

[24]For a summary and discussion of Lee's sermon, see Gary Selby, " 'Your Daughters Shall Prophesy': Rhetorical Strategy in the Nineteenth Century Debate over Women's Right to Preach," *Restoration Quarterly* 34, no. 3 (1992): 156-59.

[25]Elizabeth Gillan Muir, *Petticoats in the Pulpit* (Toronto: United Church Publishing House,

1991), pp. 2-3.

[26]Betty A. DeBerg, *Ungodly Women: Gender and the First Wave of American Fundamentalism* (Minneapolis: Fortress, 1990), pp. 18-19.

[27]Ibid., p. 19.

[28]Christopher Lasch, "Woman as Alien," in *The Woman Question in American History,* ed. Barbara Welter (Hinsdale, Ill.: Dryden, 1973), p. 152.

[29]DeBerg, *Ungodly Women,* p. 148.

[30]Ibid., p. 153.

[31]Tucker and Liefeld, *Daughters of the Church,* p. 254.

[32]Ibid., p. 276.

[33]Ibid., pp. 273-74.

[34]Cited by Muir, *Petticoats in the Pulpit,* p. 188.

[35]Ibid., pp. 188-89.

[36]Tucker and Liefeld, *Daughters of the Church,* p. 279.

[37]Ibid., p. 275.

[38]Quoted by Dayton and Dayton, "Recovering a Heritage," p. 125.

[39]Harold E. Raser, "Your Daughters Shall Prophesy: Women Ministers in the American Holiness Movements," *The Seminary Tower,* 49, no. 1 (Fall 1993): 7.

[40]Leon McBeth, *Women in Baptist Life* (Nashville: Broadman, 1979), p. 34.

[41]Tucker and Liefeld, *Daughters of the Church,* p. 290.

[42]Andrew Peiser, "The Education of Women: A Historical View," *Social Studies* 67, no. 2 (March-April 1976): 69.

[43]Anne Firor Scott, "The Everwidening Circle: The Diffusion of Feminist Values from the Troy Female Seminary, 1822-1872," *History of Education Quarterly* 19, no. 1 (Spring 1979): 3.

[44]Ibid., p. 9.

[45]Jill Conway, "Perspectives on the History of Women's Education in the United States," *History of Education Quarterly* 14, no. 1 (Spring 1974): 6.

[46]Margaret W. Rossiter, "Doctorates for American Women, 1868-1907," *History of Education Quarterly* 12, no. 2 (Summer 1972): 162, 165.

[47]Peiser, "Education of Women," p. 71.

[48]Scott, "Everwidening Circle," p. 17.

[49]Erika M. Hoerning, "Upward Mobility and Family Estrangement Among Females: What Happens When the 'Same Old Girl' Becomes the 'New Professional Woman'?" *International Journal of Oral History* 6, no. 2 (June 1985): 109.

[50]Joyce Antler, "But Can She Cook? Overcoming the Barriers to Women's Education," *American Educator* 9, no. 3 (Fall 1985): 30.

[51]Rossiter, "Doctorates for American Women," p. 176.

[52]Quoted by Antler, "But Can She Cook?" p. 30.

[53]Pamela Salazar, "Theological Education of Women for Ordination," *Religious Education* 82, no. 1 (Winter 1987): 67.

[54]D. B. Fraser, "Women with a Past: A New Look at the History of Theological Education," *Theological Education* 8, no. 4 (Summer 1972): 213.

[55]Salazar, "Theological Education of Women," p. 68.

[56]Fraser, "Women with a Past," p. 214.

[57]Salazar, "Theological Education of Women," p. 69.

[58]Ibid., p. 71.

⁵⁹Fraser, "Women with a Past," p. 218.
⁶⁰Salazar, "Theological Education of Women," pp. 70-71.
⁶¹Fraser, "Women with a Past," p. 218.

Chapter 3: Women in the Faith Community
¹Fritz Zerbst, *The Office of Woman in the Church*, trans. Albert G. Merkens (St. Louis, Mo.: Concordia, 1955), p. 82. For this conclusion Zerbst cites Adolf von Harnack, *Die Mission und Ausbreitung des Christentums in den ersten drei Jahrhunderten* (Leipzig, 1906), 2:58ff.
²For a helpful discussion of the position of women in Hebrew society by an author sympathetic to the complementarian position, see James B. Hurley, *Man and Woman in Biblical Perspective* (Grand Rapids, Mich.: Zondervan, 1981), pp. 33-53.
³Pamela J. Scalise, "Women in Ministry: Reclaiming Our Old Testament Heritage," *Review and Expositor* 83, no. 1 (Winter 1986): 8-9.
⁴Ibid., p. 8.
⁵Edmund Jacob, *Theology of the Old Testament* (London: Hodder & Stoughton, 1958), p. 251.
⁶Mary J. Evans, *Woman in the Bible* (Downers Grove, Ill.: InterVarsity Press, 1983), p. 26.
⁷It is simply erroneous to conclude that Miriam "ministered only to women" as Thomas R. Schreiner claims; see his "The Valuable Ministries of Women in the Context of Male Leadership: A Survey of Old and New Testament Examples and Teaching," in *Recovering Biblical Manhood and Womanhood: A Response to Evangelical Feminism*, ed. John Piper and Wayne Grudem (Wheaton, Ill.: Crossway, 1991), p. 216. The Miriam stories show her to be very much a public figure, a member of the trio of leaders in Israel.
⁸G. Rawlinson, *Psalms*, in *The Pulpit Commentary*, ed. H. D. M. Spence and Joseph S. Exell (New York: Funk and Wagnall, n.d.), 2:44. See also A. A. Anderson, *The Book of Psalms*, New Century Bible (London: Marshall, Morgan and Scott, 1972), p. 488. This translation is indicated in the margin of the New Revised Standard Version.
⁹Schreiner, "Valuable Ministries of Women," p. 216.
¹⁰Schreiner erroneously reads the male headship principle into the text when he remarks, "Note that Deborah did not go out and publicly proclaim the word of the Lord. Instead, individuals came to her in private for a word from the Lord." Nor is there anything in the text to warrant his citing of her command to Barak as substantiating his conclusion: "Note that even when she speaks to Barak she calls him and speaks to him individually" ("Valuable Ministries of Women," p. 216). The text is silent as to where this event took place. Schreiner's concern to harmonize the account with his male headship principle is foreign to the concern of the biblical author. Deborah commanded Barak to assemble the army. To suggest that this does not entail the exercise of authority over a man in an official capacity presses the text into a procrustean bed.
¹¹Christina Campbell, "Principles of Female Ordination in the Old Testament," *Priscilla Papers* 7, no. 2 (Spring 1993): 8.
¹²Irene W. Foulkes, "Bible and Tradition," *Midstream* 21, no. 3 (July 1982): 340-41.
¹³The text contains a translation difficulty. The verse could also read, "O Zion, bringer of good tidings . . . O Jerusalem, bringer of good tidings," the feminine construction indicating that the city is personified as the herald. Some commentators argue that only this reading makes sense of the feminine pronoun: "But unless the person addressed is Zion it is difficult to account for the fem. imperatives and the fem. participle" (R. N. Whybray, *The Book of Isaiah*, New Century Bible [London: Marshall, Morgan and Scott, 1975], 2:52; see also Edward J. Young, *The Book of Isaiah* [Grand Rapids, Mich.: Eerdmans,

1972], 3:36-37). In contrast to Isaiah, these scholars find it inconceivable that a woman might serve as the herald of God's arrival.

¹⁴For this erroneous suggestion, see Schreiner, "Valuable Ministries of Women," p. 216.

¹⁵For a detailed summary and exegesis of the relevant gospel texts, see Ben Witherington III, *Women in the Ministry of Jesus* (Cambridge: Cambridge University Press, 1984).

¹⁶Ibid., p. 126.

¹⁷C. G. Montefiore, *The Synoptic Gospels* (London: Macmillan, 1909), 1:377.

¹⁸G. N. Stanton, *Jesus of Nazareth in New Testament Preaching* (London: Cambridge University Press, 1974), p. 152.

¹⁹For a recent description see Alvin John Schmidt, *Veiled and Silenced: How Culture Shaped Sexist Theology* (Macon, Ga.: Mercer University Press, 1989).

²⁰See Sarah B. Pomeroy, *Goddesses, Whores, Wives and Slaves: Women in Classical Antiquity* (New York: Schocken, 1975), pp. 93-148.

²¹David Cohen, "Seclusion, Separation and the Status of Women in Classical Athens," *Greece and Rome* 36, no. 1 (April 1989): 6.

²²Margaret Y. MacDonald, "Early Christian Women Married to Unbelievers," *Studies in Religion* 19, no. 2 (1990): 223.

²³See Wisdom of Solomon 25:24; *Apocalypse of Moses* 9:2.

²⁴Josephus *Contra Apionem* 2.201.

²⁵Hurley, *Man and Woman in Biblical Perspective*, p. 63.

²⁶See Evans, *Woman in the Bible*, p. 35.

²⁷The temple included three courts. Ritually clean Jews could enter the first court with their wives. Within this court was the sacred court, which women were forbidden to enter. Within the sacred court was a third court to which only the priests were allowed access (Josephus *Antiquities* 15.11.5).

²⁸See Aída Besançon Spencer, *Beyond the Curse: Women Called to Ministry* (Peabody, Mass.: Hendrickson, 1985), p. 56. She notes that this prayer does not itself stand as proof of a low view of women in Judaism: "The prayer of thanksgiving is given not so much because Gentiles, women and slaves are inherently inferior but because they are not obliged to fulfill the commands to study the law." Differing obligations, however, were one factor that placed women on unequal footing with men in Jewish society.

²⁹See, for example, Philo *On the Special Laws* 3.31.169-70; *Flaccus* 11.89. Cited in Spencer, *Beyond the Curse*, p. 50.

³⁰Grant R. Osborne, "Women in Jesus' Ministry," *Westminster Theological Journal* 51 (Fall 1989): 262-63, 289; Joachim Jeremias, *Jerusalem in the Time of Jesus*, trans. F. H. Cave and C. H. Cave, 3rd ed. (Philadelphia: Fortress, 1969), pp. 361-63.

³¹Hurley, *Man and Woman in Biblical Perspective*, p. 83. Mary Evans is so impressed with the Jesus of the Gospels that she claims his valuing of women as persons was "an idea found nowhere in, and in some ways alien to, the Jewish thought of the time" (*Woman in the Bible*, p. 46).

³²For a citation, see Evans, *Woman in the Bible*, p. 48.

³³Osborne, "Women in Jesus' Ministry," p. 289.

³⁴See, for example, Foulkes, "Bible and Tradition," pp. 343-44.

³⁵Spencer, *Beyond the Curse*, p. 58.

³⁶For the theological significance of Martha's confession in the context of the Fourth Gospel, see Sandra M. Schneiders, "Women in the Fourth Gospel and the Role of Women in the Contemporary Church," *Biblical Theology Bulletin* 12, no. 2 (April 1982):

41.
[37]Witherington, *Women in the Ministry of Jesus*, p. 122.
[38]Specifically, John reports that Jesus appeared first to Mary Magdalene. On the relevance of this for the church's mission, see Teresa Okure, "The Significance Today of Jesus' Commission to Mary Magdalene," *International Review of Mission* 81, no. 322 (April 1992): 177-88.
[39]Floyd V. Filson, *The Gospel According to St. Matthew* (London: Adam & Charles Black, 1960), p. 302.
[40]Eduard Schweizer, *The Good News According to Mark*, trans. Donald H. Madvig (Atlanta: John Knox, 1970), p. 363.
[41]This seems to be the conclusion of Evans, *Woman in the Bible*, p. 54.
[42]Osborne, "Women in Jesus' Ministry," pp. 289-90.
[43]Ibid.
[44]See Paul K. Jewett, *The Ordination of Women* (Grand Rapids, Mich.: Eerdmans, 1980), p. 62.
[45]Witherington, *Women in the Ministry of Jesus*, p. 128.
[46]Ben Witherington III, *Women in the Earliest Churches* (Cambridge: Cambridge University Press, 1988), p. 148.
[47]Jewett, *The Ordination of Women*, p. 65.
[48]Witherington, *Women in the Earliest Churches*, p. 147.
[49]Ibid., p. 144.
[50]Witherington, *Women in the Ministry of Jesus*, p. 129. See his lengthier discussion in *Women in the Earliest Churches*, pp. 146-57.
[51]Witherington, *Women in the Earliest Churches*, p. 155.
[52]Some evangelical scholars argue that in this context prophecy does not involve speaking authoritative words. See, for example, Schreiner, "Valuable Ministries of Women," p. 217. However, this is a minority and historically novel position. We will discuss this in greater detail in chapter seven.
[53]See E. Earle Ellis, "The Role of the Christian Prophet in Acts," in *Apostolic History and the Gospel*, ed. W. Ward Gasque and R. P. Martin (Grand Rapids, Mich.: Eerdmans, 1971), pp. 55-56.
[54]Walter Bauer, *A Greek-English Lexicon of the New Testament and Other Early Christian Literature*, trans. and ed. William F. Arndt and F. Wilbur Gingrich (Chicago: University of Chicago Press, 1957), p. 708. See also F. F. Bruce, *Commentary on the Book of Acts* (Grand Rapids, Mich.: Eerdmans, 1971), p. 369.
[55]C. E. B. Cranfield, *The Epistle to the Romans* (Edinburgh: T & T Clark, 1979), 2:784.
[56]John Piper and Wayne Grudem, "An Overview of Central Concerns: Questions and Answers," in *Recovering Biblical Manhood and Womanhood: A Response to Evangelical Feminism*, ed. John Piper and Wayne Grudem (Wheaton, Ill.: Crossway, 1991), p. 69.
[57]As is the case with the exegesis of Piper and Grudem in ibid.
[58]Ibid., p. 85. See also Schreiner, "Valuable Ministries of Women," p. 218.
[59]Witherington, *Women in the Earliest Churches*, p. 154.
[60]E. Earle Ellis, *Prophecy and Hermeneutic in Early Christianity* (Tübingen: Mohr, 1978), pp. 6-7.
[61]Hence Witherington, *Women in the Earliest Churches*, p. 111.
[62]W. Derek Thomas, "The Place of Women in the Church at Philippi," *Expository Times* 83 (January 1972): 117-20.

[63]Victor C. Pfitzner, *Paul and the Agon Motif: Traditional Athletic Imagery in the Pauline Literature* (Leiden: Brill, 1967), p. 120.

[64]Evans, *Woman in the Bible*, p. 128.

[65]M. Goguel, *The Primitive Church*, trans. H. G. Shape (London: Allen and Unwin, 1964), p. 552.

[66]J. Daniélou, *The Ministry of Women in the Early Church*, trans. Glyn Simon (Leighton Buzzard, U.K.: Faith Press, 1961), p. 8.

[67]Ronald Y. K. Fung, "Ministry in the New Testament," in *The Church in the Bible and the World*, ed. D. A. Carson (Grand Rapids, Mich.: Baker, 1987), p. 181.

[68]Piper and Grudem, "Overview of Central Concerns," p. 68.

[69]See, for example, Witherington, *Women in the Earliest Churches*, p. 110.

[70]For a discussion of the role of church leaders as patrons, see Gerd Theissen, *The Social Setting of Pauline Christianity* (Philadelphia: Fortress, 1984), p. 105.

[71]For an example of such an invalid comparison, see Schreiner, "Valuable Ministries of Women," p. 222.

[72]Wayne A. Meeks, *The First Urban Christians: The Social World of the Apostle Paul* (New Haven, Conn.: Yale University Press, 1983), p. 119.

[73]Alvera Mickelsen, "An Egalitarian View: There Is Neither Male nor Female in Christ," in *Women in Ministry: Four Views*, ed. Bonnidell Clouse and Robert G. Clouse (Downers Grove, Ill.: InterVarsity Press, 1989), p. 189.

[74]For example, in commenting on 1 Corinthians 11:2-16, Meeks notes, "In brief, [Paul] leaves unquestioned the right of women, led by the Spirit, to exercise the same leadership roles in the assembly as men, but insists only that the conventional symbols of sexual difference, in clothing and hair styles, be retained" (*First Urban Christians*, p. 220, n. 107).

[75]Caroline F. Whelan, "Amica Pauli: The Role of Phoebe in the Early Church," *Journal of the Study of the New Testament* 49 (March 1993): 68. Whelan cites several sources. Pliny's *Epistle to Trajan* 10.96.8 refers to two slave women whom the Christians called "deaconesses." The Latin, however, is *ministrae*, which does not necessarily denote a specifically female order, but may in fact suggest an egalitarian attitude toward church offices. See Pliny, *Letters and Panegyrics*, trans. Betty Radice, Loeb Classical Library (Cambridge, Mass.: Harvard University Press, 1975), 2:288-89.

[76]For a defense of this position, see Hurley, *Man and Woman in Biblical Perspective*, pp. 229-32.

[77]See Fung, "Ministry in the New Testament," p. 181.

[78]For a helpful discussion of the role of Phoebe, see Craig S. Keener, *Paul, Women and Wives: Marriage and Women's Ministry in the Letters of Paul* (Peabody, Mass.: Hendrickson, 1992), pp. 237-40.

[79]Commentators generally see in this verse a reference to a specific office that Phoebe held in the local congregation. Cranfield, for example, writes, "It is natural . . . in view of the way in which Paul formulates his thought . . . to understand it as referring to a definite office. We regard it as virtually certain that Phoebe is being described as 'a (or possibly 'the') deacon' of the church in question" (*The Epistle to the Romans*, 2:781). Similarly, Matthew Black notes, "As a deaconess (cf. 1 Tim. 3:11) she had also an official function in the congregation at Cenchreae" (*Romans*, 2nd ed., New Century Bible [Grand Rapids, Mich.: Eerdmans, 1989], p. 208).

[80]This conclusion has gained support in recent years. See the commentaries cited in the

previous note and Whelan, "Amica Pauli," p. 82; Robert Jewett, "Paul, Phoebe and the Spanish Mission," in *The Social World of Formative Christianity*, ed. Jacob Neusner et al. (Philadelphia: Fortress, 1988), pp. 148-50.

[81]This conclusion is supported even by some who oppose women elders. See, for example, Fung, "Ministry in the New Testament," p. 180.

[82]For a summary of the main positions, see Whelan, "Amica Pauli," pp. 69-70, n. 6.

[83]Franz J. Leenhardt, *The Epistle to the Romans* (London: Lutterworth, 1961), p. 379.

[84]Hence the masculine noun can mean "leader, chief, presiding officer, or one who stands before to protect." H. G. Liddell and R. Scott, *A Greek-English Lexicon* (Oxford: Clarendon Press, 1992), p. 1526.

[85]John Murray, *The Epistle to the Romans* (Grand Rapids, Mich.: Eerdmans, 1965), 2:227, n. 1.

[86]See the helpful arguments of Schreiner, "Valuable Ministries of Women," pp. 219-20.

[87]For an argument in favor of "ruling elder," see Mickelsen, "Egalitarian View," p. 190, and Letha Scanzoni and Nancy Hardesty, *All We're Meant to Be* (Waco, Tex.: Word, 1974), p. 62.

[88]See the conclusions of Whelan, "Amica Pauli," pp. 82-85.

[89]Evans, *Woman in the Bible*, p. 124.

[90]Ibid.

[91]See J. Foster, "St. Paul and Women," *Expository Times* 62 (Summer 1951): 378.

[92]For an example, see Judith K. Applegate, "The Co-elect Woman of 1 Peter," *New Testament Studies* 38 (October 1992): 587-604.

[93]See, for example, A. E. Brooke, *A Critical and Exegetical Commentary on the Johannine Epistles*, International Critical Commentary (Edinburgh: T & T Clark, 1912), pp. lxxxi, 168-69.

[94]Hence Werner Foerster, "κυρία," in *Theological Dictionary of the New Testament*, ed. Gerhard Kittel, trans. Geoffrey W. Bromiley, 10 vols. (Grand Rapids, Mich.: Eerdmans, 1964-1976), 3:1095.

[95]H. A. Sawtelle, *Commentary on the Epistles of John*, American Commentary on the New Testament (Philadelphia: American Baptist Publication Society, 1888), 7:67, 76. For an interpretation of the epistle as addressed to an Ephesian widow, together with her physical children, see William Derry, *The Epistles of St. John*, Expositor's Bible Commentary (New York: Wilbur B. Ketcham, n.d.), 6:822.

[96]Hence Spencer, *Beyond the Curse*, pp. 109-12.

[97]Joan Morris, *The Lady Was a Bishop: The Hidden History of Women with Clerical Ordination and the Jurisdiction of Bishops* (New York: Macmillan, 1973), p. 2.

[98]Brooke, *Johannine Epistles*, p. 168.

[99]Murray writes that the apostle's remark likely suggests that "these persons were well known to the apostles and were distinguished for faith and service" (*Epistle to the Romans*, 2:230).

[100]F. F. Bruce, *The Letter of Paul to the Romans* (Grand Rapids, Mich.: Eerdmans, 1963, 1990), p. 258.

[101]Barrett, Cranfield (who notes that this seems to have been the unanimous view of the patristic commentators) and Dunn also support this interpretation. C. K. Barrett, *A Commentary on the Epistle to the Romans* (London: Adam and Charles Black, 1957), p. 283; C. E. B. Cranfield, *The Epistle to the Romans* (Edinburgh: T & T Clark, 1979), 2:789; J. G. Dunn, *Romans*, Word Biblical Commentary (Dallas: Word, 1988), 2:895.

[102]Hurley, *Man and Woman in Biblical Perspective*, p. 121.

103Piper and Grudem, "Overview of Central Concerns," p. 80.

104William Sanday and Arthur C. Headlam, *A Critical and Exegetical Commentary on the Epistle to the Romans*, 5th ed., International Critical Commentary (Edinburgh: T & T Clark, 1902), p. 423. See also Bauer, *Lexicon*, p. 298.

105For a summary of the main uses of *apostle* in the New Testament, see Witherington, *Women in the Earliest Churches*, p. 115; C. K. Barrett, *The Signs of an Apostle* (Philadelphia: Fortress, 1872), pp. 23-81; Rudolf Schnackenburg, "Apostles Before and During Paul's Time," in *Apostolic History and the Gospel*, ed. W. Ward Gasque and R. P. Martin (Grand Rapids, Mich.: Eerdmans, 1970), pp. 293-94.

106Ray R. Schulz, "Romans 16:7: Junia or Junias?" *Expository Times* 98, no. 4 (January 1987): 109.

107Piper and Grudem, "Overview of Central Concerns," p. 81.

108Ibid.

109See Schulz, "Romans 16:7?" pp. 108-10. His article effectively answers the arguments set forth by Piper and Grudem, "Overview of Central Concerns," pp. 79-80.

110Origen *Epistolam ad Romanos Commentariorum* 10.26; 39.

111John Chrysostom *Homily on the Epistle of St. Paul the Apostle to the Romans* 31, in *A Select Library of Nicene and Post-Nicene Fathers*, trans. J. P. Morris and W. H. Simcox (Grand Rapids, Mich.: Eerdmans, 1980), 11:555.

112See Mickelsen, "Egalitarian View," p. 190. For her conclusion Mickelsen cites Scott Bartchy, "Power, Submission and Sexual Identity Among the Early Christians," in *Essays on New Testament Christianity*, ed. C. Robert Wetzel (Cincinnati: Standard, 1978).

113Schulz, "Romans 16:7," p. 110.

114Hence Cranfield, *Romans*, 2:788.

115For this conclusion see Schreiner, "Valuable Ministries of Women," p. 221. He appeals to the work of Piper and Grudem, "Overview of Central Concerns," pp. 79-81.

Chapter 4: Women in the Writings of Paul

1Paul K. Jewett, *The Ordination of Women* (Grand Rapids, Mich.: Eerdmans, 1980), p. 68.

2Wilhelm C. Linss, "St. Paul and Women," *Dialog* 24 (Winter 1985): 36.

3The Pauline authorship of the Pastoral Epistles is widely questioned. However, for the purposes of our discussion, we simply assume that the verse under consideration came from the pen of Paul, or at least represents Paul's thoughts.

4Peter Richardson, *Paul's Ethic of Freedom* (Philadelphia: Westminister Press, 1979), pp. 16-17.

5See, for example, Ben Witherington III, "Rite and Rights for Women—Galatians 3.28," *New Testament Studies* 27, no. 5 (1981): 597, 603, n. 20.

6Ibid., pp. 593-94.

7F. F. Bruce, *Commentary on Galatians*, New International Greek Testament Commentary (Grand Rapids, Mich.: Eerdmans, 1982), p. 187.

8H. Wayne House, "Neither . . . Male nor Female . . . in Christ Jesus," *Bibliotheca Sacra* 145, no. 577 (1988): 54-55.

9Robert L. Saucy, "The Negative Case Against the Ordination of Women," in *Perspectives on Evangelical Theology: Papers from the Thirtieth Annual Meeting of the Evangelical Theological Society*, ed. Kenneth S. Kantzer and Stanley N. Gundry (Grand Rapids, Mich.: Baker, 1979), p. 281. See also the discussion that follows the article.

10In addition, see George W. Knight III, "Male and Female Related He Them," *Christianity*

Today 20, no. 14 (April 9, 1976): 705, 709; J. J. Davis, "Some Reflections on Galatians 3:28: Sexual Roles and Biblical Hermeneutics," *Journal of the Evangelical Theological Society* 19 (1976): 201-8.

[11]Paul K. Jewett, *Man as Male and Female: A Study in Sexual Relationships from a Theological Point of View* (Grand Rapids, Mich.: Eerdmans, 1975), p. 142.

[12]For a list of scholars who propose this idea, see Witherington, "Rite and Rights for Women," p. 602, n. 1.

[13]See, for example, Krister Stendahl, *The Bible and the Role of Women* (Philadelphia: Fortress, 1966), pp. 32-33.

[14]Klyne R. Snodgrass, "The Ordination of Women—Thirteen Years Later: Do We Really Value the Ministry of Women?" *Covenant Quarterly* 48, no. 3 (August 1990): 34-35.

[15]For a defense of this procedure, see Stephen D. Lowe, "Rethinking the Female Status/Function Question: The Jew/Gentile Relationship as Paradigm," *Journal of the Evangelical Theological Society* 34, no. 1 (March 1991): 59-61.

[16]Note: the council placed certain restrictions on Gentile converts—that they abstain from sexual immorality and eating blood. Paul enjoined the former on his readers (e.g., 1 Cor 6), for he viewed this as a universally binding moral prohibition. However, there is no evidence that he directed them to follow the latter, which was a purely dietary law.

[17]Lowe, "Rethinking the Female Status/Function Question," p. 65.

[18]Ibid., p. 67.

[19]Ibid., p. 72.

[20]Jewett, *Man as Male and Female*, p. 139.

[21]See Craig S. Keener, *Paul, Women and Wives: Marriage and Women's Ministry in the Letters of Paul* (Peabody, Mass.: Hendrickson, 1992), pp. 206-7.

[22]Harold Mattingly, *The Man in the Roman Street* (New York: W. W. Norton, 1966), p. 131.

[23]On this text see S. Scott Bartchy, *First-Century Slavery and 1 Corinthians 7:21*, SBL Dissertation Series 11 (Missoula, Mont.: Society of Biblical Literature/Seminar on Paul, 1973).

[24]Bruce, *Commentary on Galatians*, pp. 188-89.

[25]Ibid., p. 190.

[26]See A. Oepke, "ἀνήρ," in *Theological Dictionary of the New Testament*, ed. Gerhard Kittel and Gerhard Friedrich, 10 vols. (Grand Rapids, Mich.: Eerdmans, 1964-1976), 1:362.

[27]Bruce, *Commentary on Galatians*, p. 189.

[28]Ronald Y. K. Fung, "Ministry in the New Testament," in *The Church in the Bible and the World*, ed. D. A. Carson (Grand Rapids, Mich.: Baker, 1987), p. 182.

[29]Witherington, "Rite and Rights for Women," p. 595.

[30]Ibid., p. 599.

[31]Ibid., p. 600.

[32]See George W. Knight III, *The New Testament Teaching on the Role Relationship of Men and Women* (Grand Rapids, Mich.: Baker, 1977), pp. 45-46. For a response to Knight, see Keener, *Paul, Women and Wives*, pp. 110-11.

[33]Commentators agree that the Pastoral Epistles were written last. First Corinthians is generally dated during the period of Paul's third missionary journey, sometime between A.D. 55 and 58. Galatians was probably written earlier, perhaps as early as A.D. 48, but clearly by the mid-50s. See, for example, *International Bible Commentary*, ed. F. F. Bruce, rev. ed. (Grand Rapids, Mich.: Zondervan, 1986), p. 1416.

[34]Bruce, *Commentary on Galatians*, p. 190.

35See, for example, Barbara Hall, "Paul and Women," *Theology Today* 31, no. 1 (April 1974): 50-55; William O. Walker Jr., "1 Corinthians 11:2-16 and Paul's Views Regarding Women," *Journal of Biblical Literature* 94, no. 1 (1975): 94-110; Lamar Cope, "1 Cor. 11:2-16: One Step Further," *Journal of Biblical Literature* 97, no. 3 (1978): 435-36; G. W. Trompf, "On Attitudes Toward Women in Paul and Paulinist Literature: 1 Corinthians 11:2-16 and Its Context," *Catholic Biblical Quarterly* 42, no. 2 (1980): 196-215.

36For a succinct rebuttal of the arguments, see Ben Witherington III, *Women in the Earliest Churches* (Cambridge: Cambridge University Press, 1988), pp. 78-79. See also Gordon D. Fee, *The First Epistle to the Corinthians*, New International Commentary on the New Testament (Grand Rapids, Mich.: Eerdmans, 1987), p. 492.

37C. F. D. Moule, *Worship in the New Testament* (London: Lutterworth, 1961), p. 65.

38See, for example, Mary J. Evans, *Woman in the Bible* (Downers Grove, Ill.: InterVarsity Press, 1983), p. 83.

39For the defense of another alternative, see ibid., pp. 94-95.

40Keener, *Paul, Women and Wives*, pp. 28-31, 46-47.

41Thomas R. Schreiner, "Head Coverings, Prophecies and the Trinity: 1 Corinthians 11:2-16," in *Recovering Biblical Manhood and Womanhood*, ed. John Piper and Wayne Grudem (Wheaton, Ill.: Crossway, 1991), pp. 125-26.

42Witherington, *Women in the Earliest Churches*, pp. 82-83.

43See J. Keir Howard, "Neither Male nor Female: An Examination of the Status of Women in the New Testament," *Evangelical Quarterly* 55, no. 1 (January 1983): 34.

44Walter Bauer, *A Greek-English Lexicon of the New Testament and Other Early Christian Literature*, trans. and ed. William F. Arndt and F. Wilbur Gingrich (Chicago: University of Chicago Press, 1957), p. 73.

45David W. J. Gill notes, "Public marble portraits of women at Corinth, presumably members of wealthy and prestigious families, are most frequently shown bare-headed," suggesting that the appearance of women in public bare-headed was socially acceptable. Gill then indicates the circumstances in which women would cover their heads, such as when acting as priestesses ("Importance of Roman Portraiture for Head-Coverings in 1 Corinthians 11:2-16," *Tyndale Bulletin* 41, no. 2 [1990]: 251-56).

46James B. Hurley, *Man and Woman in Biblical Perspective* (Grand Rapids, Mich.: Zondervan, 1981), p. 270.

47Joachim Jeremias, *Jerusalem in the Time of Jesus*, trans. F. H. Cave and C. H. Cave, 3rd ed. (Philadelphia: Fortress, 1969), pp. 359-60.

48Gill, "Importance of Roman Portraiture," pp. 251-56.

49Hurley, *Man and Woman in Biblical Perspective*, p. 269.

50Ibid., pp. 170-71.

51See Alan Padgett, "Paul on Women in the Church: The Contradictions of Coiffure in 1 Corinthians 11.2-16," *Journal for the Study of the New Testament* 20 (1984): 70.

52Evans draws the opposite conclusion from these injunctions, arguing that they would not be necessary if women were to participate in worship with a shawl (*Women in the Bible*, pp. 87-88).

53For a recent restatement of this position, see Kenneth T. Wilson, "Should Women Wear Head Coverings?" *Bibliotheca Sacra* 148, no. 592 (October-December 1991): 442-62.

54Padgett, "Paul on Women in the Church," pp. 76-83; Thomas P. Shoemaker, "Unveiling of Equality: 1 Corinthians 11:2-16," *Biblical Theology Bulletin* 17, no. 2 (April 1987): 61-63.

⁵⁵For this interpretation, see Padgett, "Paul on Women in the Church," pp. 71, 76-83.

⁵⁶Bauer, *Lexicon*, p. 829.

⁵⁷Padgett, "Paul on Women in the Church," p. 83. Other scholars who have taken note of this apparent mistranslation, however, find different implications in Paul's comment. The "unusual practice" may have been the views of those Corinthians who held that women must wear both long hair and a veil (Hurley, *Man and Woman in Biblical Perspective*, p. 179), or again, the insistence that women pray and prophesy without a head covering (Witherington, *Women in the Earliest Churches*, p. 90).

⁵⁸Howard, "Neither Male nor Female," p. 35. Howard argues that Paul's strictures are equally directed toward Corinthian men. But scholars differ as to which problem the apostle saw in men's demeanor. Howard, for example, declares, "The men of Corinth are roundly condemned for having their hair dressed in such elaborate fashions that were generally associated with homosexuality." Gill, in contrast, sees the problem as that of wearing a Roman toga partly covering the head, which he claims set them apart as members of the socially elite and thereby caused divisions in the church ("Importance of Roman Portraiture," pp. 246-51.

⁵⁹J. Murphy-O'Connor, *1 Corinthians* (Wilmington, Del.: Michael Glazier, 1979), pp. 104-9. See also J. Murphy-O'Connor, "The Non-Pauline Character of 1 Corinthians 11:2-16," *Journal of Biblical Literature* 95 (December 1976): 615-21; "Sex and Logic in 1 Corinthians 11:2-16," *Catholic Biblical Quarterly* 42 (October 1980): 482-500. See also Howard, "Neither Male nor Female," p. 36.

⁶⁰Elisabeth Schüssler Fiorenza, *In Memory of Her* (New York: Crossroad, 1983), p. 227.

⁶¹Gail Paterson Corrington, "The 'Headless Woman': Paul and the Language of the Body in 1 Cor 11:2-16," *Perspectives in Religious Studies* 18, no. 3 (Fall 1991): 228.

⁶²Ross S. Kraemer, "Ecstasy and Possession: The Attraction of Women to the Cult of Dionysus," *Harvard Theological Review* 72 (January-April 1979): 55-80.

⁶³Eva Cantarella, *Pandora's Daughters: The Role and Status of Women in Greek and Roman Antiquity*, trans. Maureen B. Fant (Baltimore, Md.: Johns Hopkins University Press, 1967), p. 127.

⁶⁴Contemporary defenders of the traditional view include Wayne Grudem, "Does *Kephalē* ('Head') Mean 'Source' or 'Authority Over' in Greek Literature? A Survey of 2,336 Examples," *Trinity Journal* 6, n.s. (Spring 1985): 38-59; Joseph A. Fitzmyer, "Another Look at *Kephalē* in 1 Corinthians 11.3," *New Testament Studies* 35, no. 4 (1989): 503-11; Wayne Grudem, "The Meaning of *Kephalē* ('Head'): A Response to Recent Studies," *Trinity Journal* 11, n.s. (Spring 1990): 3-72.

⁶⁵Steven Bedale, "The Meaning of *Kephalē* in the Pauline Epistles," *Journal of Theological Studies* 5, n.s. (1954): 211-15.

⁶⁶Berkeley Mickelsen and Alvera Mickelsen, "The 'Head' of the Epistles," *Christianity Today* 25, no. 4 (February 20, 1981): 20-23 [264-67]; Evans, *Woman in the Bible*, pp. 66-67; Berkeley Mickelsen and Alvera Mickelsen, "What Does *Kephalē* Mean in the New Testament?" in *Women, Authority and the Bible*, ed. Alvera Mickelsen (Downers Grove, Ill.: InterVarsity Press, 1986): 97-110; Catherine Clark Kroeger, "Appendix 3: The Classical Concept of Head as 'Source,' " in *Equal to Serve: Women and Men in the Church and Home*, ed. Gretchen Gaebelein Hull (Old Tappan, N.J.: Revell, 1987), pp. 267-83; Alvera Mickelsen, "An Egalitarian View: There Is Neither Male nor Female in Christ," in *Women in Ministry: Four Views*, ed. Bonnidell Clouse and Robert G. Clouse (Downers Grove, Ill.: InterVarsity Press, 1989), pp. 192-98; Witherington, *Women in the Earliest Churches*, pp. 84-85.

[67]See, for example, Richard S. Cervin, "Does *Kephalē* Mean 'Source' or 'Authority Over' in Greek Literature? A Rebuttal," in *Trinity Journal* 10, n.s. (Spring 1989): 85-112.

[68]For this, as well as a short summary of the debate, see Keener, *Paul, Women and Wives,* pp. 33-34.

[69]George W. Knight III, "Male and Female Related He Them," *Christianity Today* 20, no. 14 (April 9, 1976), p. 709; Fred L. Fisher, *1 & 2 Corinthians* (Waco, Tex.: Word, 1975), p. 176.

[70]Evans, *Woman in the Bible,* p. 89. We will look at the question of the intent of the Genesis creation narratives in the next chapter.

[71]Ibid., p. 90.

[72]Keener, *Paul, Women and Wives,* p. 37.

[73]Morna D. Hooker, "Authority on Her Head: An Examination of 1 Corinthians 11:10," *New Testament Studies* 10 (1963-1964): 410-16; C. K. Barrett, *A Commentary on the First Epistle to the Corinthians* (London: A. & C. Black, 1968), p. 250; F. F. Bruce, *1 & 2 Corinthians,* New Century Bible (Greenwood, S.C.: Attic, 1971), p. 106; Fiorenza, *In Memory of Her,* p. 230; Witherington, *Women in the Earliest Churches,* pp. 87-88.

[74]See, for example, James B. Hurley, "Did Paul Require Veils or the Silence of Women?" *Westminister Theological Journal* 35 (Winter 1973): 206-12.

[75]Hence Thomas P. Shoemaker, "Unveiling of Equality: 1 Corinthians 11:2-16," *Biblical Theology Bulletin* 17, no. 2 (April 1987): 61.

[76]Kenneth T. Wilson, "Should Women Wear Head Coverings?" *Bibliotheca Sacra* 48, no. 592 (October-December 1991): 453.

[77]Fee, *First Epistle to the Corinthians,* pp. 520-21.

[78]Fiorenza, *In Memory of Her,* p. 229. She appeals to the exegesis of Josef Kürzinger, "Frau und Mann nach 1 Kor 11,11ff," *Biblische Zeitschrift* 22, no. 2 (1978): 270-75.

[79]Kroeger, "Appendix 3: The Classical Concept of Head as 'Source,' " pp. 282-83. See also Gilbert G. Bilezikian, *Beyond Sex Roles: A Guide for the Study of Female Roles in the Bible* (Grand Rapids, Mich.: Baker, 1985), p. 241; Richard C. Kroeger and Catherine Clark Kroeger, "Subordinationism," in *Evangelical Dictionary of Theology,* ed. Walter A. Elwell (Grand Rapids, Mich.: Baker, 1985), p. 1058.

[80]See, for example, Schreiner, "Head Coverings," pp. 128-29.

[81]Even many complementarians are willing to forgo the ancient symbol. See, for example, Hurley, *Man and Woman in Biblical Perspective,* pp. 181-84; Wilson, "Should Women Wear Headcoverings?" pp. 454, 460-62.

[82]See, for example, Schreiner, "Head Coverings," pp. 126-27.

[83]Ibid., p. 132. See also Grant R. Osborne, "Hermeneutics and Women in the Church," *Journal of the Evangelical Theological Society* 20, no. 4 (December 1977): 337-52.

[84]Hurley, for example, declares that although Paul's discussion "reflects primarily upon the situation of a married couple . . . it also affects the generic situation of women in worship" (*Man and Woman in Biblical Perspective,* p. 181).

[85]Fung, "Ministry in the New Testament," p. 186.

[86]Jeremias, *Jerusalem in the Time of Jesus,* pp. 359-60.

[87]See Fung, "Ministry in the New Testament," pp. 187-88.

[88]Fiorenza, *In Memory of Her,* p. 230.

[89]Alan Padgett, "Feminism in First Corinthians: A Dialogue with Elisabeth Schüssler Fiorenza," *Evangelical Quarterly* 58, no. 2 (April 1986): 129.

[90]For an argument in favor of this understanding, see Charles Talbert, *Reading Corinthians:*

A Literary and Theological Commentary on 1 & 2 Corinthians (New York: Crossroad, 1987), p. 91. For a response, see Witherington, *Women in the Earliest Churches*, pp. 96-97.

[91]Hurley, *Man and Woman in Biblical Perspective*, p. 193.

[92]Fee, *First Epistle to the Corinthians*, pp. 699-708. See also C. K. Barrett, *A Commentary on the First Epistle to the Corinthians* (New York: Harper & Row, 1968), pp. 330-33; Hans Conzelmann, *1 Corinthians*, trans. J. W. Leitch (Philadelphia: Fortress, 1975), p. 246; Jerome Murphy-O'Connor, *1 Corinthians* (Wilmington, Del.: Michael Glazier, 1979), p. 133; Eduard Schweizer, "The Service of Worship: An Exposition of 1 Cor. 14," *Interpretation* 13, no. 3 (July 1959): 402-3. For a response to Fee, see D. A. Carson, " 'Silent in the Churches': On the Role of Women in 1 Corinthians 14:33b-36," in *Recovering Biblical Manhood and Womanhood*, pp. 141-45.

[93]Bilezikian, *Beyond Sex Roles*, pp. 286-88; Evans, *Women in the Bible*, pp. 99-100; David W. Odell-Scott, "Let the Women Speak in Church: An Egalitarian Interpretation of 1 Cor 14:33b-36," *Biblical Theology Bulletin* 13, no. 3 (July 1983): 90-93; David W. Odell-Scott, "In Defense of an Egalitarian Interpretation of 1 Cor 14:34-36: A Reply to Murphy-O'Connor's Critique," *Biblical Theology Bulletin* 17, no. 3 (July 1987); 100-103; N. M. Flanagan and E. H. Snyder, "Did Paul Put Down Women in 1 Cor. 14:34-36?" *Biblical Theology Bulletin* 11 (January 1981): 10-12. For a rebuttal, see Carson, "Silent in the Churches," pp. 147-51; Keener, *Paul, Women and Wives*, pp. 75-76; Witherington, *Women in the Earliest Churches*, pp. 98-99.

[94]For an evangelical scholar who holds to this position, see Howard, "Neither Male nor Female," pp. 37-38.

[95]Padgett, "Feminism in First Corinthians," p. 132.

[96]See, for example, Witherington, *Women in the Earliest Churches*, p. 92.

[97]See, for example, Virginia Mollenkott, *Women, Men and the Bible* (Nashville: Abingdon, 1977), p. 96.

[98]Fung, "Ministry in the New Testament," p. 192.

[99]Heikki Räisänen, *Paul and the Law* (Philadelphia: Fortress, 1983), p. 16.

[100]Bauer, *Lexicon*, 542.

[101]Richard C. Kroeger and Catherine Clark Kroeger, "Pandemonium and Silence at Corinth," in *Women and the Ministries of Christ*, ed. Roberta Hestenes and Lois Curley (Pasadena, Calif.: Fuller Theological Seminary, 1979), pp. 51-52.

[102]Fung, "Ministry in the New Testament," p. 192.

[103]Susan T. Foh, *Women and the Word of God* (Phillipsburg, N.J.: Presbyterian and Reformed, 1979), p. 118; J. Paul Sampley, *And the Two Shall Become One Flesh* (Cambridge: Cambridge University Press, 1971), p. 99.

[104]D. A. Carson, *Exegetical Fallacies* (Grand Rapids, Mich.: Baker, 1984), pp. 39-40.

[105]George W. Knight III, *The Role Relationship of Men and Women*, rev. ed. (Chicago: Moody Press, 1985), pp. 25, 45. See also Bruce, *1 & 2 Corinthians*, p. 136.

[106]Even several complementarians agree with this conclusion. See, for example, Fung, "Ministry in the New Testament," p. 192; James I. Packer, "Postscript: I Believe in Women's Ministry," in *Why Not? Priesthood and the Ministry of Women*, ed. Michael Bruce and G. E. Duffield, rev. and aug. R. T. Beckwith (Appleford, U.K.: Marcham Books, 1976), p. 171; Stephen B. Clark, *Man and Woman in Christ* (Ann Arbor, Mich.: Servant, 1980), p. 187.

[107]Hurley, *Man and Woman in Biblical Perspective*, p. 192.

[108]Witherington, *Women in the Earliest Churches*, pp. 102-3.

[109]Ibid.

[110]For summaries of the major interpretations, see J. W. MacGorman, "Glossolalic Error and Its Correction: 1 Corinthians 12-14," *Review and Expositor* 80 (Summer 1983): 399. See also Fung, "Ministry in the New Testament," pp. 193-95.

[111]Fung, "Ministry in the New Testament," p. 191.

[112]See, for example, F. W. Grosheide, *The First Epistle to the Corinthians* (Grand Rapids, Mich.: Eerdmans, 1953), p. 342.

[113]For examples see Alvin John Schmidt, *Veiled and Silenced: How Culture Shaped Sexist Theology* (Macon, Ga.: Mercer University Press, 1989), pp. 149-61.

[114]Luther, for example, allowed women to sing. Nevertheless, Calvin may have been "the only reformer to place Paul's advice for women to be silent in the church among the indifferent things in which the Christian is free" (Jane Dempsey Douglas, "Christian Freedom: What Calvin Learned at the School of Women," *Church History* 53, no. 2 [June 1984]: 155).

[115]Schmidt, *Veiled and Silenced*, p. 154, quoting from *Lutheran Witness*, January 21, 1900, p. 126.

[116]In fact, Missouri Synod Lutherans did not lift the ban until 1969 (Schmidt, *Veiled and Silenced*, pp. 160-61).

[117]Evans, *Woman in the Bible*, pp. 96-97.

[118]For a helpful summary and succinct evaluation of the major proposals written by a complementarian, see Fung, "Ministry in the New Testament," pp. 195-97. See also Hurley, *Man and Woman in Biblical Perspective*, pp. 185-88.

[119]Charles Caldwell Ryrie, *The Role of Women in the Church* (Chicago: Moody Press, 1958), pp. 76-78.

[120]Herman Ridderbos, *Paul: An Outline of His Ministry*, trans. John Richard DeWitt (Grand Rapids, Mich.: Eerdmans, 1975), p. 462; Gerald L. Almlie, "Women's Church and Communion Participation," *Christian Brethren Review* 33 (1982): 44.

[121]Jean Héring, *The First Epistle of St. Paul to the Corinthians*, trans. A. W. Heathcote and P. J. Allcock (London: Epworth, 1962), p. 154; Peter Richardson, *Paul's Ethic of Freedom* (Philadelphia: Westminster Press, 1979), p. 157. See also Heinrich Schlier, "κεφαλή κτλ," in *Theological Dictionary of the New Testament*, ed. Gerhard Kittel, trans. Geoffrey W. Bromiley, 10 vols. (Grand Rapids, Mich.: Eerdmans, 1964-1976), 3:680.

[122]Fisher, *1 & 2 Corinthians*, p. 231.

[123]On this possibility see Héring, *First Epistle of St. Paul to the Corinthians*, p. 154.

[124]W. J. Dumbrell, "The Role of Women: A Reconsideration of the Biblical Evidence," *Interchange* 21 (1977): 14-22; Fung, "Ministry in the New Testament," p. 194; Wayne Grudem, *The Gift of Prophecy in 1 Corinthians* (Washington, D.C.: University Press of America, 1982), pp. 245-55; Hurley, *Man and Woman in Biblical Perspective*, pp. 188-93; M. E. Thrall, *I and II Corinthians* (Cambridge: Cambridge University Press, 1965), p. 102.

[125]Keener, *Paul, Women and Wives*, p. 79.

[126]Fung, "Ministry in the New Testament," p. 197. Fortunately, Fung returns to this question later in the essay.

[127]Carson, "Silent in the Churches," pp. 151-52.

[128]Knight, *New Testament Teaching*, pp. 33-34.

[129]Keener, *Paul, Women and Wives*, pp. 79-80.

[130]Witherington, *Women in the Earliest Churches*, pp. 92-96.

[131]E. Earle Ellis, "The Silenced Wives of Corinth (1 Cor. 14.34-35)," in *New Testament*

Textual Criticism: Its Significance for Exegesis, ed. E. J. Epp and Gordon D. Fee (New York: Oxford University Press, 1981), p. 218; Evans, *Woman in the Bible,* pp. 99-100, 107.

[132]Evans, *Woman in the Bible,* p. 100.

[133]David Hill, *New Testament Prophecy* (Atlanta: John Knox, 1979), pp. 134-35. See also Clark, *Man and Woman in Christ,* p. 184; H. H. Esser, *"nomos,"* in *New International Dictionary of New Testament Theology,* ed. Colin Brown (Grand Rapids, Mich.: Zondervan, 1976), 2:446.

[134]Ralph P. Martin, *The Spirit and the Congregation* (Grand Rapids, Mich.: Eerdmans, 1984), p. 84.

[135]Letha Scanzoni and Nancy Hardesty, *All We're Meant to Be* (Waco, Tex.: Word, 1974), pp. 68-69.

[136]Keener, *Paul, Women and Wives,* p. 70.

[137]Howard, "Neither Male nor Female," p. 38.

[138]Keener, *Paul, Women and Wives,* p. 81.

[139]J. D. G. Dunn, *Jesus and the Spirit* (Philadelphia: Westminster Press, 1975), p. 435 n. 115; J. D. G. Dunn, *Unity and Diversity in the New Testament,* 2nd ed. (London: SCM Press, 1990), p. 10.

[140]Wither, *Women in the Earliest Churches,* p. 103.

[141]Roger L. Omanson, "The Role of Women in the New Testament Church," *Review and Expositor* 83, no. 1 (Winter 1986): 21.

[142]Keener, *Paul, Women and Wives,* pp. 81-85.

[143]Padgett, "Feminism in First Corinthians," p. 131.

[144]Keener, *Paul, Women and Wives,* p. 72.

[145]Witherington, *Women in the Earliest Churches,* p. 104.

[146]Howard, "Neither Male nor Female," p. 39.

[147]Evans, *Woman in the Bible,* p. 107.

[148]See Gordon D. Fee, *1 & 2 Timothy, Titus,* New International Biblical Commentary (Peabody, Mass.: Hendrickson, 1988), pp. 5-14.

[149]Ann L. Bowman, "Women in Ministry: An Exegetical Study of 1 Timothy 2:11-15," *Bibliotheca Sacra* 149, no. 594 (April-June 1992): 195.

[150]See ibid., p. 194.

[151]Hurley, *Man and Woman in Biblical Perspective,* p. 202.

[152]Philip B. Payne, "Libertarian Women in Ephesus: A Response to Douglas J. Moo's Article '1 Timothy 2:11-15: Meaning and Significance,'" *Trinity Journal* n.s. 2 (Fall 1981): 183.

[153]Aída Besançon Spencer, *Beyond the Curse: Women Called to Ministry* (Peabody, Mass.: Hendrickson, 1985), p. 84.

[154]Mickelsen, "Egalitarian View," pp. 201-2.

[155]J. N. D. Kelly, *The Pastoral Epistles,* Harper's New Testament Commentaries (San Francisco: Harper & Row, 1960), p. 12; A. T. Hanson, *The Pastoral Epistles,* New Century Bible Commentary (Grand Rapids, Mich.: Eerdmans, 1982), p. 25.

[156]See Payne, "Libertarian Women," p. 185.

[157]Spencer, *Beyond the Curse,* p. 81.

[158]Snodgrass, "Ordination of Women," p. 38.

[159]Mickelsen, "Egalitarian View," p. 200. See also Evans, *Woman in the Bible,* p. 101; Martin Dibelius and Hans Conzelmann, *The Pastoral Epistles,* trans. Philip Buttolph and Adela Yarbro (Philadelphia: Fortress, 1972), pp. 44-46; Donald Guthrie, *The Pastoral Epistles*

(Grand Rapids, Mich.: Eerdmans, 1990), pp. 84-85.

[160]Evans, *Woman in the Bible*, p. 101.

[161]K. H. Rengstorf, "μανθάνω κτλ.," in *Theological Dictionary of the New Testament*, ed. Gerhard Kittel and Gerhard Friedrich, trans. Geoffrey W. Bromiley, 10 vols. (Grand Rapids, Mich.: Eerdmans, 1964-1976), 4:410.

[162]G. Abbott-Smith, *A Manual Greek Lexicon of the New Testament*, 3rd ed. (Edinburgh: T & T Clark, 1937), p. 277. See also Bauer, *Greek-English Lexicon*, p. 491.

[163]Spencer, *Beyond the Curse*, p. 74.

[164]For examples from the rabbinical writings, see ibid., pp. 77-80.

[165]Ibid., p. 77.

[166]For example, Douglas Moo, "What Does It Mean Not to Teach or Have Authority over Men? 1 Timothy 2:11-15," in *Recovering Biblical Manhood and Womanhood*, ed. John Piper and Wayne Grudem (Wheaton, Ill.: Crossway, 1991), p. 183.

[167]Howard, "Neither Male Nor Female," p. 40.

[168]Of course the orthodox teachers in the congregation may be men (Dibelius and Conzelmann, *Pastoral Epistles*, p. 47).

[169]Gloria Neufeld Redekop, "Let the Women Learn: 1 Timothy 2:8-15 Reconsidered," *Studies in Religion* 19, no. 2 (1990): 241-42; Walter Lock, *A Critical and Exegetical Commentary on the Pastoral Epistles* (Edinburgh: T & T Clark, 1924), p. 32.

[170]For example, Fung and Spencer argue for two prohibitions, whereas the Kroegers and Moo agree that Paul intended only one prohibition.

[171]See, for example, Catherine Clark Kroeger and Richard C. Kroeger, *I Suffer Not a Woman: Rethinking 1 Timothy 2:11-15 in Light of Ancient Evidence* (Grand Rapids, Mich.: Baker, 1992), pp. 83-84.

[172]For a succinct summary of the arguments favoring this interpretation, see Fung, "Ministry in the New Testament," pp. 198-99.

[173]Spencer, *Beyond the Curse*, p. 87.

[174]Payne, "Libertarian Women," p. 175.

[175]Moo, "What Does It Mean," p. 197 n. 16.

[176]Kroeger and Kroeger, *I Suffer Not a Woman*, p. 80.

[177]Roy B. Zuck, "Greek Words for Teach," *Bibliotheca Sacra* 122 (April-June 1965): 159-60.

[178]Moo, "What Does It Mean," p. 185.

[179]Timothy J. Harris, "Why Did Paul Mention Eve's Deception? A Critique of P. W. Barnett's Interpretation of 1 Timothy 2," *Evangelical Quarterly* 62, no. 4 (1990): 341.

[180]Payne, "Libertarian Women," pp. 172-73. See also John Toews, "Women in Church Leadership: 1 Timothy 2:11-15, a Reconsideration," in *The Bible and the Church: Essays in Honor of Dr. David Ewert*, ed. A. J. Dueck, H. J. Giesbrecht and V. G. Shillington (Hillsboro, Kans.: Kindred, 1983), p. 84.

[181]For one possible counterexample, see Kroeger and Kroeger, *I Suffer Not a Woman*, p. 226 n. 6.

[182]John Piper, "The Order of Creation," *The Standard*, April 1984, p. 38.

[183]N. J. Hommes, "Let Women Be Silent in the Church," *Calvin Theological Journal* 4, no. 1 (1969): 10.

[184]Bruce Barron, "Putting Women in Their Place: 1 Timothy 2 and Evangelical Views of Women in Church Leadership," *Journal of the Evangelical Theological Society* 33, no. 4 (December 1990): 456. Although plausible, this suggestion is not likely. Paul did call individuals to sacrifice their rights for the sake of the gospel reputation, in order to

silence slanderous accusations from the opponents of the faith. But this would be the only case in which he diminished the role of a specific group as a way of combating erroneous understandings within the church.

185See, for example, David L. Balch, *Let Wives Be Submissive: The Domestic Code in 1 Peter* (Chico, Calif.: Scholars Press, 1981), pp. 65-76. For information about the cultural restriction of women, see also David C. Verner, *The Household of God: The Social World of the Pastoral Epistles* (Chico, Calif.: Scholars Press, 1983).

186For a discussion of the larger context of concern for church order and the reputation of the gospel, see Peter Lippert, *Leben als Zeugnis* (Stuttgart: Katholisches Bibelwerk, 1968), pp. 17-87.

187For a discussion of this problem, see James G. Sigountos and Myron Shank, "Public Roles for Women in the Pauline Church: A Reappraisal of the Evidence," *Journal of the Evangelical Theological Society* 26, no. 3 (September 1983): 283-95.

188This view suffers under the same liability as the previous suggestion. It would mark the only occasion in which Paul diminished the role of a specific group as a way of combating difficulties within the church.

189For examples of scholars who hold this position, see Keener, *Paul, Women and Wives*, p. 127 n. 82.

190Alan Padgett, "Wealthy Women at Ephesus: 1 Timothy 2:8-15 in Social Context," *Interpretation* 41, no. 1 (January 1987): 25.

191Spencer, *Beyond the Curse*, p. 84.

192For a discussion of the range of meanings it could carry, see Kroeger and Kroeger, *I Suffer Not a Woman*, pp. 84-104.

193Ibid., p. 103; see also pp. 99-113.

194This supposition finds support from the lexicons. See, for example, H. G. Liddell and R. Scott, *A Greek-English Lexicon* (Oxford: Clarendon, 1841, 1992), p. 275; Joseph Henry Thayer, *A Greek-English Lexicon of the New Testament*, rev. ed. (orig. 1889; Wheaton, Ill.: Evangel, 1974), p. 84. For the resultant idea of "domineer," see Bauer, *Greek-English Lexicon*, p. 121.

195Hommes, "Let Women Be Silent," p. 19.

196Witherington, *Women in the Earliest Churches*, pp. 121-22.

197George W. Knight III, "*Authenteō* in Reference to Women in 1 Timothy 2.12," *New Testament Studies* 30, no. 1 (January 1984): 143-57. See also Douglas J. Moo, "1 Timothy 2:11-15: Meaning and Significance," *Trinity Journal* 1, n.s., no. 1 (1980): 66-67.

Knight's conclusion, however, is challenged by Leland E. Wilshire, "The TLG Computer and Further Reference to *Authenteō* in 1 Timothy 2:12," *New Testament Studies* 34, no. 1 (1988): 120-34. He writes, "The 314 literary citations of the TLG Computer . . . may be of help in understanding the meaning of 1 Tim. 2:12. Sometime during the spread of koinē, the word *authenteō* went beyond the predominant Attic meaning connecting it with murder and suicide and into the broader concept of criminal behavior. It also began to take on the additional meanings of 'to exercise authority/power/rights' which became firmly established in the Greek Patristic writers to mean 'to exercise authority.' " However, Wilshire disagrees with Knight's conclusion that "the recognized meaning of the word in the first century B.C. and A.D. documents would remain, and that the recognized meaning is 'to have authority over.' " See Leland E. Wilshire, "1 Timothy 2:12 Revisited: A Reply to Paul W. Barnett and Timothy J. Harris," *Evangelical Quarterly* 65, no. 1 (1993): 44.

In an address to a conference on "Women, Abuse and the Bible" (April 1994) sponsored by Christians for Biblical Equality, David Scholer argues that Wilshire's data actually militates against Knight's position.

[198]Andrew C. Perriman, "What Eve Did, What Women Shouldn't Do: The Meaning of *Authenteō* in 1 Timothy 2:12," *Tyndale Bulletin* 44, no. 1 (1993): 138.

[199]Harris, "Why Did Paul Mention Eve's Deception?" p. 342.

[200]Wilshire, "1 Timothy 2:12 Revisited," p. 48.

[201]Perriman, "What Eve Did," p. 141.

[202]Spencer, *Beyond the Curse*, p. 88.

[203]Perriman, "What Eve Did," p. 142.

[204]Kroeger and Kroeger, *I Suffer Not a Woman*, pp. 117-70.

[205]Ibid., p. 151.

[206]Ibid., p. 125.

[207]John Piper and Wayne Grudem, "An Overview of Central Concerns: Questions and Answers," in *Recovering Biblical Manhood and Womanhood: A Response to Evangelical Feminism*, ed. John Piper and Wayne Grudem (Wheaton, Ill.: Crossway, 1991), p. 82.

[208]Hurley, *Man and Woman in Biblical Perspective*, p. 203.

[209]See, for example, Walter C. Kaiser Jr., *Toward an Exegetical Theology: Biblical Exegesis for Preaching and Teaching* (Grand Rapids, Mich.: Baker, 1981), pp. 119-20; David M. Scholer, "1 Timothy 2:9-15 and the Place of Women in the Church's Ministry," in *Women, Authority and the Bible*, ed. Alvera Mickelsen (Downers Grove, Ill.: InterVarsity Press, 1986), p. 208.

[210]Payne, "Libertarian Women," p. 176.

[211]Moo, "What Does It Mean," p. 190.

[212]See, for example, Hurley, *Man and Woman in Biblical Perspective*, pp. 207-8.

[213]Ibid., p. 209.

[214]E. Margaret Howe, *Woman and Church Leadership* (Grand Rapids, Mich.: Zondervan, 1982), p. 47.

[215]Kelly, *Pastoral Epistles*, p. 68. See also Moo, "1 Timothy 2:11-15," p. 70.

[216]Alan M. Stibbs, "1 Timothy," in *New Bible Commentary*, ed. F. Davidson, A. M. Stibbs and E. F. Kevan, 2nd ed. (London: Inter-Varsity Press, 1954), p. 1068; and in *New Bible Commentary*, rev. ed., ed. Donald Guthrie and J. A. Motyer (London: Inter-Varsity Press, 1970), p. 1171.

[217]See, for example, Fung, "Ministry in the New Testament," pp. 201-2.

[218]Evans, *Woman in the Bible*.

[219]Hurley, *Man and Woman in Biblical Perspective*, p. 216.

[220]Mickelsen, "Egalitarian View," p. 203.

[221]Padgett, "Wealthy Women at Ephesus," pp. 26-27.

[222]Harris, "Why Did Paul Mention Eve's Deception?" p. 349. See also Scholer, "1 Timothy 2:9-15 and the Place of Women," p. 211.

[223]Spencer, *Beyond the Curse*, p. 91; see also Perriman, "What Eve Did," p. 139.

[224]Keener, *Paul, Women and Wives*, p. 116.

[225]See Stanley J. Grenz, *Sexual Ethics* (Dallas: Word, 1990), pp. 29-30.

[226]For a summary and representative adherents of each position, see Fung, "Ministry in the New Testament," pp. 203-4.

[227]Ibid., p. 203.

[228]Hanson, *Pastoral Epistles*, p. 74.

229Bowman, "Women in Ministry," p. 212. Some egalitarians share the basic understanding that "childbearing" represents the specifically female role in reproduction or refers to a woman's role, while disagreeing with the complementarian conclusion that male headship is in view here. For an example of a more speculative egalitarian interpretation, see Mark D. Roberts, "Woman Shall Be Saved: A Closer Look at 1 Timothy 2:15," *TSF Bulletin* 5, no. 2 (November-December 1981): 4-7.

230Paul W. Barnett, "Wives and Women's Ministry (1 Timothy 2:11-15)," *Evangelical Review of Theology* 15, no. 4 (January 1991): 332.

231For a variation of this ancient idea, see Padgett, "Wealthy Women at Ephesus," pp. 28-30.

232For a recent defense of this view, see Keener, *Paul, Women and Wives*, pp. 118-20.

233Witherington, *Women in the Earliest Churches*, pp. 123-24.

234Stanley E. Porter, "What Does It Mean to Be 'Saved by Childbirth' (1 Timothy 2.15)?" *Journal for the Study of the New Testament* 49 (March 1993): 101. See also David R. Kimberley, "1 Tim. 2:15: A Possible Understanding of a Difficult Text," *Journal of the Evangelical Theological Society* 35, no. 4 (December 1992): 481-86.

235Kroeger and Kroeger, *I Suffer Not a Woman*, p. 176.

236For a similar idea, see Keener, *Paul, Women and Wives*, p. 117.

237Spencer, *Beyond the Curse*, p. 95.

238James I. Packer, "Understanding the Differences," in *Women, Authority and the Bible*, ed. Alvera Mickelsen (Downers Grove, Ill.: InterVarsity Press, 1986), p. 296.

239James I. Packer, "Let's Stop Making Women Presbyters," *Christianity Today* 35, no. 2 (February 11, 1991): 20.

240Hence Keener, *Paul, Women and Wives*, p. 113.

241Sigountos and Shank, "Public Roles for Women," p. 294.

Chapter 5: Women in Creation

1Paul K. Jewett, "Why I Favor the Ordination of Women," *Christianity Today* 19, no. 18 (June 6, 1975): 7 [873].

2For a helpful discussion of the significance of the dominance of paternal rather than maternal metaphors to speak of the nature of God, see Samuel L. Terrien, *Till the Heart Sings* (Philadelphia: Fortress, 1985), pp. 59-70.

3The basically masculine orientation of the trinitarian actions is noted by Urban T. Holmes, "The Sexuality of God," in *Male and Female: Christian Approaches to Sexuality*, ed. Ruth Tiffany Barnhouse and Urban T. Holmes III (New York: Seabury, 1976), pp. 264-65.

4C. S. Lewis, "Priestesses in the Church?" in *God in the Dock*, ed. Walter Hooper (Grand Rapids, Mich.: Eerdmans, 1970), p. 236.

5See David Walker, "Are Opponents of Women Priests Sexists?" *Churchman* 105, no. 4 (1991): 329.

6Phyllis Trible, "Depatriarchalizing in Biblical Interpretation," *Journal of the American Academy of Religion* 41 (March 1973): 31. Conclusions similar to Trible's are often cited by evangelical feminists. See, for example, Mary J. Evans, *Woman in the Bible* (Downers Grove, Ill.: InterVarsity Press, 1983), p. 21.

7The significance of the Hebrew assertion of the celibacy of God in contrast to the outlook of the surrounding religions is put forth by Joseph Blenkinsop, *Sexuality and the Christian Tradition* (Dayton, Ohio: Pflaum, 1969), pp. 24-27. See also Tikva Frymer-

Kensky, "Law and Philosophy: The Case of Sex in the Bible," *Semeia* 45 (1989): 90-91. Nevertheless, the situation may not have been so simple, as is argued by Mark S. Smith, "God Male and Female in the Old Testament: Yahweh and His 'Asherah,' " *Theological Studies* 48 (June 1987): 333-40.

[8]Pamela J. Scalise, "Women in Ministry: Reclaiming Our Old Testament Heritage," *Review and Expositor* 83, no. 1 (Winter 1986): 8.

[9]Gretchen Gaebelein Hull, *Equal to Serve* (Old Tappan, N.J.: Revell, 1987), p. 221.

[10]Stephen C. Barton, "Impatient for Justice: Five Reasons Why the Church of England Should Ordain Women to the Priesthood," *Theology* 92, no. 749 (September 1989): 404.

[11]Jewett, "Why I Favor the Ordination of Women," p. 10 [876].

[12]Ibid.

[13]Barton, "Impatient for Justice," p. 404.

[14]Madeleine Boucher, "Ecumenical Documents: Authority in Community," *Midstream* 21, no. 3 (July 1982): 409.

[15]Sara Butler, "Forum: Some Second Thoughts on Ordaining Women," *Worship* 63, no. 2 (March 1989): 160.

[16]See, for example, Elizabeth Achtemeier, "Exchanging God for 'No Gods': A Discussion of Feminist Language for God," in *Speaking the Christian God*, ed. Alvin F. Kimel Jr. (Grand Rapids, Mich.: Eerdmans, 1992), pp. 1-16.

[17]One feminine motif is foreign to the Bible, however. In contrast to masculine metaphors that speak of Yahweh as husband to Israel, the authors of Scripture never use imagery of God as wife.

[18]Terrien, *Till the Heart Sings*, p. 57.

[19]The feminine images of the divine have been the subject of several studies. For a short summary of these images, see Aída Besançon Spencer, *Beyond the Curse: Women Called to Ministry* (Peabody, Mass.: Hendrickson, 1985), pp. 122-31.

[20]Hannah Whitall Smith, *The God of All Comfort* (Chicago: Moody Press, 1956), p. 69.

[21]Spencer, *Beyond the Curse*, p. 122.

[22]S. M. Hutchens, "God, Gender and the Pastoral Office," *Touchstone* 15, no. 4 (Fall 1992): 15.

[23]Thomas R. Schreiner, "Head Coverings, Prophecies and the Trinity: 1 Corinthians 11:2-16," in *Recovering Biblical Manhood and Womanhood: A Response to Evangelical Feminism*, ed. John Piper and Wayne Grudem (Wheaton, Ill.: Crossway, 1991), p. 128.

[24]Erroll Hulse, "The Man-Woman Controversy," *Reformation Today* 119 (January-February 1991): 20.

[25]Richard N. Longenecker, "Authority, Hierarchy and Leadership Patterns in the Bible," in *Women, Authority and the Bible*, ed. Alvera Mickelsen (Downers Grove, Ill.: InterVarsity Press, 1986), p. 76.

[26]Jürgen Moltmann, *Trinity and the Kingdom* (San Francisco: Harper & Row, 1981), pp. 68-69.

[27]See, for example, Bernard Cooke, "Non-patriarchal Salvation," *Horizons* 10, no. 1 (1983): 22-31.

[28]Wolfhart Pannenberg is an important contemporary proponent of this idea. For a summary statement of his position, see Stanley J. Grenz, *Reason for Hope: The Systematic Theology of Wolfhart Pannenberg* (New York: Oxford University Press, 1990), p. 50.

[29]See, for example, Robert W. Jenson, *The Triune Identity: God According to the Gospel* (Philadelphia: Fortress, 1982), pp. 143-44.

[30]See Geoffrey R. Lilburne, "Christology: In Dialogue with Feminism," *Horizons* 11, no. 1 (Spring 1984): 22.

[31]Robert L. Saucy, "The Negative Case Against the Ordination of Women," in *Perspectives on Evangelical Theology: Papers from the Thirtieth Annual Meeting of the Evangelical Theological Society,* ed. Kenneth S. Kantzer and Stanley N. Gundry (Grand Rapids, Mich.: Baker, 1979), pp. 279-80.

[32]For an example of this position's receiving official sanction in a church body, see Samuel H. Nafzger, "The Doctrinal Position of the LCMS on the Service of Women in the Church," *Concordia Journal* 18, no. 2 (April 1992): 125-29.

[33]Alvera Mickelsen, "An Egalitarian View: There Is Neither Male nor Female in Christ," in *Women in Ministry: Four Views,* ed. Bonnidell Clouse and Robert G. Clouse (Downers Grove, Ill.: InterVarsity Press, 1989), p. 173.

[34]John Calvin, *Commentaries on the First Book of Moses Called Genesis,* trans. John King (orig. 1847; Grand Rapids, Mich.: Baker, 1979), 1:129-30, 172.

[35]Martin Luther, *Lectures on Genesis: Chapters 1-5,* trans. George V. Schick, in *Luther's Works,* ed. Jaroslav Pelikan (St. Louis, Mo.: Concordia Publishing House, 1958), 1:137-38, 202-3.

[36]John Piper, "A Vision of Biblical Complementarity: Manhood and Womanhood Defined According to the Bible," in *Recovering Biblical Manhood and Womanhood: A Response to Evangelical Feminism,* ed. John Piper and Wayne Grudem (Wheaton, Ill.: Crossway, 1991), p. 36.

[37]Ibid.

[38]James I. Packer, "Let's Stop Making Women Presbyters," *Christianity Today* 35, no. 2 (February 11, 1991): 20.

[39]Piper, "Vision of Biblical Complementarity," p. 53.

[40]Packer, "Let's Stop Making Women Presbyters," p. 20.

[41]George H. Tavard, "Theology and Sexuality," in *Women in the World's Religions, Past and Present,* ed. Ursula King (New York: Paragon, 1987), pp. 78-79. He develops this thesis more fully in *Woman in Christian Tradition* (South Bend, Ind.: University of Notre Dame Press, 1973).

[42]Marianne H. Micks notes that one feminist's writings took this point so far as to be accused "of thinking that if we ignored our different reproductive organs we would all be the same" (*Our Search for Identity* [Philadelphia: Fortress, 1982], p. 18).

[43]This difficulty has been noted even by proponents of the concept of androgyny. Some have moved beyond the older goal of establishing a single ideal for everyone (termed "monoandrogynism") to advocating a variety of options ("polyandrogynism"). See Joyce Trebilcot, "Two Forms of Androgynism," in *Femininity, Masculinity and Androgyny,* ed. Mary Vetterling-Braggin (Totowa, N.J.: Rowman and Allanheld, 1982), pp. 161-69. Others such as Mary Ann Warren look forward to the day when the concept of androgyny will "become obsolete" and "we will be comfortable with our natural human differences" ("Is Androgyny the Answer to Sexual Stereotyping?" in *Femininity, Masculinity and Androgyny,* pp. 184-85). A critique of the two types of androgyny is presented in James B. Nelson, *The Intimate Connection* (Philadelphia: Westminster Press, 1988), pp. 98-99.

[44]Psychologists Janet T. Spence and Robert L. Helmreich note that gender roles are present in some form in all societies, even though their exact forms vary (*Masculinity and Femininity* [Austin, Tex.: University of Texas Press, 1978], pp. 4-5).

⁴⁵Nelson, *Intimate Connection*, p. 75.

⁴⁶The importance of this difference for women's development is explored in Carol Gilligan, *In a Different Voice* (Cambridge, Mass.: Harvard University Press, 1982).

⁴⁷Like Jung, however, they find both traits present to varying degrees in all males and females (Spence and Helmreich, *Masculinity and Femininity*, p. 18).

⁴⁸Milton Diamond and Arno Karlen, *Sexual Decisions* (Boston: Little, Brown, 1980), pp. 447-48. A lengthier list of gender differences and their application to psychological therapy is found in Ron Johnson and Deb Brock, "Gender-Specific Therapy," *Journal of Psychology and Christianity* 7, no. 4 (Winter 1988): 56-57. See also Vance Packard, *The Sexual Wilderness* (New York: David McKay, 1968), pp. 338-60.

⁴⁹Jerome Kagan, "Psychology of Sex Differences," in *Human Sexuality in Four Perspectives*, ed. Frank A. Beach (Baltimore, Md.: Johns Hopkins University Press, 1976).

⁵⁰For a summary of the differences in brain development, see Milton Diamond, "Human Sexual Development: Biological Foundations for Social Development," in *Human Sexuality in Four Perspectives*, ed. Frank A. Beach (Baltimore, Md.: Johns Hopkins University Press, 1976), pp. 51-52.

⁵¹Johnson and Brock, "Gender-Specific Therapy," p. 56.

⁵²The work of neuropsychologists Jerre Levy and Roger Sperry is summarized by John C. Dwyer, *Human Sexuality: A Christian View* (Kansas City, Mo.: Sheed and Ward, 1987), pp. 142-44. The implications for theology of such research is sketched out in James B. Ashbrook, "Ways of Knowing God: Gender and the Brain," *Christian Century* 106 (January 4-11, 1989): 14-15.

⁵³For an intriguing discussion of "womanly" versus "manly" existence based on recent findings in neuropsychology, see Dwyer, *Human Sexuality*, pp. 145-48.

⁵⁴Lisa Cowle Cahill, *Between the Sexes* (Philadelphia: Fortress, 1985), p. 91.

⁵⁵Raymond C. Ortlund Jr., "Male-Female Equality and Male Headship," in *Recovering Biblical Manhood and Womanhood: A Response to Evangelical Feminism*, ed. John Piper and Wayne Grudem (Wheaton, Ill.: Crossway, 1991), p. 98.

⁵⁶Elton M. Eenigenburg, "The Ordination of Women," *Christianity Today* 3, no. 15 (April 27, 1959): 16.

⁵⁷Advertisement in *Christianity Today*, 33, no. 1 (January 13, 1989). See also Gene A. Getz, *The Measure of a Family* (Glendale, Calif.: Regal Books, 1976), pp. 41-43. Getz attempts to chart a middle position by concluding, "Woman's submissive role to man, then, antedates the Fall, but was *complicated by the Fall*" (p. 43).

⁵⁸Susan T. Foh, "Woman Preachers: Why Not?" *Fundamentalist Journal*, January 1985, p. 18.

⁵⁹Mary J. Evans, *Women in the Bible* (Downers Grove, Ill.: InterVarsity Press, 1983), p. 14.

⁶⁰Elisabeth Elliot, "Why I Oppose the Ordination of Women," *Christianity Today* 19, no. 18 (June 6, 1975): 16.

⁶¹Ibid., p. 13.

⁶²This point is argued successfully in the classic evangelical work by Jewett, *Man as Male and Female*, pp. 120-28.

⁶³See, for example, Rosemary Nixon, "The Priority of Perfection," *The Modern Churchman* 27, no. 1 (1984): 36. Even Karl Barth hints in this direction in his discussion of this text in *Church Dogmatics* 3/1, trans. J. W. Edwards, O. Bussey and Harold Knight (Edinburgh: T & T Clark, 1958), p. 294. For a discussion and critique of Barth's position, see Jewett, *Man as Male and Female*, pp. 33-40, 82-86.

⁶⁴For an interesting example of an egalitarian exegesis of Genesis 2, see Terrien, *Till the*

Heart Sings, pp. 7-17.

[65]Marianne Meye Thompson, "Response to Richard Longenecker," in *Women, Authority and the Bible*, ed. Alvera Mickelsen (Downers Grove, Ill.: InterVarsity Press, 1986), p. 96.

[66]For a rebuttal of this conclusion, however, see Ortlund, "Male-Female Equality and Male Headship," p. 103.

[67]Ibid., p. 102.

[68]See Evans, *Woman in the Bible*, p. 16.

[69]Phyllis Trible, *God and the Rhetoric of Sexuality* (Philadelphia: Fortress, 1978), p. 100.

[70]See Stanley J. Grenz, *Sexual Ethics* (Dallas: Word, 1990), pp. 5, 19, 223.

[71]As the text indicates, "Eve" is connected with the woman's role in reproduction. Some see the naming of Eve as an indication of the arrogance of Adam after the Fall. See, for example, Donald M. Joy, *Men Under Construction* (Wheaton, Ill.: Victor Books, 1989), pp. 115-16, 120.

[72]Mary Stewart Van Leeuwen, *Gender and Grace* (Downers Grove, Ill.: InterVarsity Press, 1990), p. 41.

[73]Trible, *God and the Rhetoric of Sexuality*, p. 100.

[74]Elliot, "Why I Oppose the Ordination of Women," p. 14.

[75]Ortlund, "Male-Female Equality and Male Headship," p. 102.

[76]Mickelsen, "Egalitarian View," p. 183.

[77]David Freedman, "Woman, a Power Equal to Man," *Biblical Archaeology Review* 9, no. 1 (January-February 1983): 58.

[78]John Piper and Wayne Grudem, "An Overview of Central Concerns: Questions and Answers," in *Recovering Biblical Manhood and Womanhood: A Response to Evangelical Feminism*, ed. John Piper and Wayne Grudem (Wheaton, Ill.: Crossway, 1991), p. 87.

[79]Ortlund, "Male-Female Equality and Male Headship," p. 108.

[80]Ibid., p. 107.

[81]Ibid., p. 110.

[82]Peggy Reeves Sanday, *Female Power and Male Dominance* (New York: Cambridge University Press, 1981), p. 172. Sanday's study is noted by Cahill, *Between the Sexes*, p. 95.

[83]Robert L. Saucy, "The Negative Case Against the Ordination of Women," in *Perspectives on Evangelical Theology: Papers from the Thirtieth Annual Meeting of the Evangelical Theological Society*, ed. Kenneth S. Kantzer and Stanley N. Gundry (Grand Rapids, Mich.: Baker, 1979), p. 280.

[84]Evans, *Woman in the Bible*, p. 19.

[85]Claus Westermann, *Creation*, trans. John J. Scullion (Philadelphia: Fortress, 1974), p. 98.

[86]Cahill, *Between the Sexes*, p. 55.

[87]See Ruth Tucker, *Women in the Maze: Questions and Answers on Biblical Equality* (Downers Grove, Ill.: InterVarsity Press, 1992), p. 36.

[88]John M. Frame, "Men and Women in the Image of God," in *Recovering Biblical Manhood and Womanhood: A Response to Evangelical Feminism*, ed. John Piper and Wayne Grudem (Wheaton, Ill.: Crossway, 1991), p. 231.

[89]Roger Beckwith, "The Bearing of Holy Scripture," in *Man, Woman and Priesthood*, ed. Peter Moore (London: SPCK, 1978), p. 57.

[90]For the egalitarian reading of the creation narratives, see Spencer, *Beyond the Curse*, pp. 17-29, and Evans, *Woman in the Bible*, pp. 11-17.

[91]For a development of the philosophical basis for the social understanding of personhood, see Alistair I. McFadyen, *The Call to Personhood: A Christian Theory of the Individual in*

Social Relationships (Cambridge: Cambridge University Press, 1990).
92For a fuller discussion of the relationship of sexuality and community, see Grenz, *Sexual Ethics*, pp. 35-37.

Chapter 6: Women in the Church & the Priesthood
1Hence John Piper and Wayne Grudem, "An Overview of Central Concerns: Questions and Answers," in *Recovering Biblical Manhood and Womanhood: A Response to Evangelical Feminism*, ed. John Piper and Wayne Grudem (Wheaton, Ill.: Crossway, 1991), p. 65.
2Ibid.
3Klyne R. Snodgrass, "The Ordination of Women—Thirteen Years Later: Do We Really Value the Ministry of Women?" *Covenant Quarterly* 48, no. 3 (August 1990): 34-35.
4That the apostle is thinking about the Genesis story here is indicated by his use of Eve to introduce this theme.
5See "Agenda for Synod 1990" (Christian Reformed Church Report 26).
6Stephen C. Barton, "Impatient for Justice: Five Reasons Why the Church of England Should Ordain Women to the Priesthood," *Theology* 92, no. 749 (September 1989): 403.
7Willmore Eva, "Should Our Church Ordain Women? Yes," *Ministry* 58, no. 3 (March 1985): 18.
8See Madeleine Boucher, "Ecumenical Documents: Authority in Community," *Midstream* 21, no. 3 (July 1982): 415.
9C. S. Lewis, "Priestesses in the Church?" in *God in the Dock*, ed. Walter Hooper (Grand Rapids, Mich: Eerdmans), pp. 234-39.
10See, for example, Michael Novak, "Women, Ordination and Angels," *First Things* 32 (April 1993): 25-32.
11See the summary of the position of Canon Geddes MacGregor in Paul K. Jewett, *The Ordination of Women* (Grand Rapids, Mich: Eerdmans, 1980), pp. 15-16.
12See, for example, Bernard E. Seton, "Should Our Church Ordain Women? No," *Ministry* 58, no. 3 (March 1985): 16. Seton is a former associate secretary of the General Council of the Seventh-day Adventists.
13Ibid.
14Ibid.
15Ibid.
16Snodgrass, "Ordination of Women," p. 33.
17See Eileen Vennum, "Do Male Old Covenant Priests Exclude Female New Covenant Pastors?" *Priscilla Papers* 7, no. 2 (Spring 1993): 6-7.
18Ibid., p. 7.
19For a rebuttal of this thesis, see E. Margaret Howe, *Women and Church Leadership* (Grand Rapids, Mich.: Eerdmans, 1982), p. 100.
20Pamela J. Scalise, "Women in Ministry: Reclaiming Our Old Testament Heritage," *Review and Expositor* 83, no. 1 (Winter 1986): 8.
21See, for example, Howe, *Women and Church Leadership*, p. 100.
22Paul D. L. Avis, however, concludes that the principle would lead us in the opposite direction today: "If we allow Luther's doctrine of the universal priesthood to determine the answers we give to current questions concerning the ministry, we are likely to reach a different conclusion from that of the Reformer himself on this particular issue" ("Luther's Theology of the Church," *Churchman* 97, no. 2 [1983]: 111).
23Susan T. Foh, "A Male Leadership View," in *Women in Ministry: Four Views*, ed. Bonnidell

Clouse and Robert G. Clouse (Downers Grove, Ill.: InterVarsity Press, 1989), p. 93.
²⁴Ibid., pp. 93-94.
²⁵This position has enjoyed adherents throughout church history. See Ida Raming, "The Twelve Apostles Were Men," *Theology Digest* 40, no. 1 (Spring 1993): 24.
²⁶Mary J. Evans, *Woman in the Bible* (Downers Grove, Ill.: InterVarsity Press, 1983), p. 110.
²⁷Paul K. Jewett, "Why I Favor the Ordination of Women," *Christianity Today* 19, no. 18 (June 6, 1975): 9.
²⁸Marianne Meye Thompson, "Response to Richard Longenecker," in *Women, Authority and the Bible*, ed. Alvera Mickelsen (Downers Grove, Ill.: InterVarsity Press, 1986), p. 94.
²⁹For a helpful study that provides the exegetical foundations of a two-category summarization, see Ronald Y. K. Fung, "Ministry in the New Testament," in *The Church in the Bible and the World*, ed. D. A. Carson (Grand Rapids, Mich.: Baker, 1987), pp. 156-57.
³⁰See, for example, Ernst Käsemann, *Essays on New Testament Themes*, trans. W. J. Montague (London: SCM Press, 1964), pp. 63-94. For a rebuttal of this position, see Fung, "Ministry in the New Testament," pp. 167-71, 176.
³¹Ibid., p. 173. See also p. 176.
³²Ibid., p. 172.
³³Ibid., p. 178.
³⁴Alvera Mickelsen, "An Egalitarian View: There Is Neither Male nor Female in Christ," in *Women in Ministry: Four Views*, ed. Bonnidell Clouse and Robert G. Clouse (Downers Grove, Ill.: InterVarsity Press, 1989), p. 191.
³⁵E. Margaret Howe, "The Positive Case for the Ordination of Women," in *Perspectives on Evangelical Theology: Papers from the Thirtieth Annual Meeting of the Evangelical Theological Society*, ed. Kenneth S. Kantzer and Stanley N. Gundry (Grand Rapids, Mich.: Zondervan, 1979), p. 275.
³⁶Fung, "Ministry in the New Testament," p. 179.
³⁷Ibid., p. 209.
³⁸Ibid.
³⁹Samuel H. Nafzger, "The Doctrinal Position of the LCMS on the Service of Women in the Church," *Concordia Journal* 18, no. 2 (April 1992): 114.
⁴⁰See, for example, Eduard Schweizer, *Church Order in the New Testament* (London: SCM Press, 1961), pp. 186-87.
⁴¹In the context of their rejection of the concept of apostolic succession, many Protestants claim that the apostolic office was for the first century only. Hence Bruce Milne writes, "To claim apostolic *office* today is a misunderstanding of biblical teaching and in practice offers a serious challenge to the authority and finality of the divine revelation of the New Testament" (*Know the Truth* [Downers Grove, Ill.: InterVarsity Press, 1982], p. 218). Dispensationalists sometimes argue that the offices of apostle, prophet and evangelist were given for the stage of church history prior to the fixing of the canon. Recent charismatic scholarship, however, has revived the idea that all of these offices are present in the contemporary church. See J. Rodman Williams, *Renewal Theology: Systematic Theology from a Charismatic Perspective* (Grand Rapids, Mich.: Zondervan, 1992), 3:164-77.
⁴²Writing in a Presbyterian context, Donald J. MacNair in *The Living Church: A Guide for Revitalization* (Philadelphia: Great Commission, 1980), p. 64, defines four central tasks in pastoral ministry: being an example (1 Tim 4:12; Tit 2:7; Heb 13:7), being a "shepherd" (Acts 20:28; 1 Pet 5:1-4), overseeing (Acts 20:28; 1 Tim 3:2; 5:17; Heb 13:17) and guarding (Acts 20:28; 2 Tim 4:2-3; Tit 2:15; 2 Jn 10-11).

43See, for example, Marjorie Warkentin, *Ordination: A Biblical-Historical View* (Grand Rapids, Mich.: Eerdmans, 1982).

44H. E. Dana, "Ordination in the New Testament," *Baptist Program*, April 1970, p. 8.

45This Reformed and Free Church emphasis has gained wide recognition among the various church traditions. See, for example, *Baptism, Eucharist and Ministry*, Faith and Order Paper 111 (Geneva: World Council of Churches, 1982), p. 31. See also Daniel L. Migliore, *Faith Seeking Understanding: An Introduction to Christian Theology* (Grand Rapids, Mich.: Eerdmans, 1991), p. 227.

46*Baptism, Eucharist and Ministry*, p. 30.

47Ibid., p. 22.

48Ibid.

49Migliore, *Faith Seeking Understanding*, p. 228.

50Piper and Grudem, "Overview of Central Concerns," p. 77.

Chapter 7: Women in the Ordained Ministry

1R. C. H. Lenski, *The Interpretation of St. John's Revelation* (Minneapolis: Augsburg, 1963), p. 68. See also Philip E. Hughes, *The Book of Revelation: A Commentary* (Leicester, England: Inter-Varsity Press, 1990), p. 31.

2Paul K. Jewett, "Why I Favor the Ordination of Women," *Christianity Today* 19, no. 18 (June 6, 1975): 9.

3This argument is cited in Madeleine Boucher, "Ecumenical Documents: Authority in Community," *Midstream* 21, no. 3 (July 1982): 412.

4Michael Novak, "Women, Ordination and Angels," *First Things* 32 (April 1993): 32.

5James I. Packer, "Let's Stop Making Women Presbyters," *Christianity Today* 35, no. 2 (February 11, 1991): 20.

6Kenneth Untener, "Forum: The Ordination of Women—Can the Horizons Widen?" *Worship* 65, no. 1 (January 1991): 53.

7Thomas Aquinas *Summa Theologica* 3.78.4, trans. Fathers of the English Dominican Province (Westminster, Md.: Christian Classics, 1981), 5:2470.

8John Austin Baker (bishop of Salisbury), "Eucharistic Presidency and Women's Ordination," *Theology* 88, no. 725 (September 1985): 355.

9Congregation for the Doctrine of the Faith, "Declaration on the Admission of Women to the Ministerial Priesthood," as cited in Untener, "Forum: The Ordination of Women," p. 52.

10Mark E. Chapman, "The Ordination of Women: Evangelical and Catholic," *Dialog* 28 (Spring 1989): 135. Compare Martin Luther, *Book of Concord*, ed. T. Tappert (Philadelphia: Fortress, 1959), p. 448. For a similar position see Gretchen Gaebelein Hull, *Equal to Serve* (Old Tappan, N.J.: Revell, 1987), p. 220.

11Baker, "Eucharistic Presidency," p. 357.

12Ibid.

13See, for example, Sara Butler, "Forum: Some Second Thoughts on the Ordination of Women," *Worship* 63, no. 2 (March 1989): 165.

14S. M. Hutchens, for example, sees Jesus' maleness as indicating a cosmic priority of the male in "God, Gender and the Pastoral Office," *Touchstone* 5, no. 4 (Fall 1992): 16-17.

15Constance F. Parvey, "Where Are We Going? The Threefold Ministry and the Ordination of Women," *Word and World* 5, no. 1 (Winter 1985): 9.

16Stephen C. Barton, "Impatient for Justice: Five Reasons Why the Church of England

Should Ordain Women to the Priesthood," *Theology* 92, no. 749 (September 1989): 404.
[17]This principle dates back at least to Irenaeus. See Irenaeus *Adversus Haereses* 5.14, in *The Ante-Nicene Fathers*, ed. Alexander Roberts and James Donaldson, 10 vols. (Grand Rapids, Mich.: Eerdmans, 1975), 1:541. It played an important role in the christological controversies. Against Apolliniarius, for example, Gregory of Nazianzus asserted: "If any one has put his trust in him as a man without a human mind, he is himself devoid of mind and unworthy of salvation. For what he has not assumed he has not healed; it is united to his Deity that is saved" ("An Examination of Apollinarianism," in *Documents of the Christian Church*, ed. Henry Bettennson, 2nd ed. [London: Oxford University Press, 1963], p. 45). See also J. N. D. Kelly, *Early Christian Doctrines*, 5th rev. ed. (London: Adam and Charles Black, 1977), p. 297.
[18]Barton, "Impatient for Justice," p. 404. See also Untener, "Forum: The Ordination of Women," p. 57.
[19]Boucher, "Ecumenical Documents," p. 413.
[20]Butler, "Forum: Some Second Thoughts," pp. 157-65.
[21]Boucher, "Ecumenical Documents," p. 412.
[22]Ibid., p. 413.
[23]Parvey, "Where Are We Going?" p. 9.
[24]E. J. Kilmartin, "Apostolic Office: Sacrament of Christ," *Theological Studies* 36, no. 2 (1975): 263.
[25]Butler, "Forum: Some Second Thoughts," p. 165.
[26]Suzanne Heine, *Matriarchs, Goddesses and Images of God*, trans. John Bowden (Minneapolis: Augsburg, 1989), pp. 137-45.
[27]Thomas R. Schreiner, "The Valuable Ministries of Women in the Context of Male Leadership: A Survey of Old and New Testament Examples and Teaching," in *Recovering Biblical Manhood and Womanhood: A Response to Evangelical Feminism*, ed. John Piper and Wayne Grudem (Wheaton, Ill.: Crossway, 1991), p. 215.
[28]"Role of Women in the Church: A Report of the Study Panel of the Free Church of Scotland," *Diakonia* 4, no. 3 (March 1991): 78.
[29]James A. Borland, "Women in the Life and Teaching of Jesus," in *Recovering Biblical Manhood and Womanhood: A Response to Evangelical Feminism*, ed. John Piper and Wayne Grudem (Wheaton, Ill.: Crossway, 1991), p. 121.
[30]Ibid.
[31]Even certain contemporary Roman Catholic thinkers such as Karl Rahner agree with this conclusion. See Ida Raming, "The Twelve Apostles Were Men," *Theology Digest* 40, no. 1 (Spring 1993): 22.
[32]Ibid., p. 21.
[33]William Lane, *The Gospel According to Mark*, New International Commentary on the New Testament (Grand Rapids, Mich.: Eerdmans, 1974), p. 133.
[34]Jewett, "Why I Favor the Ordination of Women," p. 10.
[35]For a rebuttal, see Borland, "Women in the Life and Teaching of Jesus," p. 121.
[36]For a listing and discussion of common definitions, see Gary A. Yukl, *Leadership in Organizations*, 2nd ed. (Englewood Cliffs, N.J.: Prentice-Hall, 1989), pp. 2-5.
[37]Ibid., p. 3.
[38]John W. Gardner, *On Leadership* (New York: Macmillan/Free Press, 1990), p. 1.
[39]The following enumeration builds from Gardner's discussion in ibid., pp. 11-22.
[40]Ibid., p. 14.

41Ibid., p. 21.

42Ibid., pp. 21-22.

43W. Warner Burke, "Leadership as Empowering Others," in *Executive Power*, ed. Suresh Srivastva and Associates (San Francisco: Jossey-Bass, 1986), p. 75.

44The interchangeability of *bishop* and *elder* in certain New Testament texts (e.g., Acts 20:17-28; Tit 1:5, 7) suggests that in the early church they were likely not two offices, but merely alternate designations for the same position. See Joachim Rohde, *"episkopos,"* in *Exegetical Dictionary of the New Testament*, ed. Horst Balz and Gerhard Schneider (Grand Rapids, Mich.: Eerdmans, 1991), 2:36. As Bruce Milne notes, "It is now generally accepted among scholars of all traditions that the Greek words *episkopos* (bishop) and *presbyteros* (elder) are equivalents in the NT" (*Know the Truth* [Downers Grove, Ill.: InterVarsity Press, 1982], p. 241).

45Rohde, *"episkopos,"* 2:36.

46William Barclay, *The Letters to Timothy, Titus and Philemon* (Edinburgh: St. Andrews Press, 1960), p. 82.

47John Piper and Wayne Grudem, "An Overview of Central Concerns: Questions and Answers," in *Recovering Biblical Manhood and Womanhood: A Response to Evangelical Feminism*, ed. John Piper and Wayne Grudem (Wheaton, Ill.: Crossway, 1991), p. 64.

48Robert Greenleaf, *Servant Leadership* (New York: Paulist, 1977), p. 10.

49*Baptism, Eucharist and Ministry*, Faith and Order Paper 111 (Geneva: World Council of Churches, 1982), p. 23.

50For a recent example, see Daniel L. Migliore, *Faith Seeking Understanding: An Introduction to Christian Theology* (Grand Rapids, Mich.: Eerdmans, 1991), p. 229.

51Piper and Grudem, "Overview of Central Concerns," p. 64.

52Ibid., p. 69.

53George W. Knight III, "The Family and the Church: How Should Biblical Manhood and Womanhood Work Out in Practice?" in *Recovering Biblical Manhood and Womanhood: A Response to Evangelical Feminism*, ed. John Piper and Wayne Grudem (Wheaton, Ill.: Crossway, 1991), pp. 352-53.

54Piper and Grudem, "Overview of Central Concerns," p. 70.

55Susan T. Foh, "A Male Leadership View," in *Women in Ministry: Four Views*, ed. Bonnidell Clouse and Robert G. Clouse (Downers Grove, Ill.: InterVarsity Press, 1989), p. 99.

56Klyne R. Snodgrass, "The Ordination of Women—Thirteen Years Later: Do We Really Value the Ministry of Women?" *Covenant Quarterly* 48, no. 3 (August 1990): 40.

57James B. Hurley, *Man and Woman in Biblical Perspective* (Grand Rapids, Mich.: Zondervan, 1981), pp. 120-21; Douglas J. Moo, "1 Timothy 2:11-15: Meaning and Significance," *Trinity Journal* 1 (1980): 73-75; "The Interpretation of 1 Timothy 2:11-15: A Rejoinder," *Trinity Journal* 2 (Fall 1981): 206-7.

58Foh, "Male Headship View," p. 94.

59Schreiner, "Valuable Ministries of Women," p. 217.

60David M. Scholer, "1 Timothy 2:9-15 and the Place of Women in the Church's Ministry," in *Women, Authority and the Bible*, ed. Alvera Mickelsen (Downers Grove, Ill.: InterVarsity Press, 1986), p. 207. Scholer refers to D. Hill, *New Testament Prophecy*, New Foundations Theological Library (Atlanta: John Knox, 1981), and David E. Aune, *Prophecy in Early Christianity and the Ancient Mediterranean World* (Grand Rapids, Mich.: Eerdmans, 1983).

61See, for example, H. Wayne House, "Distinctive Roles for Women in the Second and

Third Centuries," *Bibliotheca Sacra* 146, no. 581 (January-March 1989): 53.

[62]Thomas Schreiner, for example, suggests that women can instruct mixed-gender groups so long as "the function of authoritative teaching to men is not involved" ("Valuable Ministries of Women," p. 223).

[63]Knight, "Family and the Church," p. 354.

[64]*Baptism, Eucharist and Ministry*, p. 22.

[65]Yukl, *Leadership in Organizations*, p. 12.

[66]*The Doubleday Dictionary for Home, School and Office*, ed. Sidney I. Landau (Garden City, N.Y.: Doubleday, 1975), p. 48.

[67]*Funk and Wagnall's New Standard Dictionary of the English Language* (New York: Funk and Wagnall's, 1965), 1:193.

[68]Ibid., 2:1946.

[69]*Doubleday Dictionary*, p. 569.

[70]Yukl, *Leadership in Organizations*, p. 14.

[71]Hence John F. O'Grady, "Authority and Power: Issues for the Contemporary Church," *Louvain Studies* 10, no. 2 (1984): 123. See also Boucher, "Ecumenical Documents," p. 405.

[72]John Kenneth Galbraith, *The Anatomy of Power* (Boston: Houghton Mifflin, 1983), pp. 4-6, 14-37.

[73]Ibid., p. 3.

[74]Ibid., pp. 5-6.

[75]Yukl, *Leadership in Organizations*, pp. 14-15. For an alternative summary, see Galbraith, *Anatomy of Power*, pp. 6-7.

[76]Max Weber, *Max Weber on Law in Economy and Society*, ed. Max Rheinstein, trans. Edward Shils and Max Rheinstein (New York: Simon & Schuster, 1967), p. 323.

[77]Max Weber, *The Theory of Social and Economic Organization* (Glencoe, Ill.: Free Press, 1947), p. 152.

[78]Karl Rahner, *Theological Investigations*, trans. Kevin Smyth (New York: Crossroad, 1982), 4:409.

[79]Richard Sennett, *Authority* (London: Secker and Warburg, 1980), p. 10.

[80]For this definition, see Rollo May, *Power and Innocence: A Search for the Sources of Violence* (New York: W. W. Norton, 1972), p. 99.

[81]Ibid., pp. 105-13.

[82]Boucher, "Ecumenical Documents," p. 404.

[83]Werner Foerster, "ἔξεστιν κτλ.," in *Theological Dictionary of the New Testament*, ed. Gerhard Kittel, trans. Geoffrey W. Bromiley, 10 vols. (Grand Rapids, Mich.: Eerdmans, 1964-1976), 2:562.

[84]Ibid.

[85]Ibid., p. 564.

[86]Ibid., p. 565.

[87]Ibid., pp. 566-67.

[88]Ibid., p. 568.

[89]Ibid., p. 569.

[90]Walter Grundmann, "δύναμαι κτλ.," in *Theological Dictionary of the New Testament*, ed. Gerhard Kittel, trans. Geoffrey W. Bromiley, 10 vols. (Grand Rapids, Mich.: Eerdmans, 1964-1976), 2:284.

[91]Ibid., p. 301.

[92]Ibid, pp. 316-17.

93Ibid., p. 300.

94Ibid.

95See Boucher, "Ecumenical Documents," p. 416.

96Piper and Grudem, "Overview of Central Concerns," p. 78.

97Ibid., p. 79.

98Ibid., p. 78.

99Ibid.

100Walter L. Liefeld, "A Plural Ministry View," in *Women in Ministry: Four Views*, ed. Bonnidell Clouse and Robert C. Clouse (Downers Grove, Ill.: InterVarsity Press, 1989), p. 147.

101Marjorie Warkentin, *Ordination: A Biblical-Historical View* (Grand Rapids, Mich.: Eerdmans, 1982), p. 171.

102E. Margaret Howe, *Women and Church Leadership* (Grand Rapids, Mich.: Zondervan, 1982), p. 231.

103Gardner, *On Leadership*, 187.

104Edgar H. Schein, *Organizational Psychology* (Englewood Cliffs, N.J.: Prentice-Hall, 1980), p. 128.

105*Baptism, Eucharist and Ministry*, p. 26.

106See, for example, the discussion of Gardner, *On Leadership*, p. 150.

107Ibid.

108See, for example, recent studies by feminist scholars such as Nancy Chodorow, *The Reproduction of Mothering: Essays in Feminist Theory*, ed. Joyce Trebilcot (Towana, N.J.: Rowman and Allanheld, 1983); Carol Gilligan, *In a Different Voice* (Cambridge, Mass.: Harvard University Press, 1982).

109We admit that it remains debatable whether women exercise a distinctive leadership or managerial style in business organizations. For a discussion of recent research, see Ann M. Morrison, Randall P. White and Ellen Van Volsor, "The Narrow Band," *Issues and Observations* (Center for Creative Leadership, Greensboro, N.C.), Spring 1987. More important for our purposes, however, is that women and men tend to see the world differently, whether because of innate gender differences or because of differing life experiences.

110Mary Stewart Van Leeuwen et al., *After Eden: Facing the Challenge of Gender Reconciliation* (Grand Rapids, Mich.: Eerdmans, 1993), p. 585.

111See Warkentin, *Ordination*, p. 182.

Works Cited

Abbott-Smith, G. *A Manual Greek Lexicon of the New Testament.* 3rd ed. Edinburgh: T & T Clark, 1937.

Achtemeier, Elizabeth. "Exchanging God for 'No Gods': A Discussion of Feminist Language for God." In *Speaking the Christian God,* edited by Alvin F. Kimel Jr. Grand Rapids, Mich.: Eerdmans, 1992.

Almlie, Gerald L. "Women's Church and Communion Participation." *Christian Brethren Review* 33 (1982): 41-55.

Anderson, A. A. *The Book of Psalms.* Edited by Ronald E. Clements and Matthew Black. New Century Bible. London: Marshall, Morgan and Scott, 1972.

Antler, Joyce. "But Can She Cook? Overcoming the Barriers to Women's Education." *American Educator* 9, no. 3 (Fall 1985).

Applegate, Judith K. "The Co-elect Woman of 1 Peter." *New Testament Studies* 38 (October 1992): 587-604.

Ashbrook, James B. "Ways of Knowing God: Gender and the Brain." *Christian Century* 106 (January 4-11, 1989): 14-15.

Aune, David. "Prophecy." In *Early Christianity and the Ancient Mediterranean World.* Grand Rapids, Mich.: Eerdmans, 1983.

Avis, Paul D. L. "Luther's Theology of the Church." *Churchman* 97, no. 2 (1983).

Baker, John Austin. "Eucharistic Presidency and Women's Ordination." *Theology* 88, no. 725 (September 1985).

Balch, David L. *Let Wives Be Submissive: The Domestic Code in 1 Peter.* Chico, Calif.: Scholars Press, 1981.

Balz, Horst, and Gerhard Schneider, eds. *Exegetical Dictionary of the New Testament.* 3 vols. Grand Rapids, Mich.: Eerdmans, 1990-1993.

Baptism, Eucharist and Ministry. Faith and Order Paper 111. Geneva: World Council of Churches, 1982.

Barclay, William. *The Letters to Timothy, Titus and Philemon.* Edinburgh: St. Andrews University Press, 1960.

Barnett, Paul W. "Wives and Women's Ministry (1 Timothy 2:11-15)." *Evangelical Review of Theology* 15, no. 4 (January 1991).

Barrett, C. K. *A Commentary on the Epistle to the Romans.* London: Adam and Charles Black, 1957.

————. *A Commentary on the First Epistle to the Corinthians.* London: Adam and Charles Black, 1968.

————. *The Signs of an Apostle.* Philadelphia: Fortress, 1972.

Barron, Bruce. "Putting Women in Their Place: 1 Timothy 2 and Evangelical Views of Women in Church Leadership." *Journal of the Evangelical Theological Society* 33, no. 4 (December 1990).

Bartchy, Scott. *First Century Slavery and 1 Corinthians 7:21.* SBL Dissertation Series 11. Missoula, Mont.: Society of Biblical Literature/Seminar on Paul, 1973.

————. "Power, Submission and Sexual Identity Among the Early Christians." In *Essays on New Testament Christianity,* edited by C. Robert Wetzel. Cincinnati: Standard, 1978.

Barth, Karl. *Church Dogmatics* 3/1. Translated by J. W. Edwards, O. Bussey and Harold Knight. Edinburgh: T & T Clark, 1958.

Barton, Stephen C. "Impatient for Justice: Five Reasons Why the Church of England Should Ordain Women to the Priesthood." *Theology* 92, no. 749 (September 1989).

Bauer, Walter. *A Greek-English Lexicon of the New Testament and Other Early Christian Literature.* Translated and edited by William F. Arndt and F. Wilbur Gingrich. Chicago: University of Chicago Press, 1957.

Beckwith, Roger. "The Bearing of Holy Scripture." In *Man, Woman and Priesthood,* edited by Peter Moore. London: SPCK, 1978.

Bedale, Steven. "The Meaning of *Kephalē* in the Pauline Epistles." *Journal of Theological Studies* n.s. 5 (October 1954): 211-16.

Bilezikian, Gilbert G. *Beyond Sex Roles: A Guide for the Study of Female Roles in the Bible.* Grand Rapids, Mich.: Baker Book House, 1985.

Blenkinsop, Joseph. *Sexuality and the Christian Tradition.* Dayton, Ohio: Pflaum, 1969.

Boccia, Maria L. "Hidden History of Women Leaders of the Church." *Journal of Biblical Equality,* September 1990.

Bolt, John. "Eschatological Hermeneutics, Women's Ordination and the Reformed Tradition." *Calvin Theological Journal* 26, no. 2 (1991).

Boucher, Madeleine. "Ecumenical Documents: Authority in Community." *Midstream* 21, no. 3 (July 1982).

Bowman, Ann L. "Women in Ministry: An Exegetical Study of 1 Timothy 2:11-15." *Bibliotheca Sacra* 149, no. 594 (April-June 1992).

Brooke, A. E. *A Critical and Exegetical Commentary on the Johannine Epistles.* International Critical Commentary. Edinburgh: T & T Clark, 1912.

Brown, Colin, ed. *New International Dictionary of New Testament Theology.* Grand Rapids, Mich.: Zondervan, 1976.

Bruce, F. F. *Commentary on Galatians.* New International Greek Testament Commentary. Grand Rapids, Mich.: Eerdmans, 1982.

————. *Commentary on the Book of Acts.* Grand Rapids, Mich.: Eerdmans, 1971.

————. *1 & 2 Corinthians.* New Century Bible. Greenwood, S.C.: Attic, 1971.

————. *The Letter of Paul to the Romans.* Grand Rapids, Mich.: Eerdmans, 1963, 1990.

————, ed. *International Bible Commentary.* Rev. ed. Grand Rapids, Mich.: Zondervan, 1986.

Burke, Warner. "Leadership as Empowering Others." In *Executive Power,* edited by Suresh Srivastva and associates. San Francisco: Jossey-Bass, 1986.

Butler, Sara. "Forum: Some Second Thoughts on Ordaining Women." *Worship* 63, no. 2

(March 1989).

Cahill, Lisa. *Between the Sexes.* Philadelphia: Fortress, 1985.

Calvin, John. *Commentaries on the First Book of Moses Called Genesis.* Translated by John King. Grand Rapids, Mich.: Baker Book House, 1979. (Reprint of the 1847 edition.)

Campbell, Christina. "Principles of Female Ordination in the Old Testament." *Priscilla Papers* 7, no. 2 (Spring 1993).

Cantarella, Eva. *Pandora's Daughters: The Role and Status of Women in Greek and Roman Antiquity.* Translated by Maureen B. Fant. Baltimore: Johns Hopkins University Press, 1967.

Carson, D. A. *Exegetical Fallacies.* Grand Rapids, Mich.: Baker Book House, 1984.

Cervin, Richard S. "Does *Kephalē* Mean 'Source' or 'Authority Over' in Greek Literature? A Rebuttal." *Trinity Journal* n.s. 10 (Spring 1989): 85-112.

Chapman, Mark E. "The Ordination of Women: Evangelical and Catholic." *Dialog* 28, no. 2 (Spring 1989).

Chodorow, Nancy. *The Reproduction of Mothering: Essays in Feminist Theory.* Edited by Joyce Trebilcot. Towana, N.J.: Rowman and Allanheld, 1983.

Chrysostom, John. "Homily on the Epistle of St. Paul the Apostle to the Romans." In *A Select Library of Nicene and Post-Nicene Fathers,* translated by J. P. Morris and W. H. Simcox. Grand Rapids, Mich.: Eerdmans, 1980.

Clark, Stephen B. *Man and Woman in Christ.* Ann Arbor, Mich.: Servant, 1980.

Clouse, Bonnidell, and Robert G. Clouse, eds. *Women in Ministry: Four Views.* Downers Grove, Ill.: InterVarsity Press, 1989.

Cohen, David. "Seclusion, Separation and the Status of Women in Classical Athens." *Greece and Rome* 36, no. 1 (April 1989).

Conway, Jill. "Perspectives on the History of Women's Education in the United States." *History of Education Quarterly* 14, no. 1 (Spring 1974).

Conzelmann, Hans. *1 Corinthians.* Translated by J. W. Leitch. Philadelphia: Fortress, 1975.

Cooke, Bernard. "Non-patriarchal Salvation." *Horizons* 10, no. 1 (1983).

Cope, Lamar. "1 Cor. 11:2-16 One Step Further." *Journal of Biblical Literature* 97, no. 3 (1978).

Corrington, Gail Paterson. "The 'Headless Woman': Paul and the Language of the Body in 1 Cor. 11:2-16." *Perspectives in Religious Studies* 18, no. 3 (Fall 1991).

Cranfield, C. E. B. *The Epistle to the Romans.* Edinburgh: T & T Clark, 1979.

Dana, H. E. "Ordination in the New Testament." *Baptist Program,* April 1970.

Danielou, J. *The Ministry of Women in the Early Church.* Translated by Glyn Simon. Leighton Buzzard, U.K.: Faith, 1961.

Davidson, F., A. M. Stibbs and E. F. Kevan, eds. *New Bible Commentary.* 2nd ed. London: Inter-Varsity Press, 1954.

Davis, J. J. "Some Reflections on Galatians 3:28—Sexual Roles and Biblical Hermeneutics." *Journal of the Evangelical Theological Society* 19, no. 14 (April 9, 1976).

Dayton, Donald. *Discovering an Evangelical Heritage.* New York: Harper & Row, 1976.

DeBerg, Betty A. *Ungodly Women: Gender and the First Wave of American Fundamentalism.* Minneapolis: Fortress, 1990.

Derry, William. "The Epistles of St. John." In *Expositor's Bible,* edited by W. Robertson Nicoll. New York: Wilbur B. Ketcham.

Diamond, Milton. "Human Sexual Development: Biological Foundations for Social Development." In *Human Sexuality in Four Perspectives,* edited by Frank A. Beach. Baltimore: Johns Hopkins University Press, 1976.

Diamond, Milton, and Arno Karlen. *Sexual Decisions.* Boston: Little, Brow, 1980.

Dibelius, Martin, and Hans Conzelmann. *The Pastoral Epistles.* Translated by Philip Buttolph and Adela Yarbro. Philadelphia: Fortress, 1972.

Douglas, Jane Dempsey. "Christian Freedom: What Calvin Learned at the School of Women." *Church History* 53, no. 2 (June 1984).

Dumbrell, W. J. "The Role of Women: A Reconsideration of the Biblical Evidence." *Interchange* 21 (1977): 14-22.

Dunn, J. D. G. *Jesus and the Spirit.* Philadelphia: Westminster Press, 1975.

————. *Romans.* Word Biblical Commentary. Dallas: Word, 1988.

————. *Unity and Diversity in the New Testament.* 2nd ed. London: SCM Press, 1990.

Dwyer, John C. *Human Sexuality: A Christian View.* Kansas City, Mo.: Sheed and Ward, 1987.

Eenigenburg, Elton M. "The Ordination of Women." *Christianity Today,* April 27, 1959.

Elliot, Elisabeth. "Why I Oppose the Ordination of Women." *Christianity Today* 19, no. 18 (June 6, 1975).

Ellis, E. Earle. "The Role of the Christian Prophet in Acts." In *Apostolic History and the Gospel,* edited by W. Ward Gasque and Ralph P. Martin. Grand Rapids, Mich.: Eerdmans, 1971.

————. "The Silenced Wives of Corinth (1 Cor. 14:34-35)." In *New Testament Textual Criticism: Its Significance for Exegesis,* edited by E. J. Epp and Gordon D. Fee. New York: Oxford University Press, 1981.

Evans, Mary J. *Woman in the Bible.* Downers Grove, Ill.: InterVarsity Press, 1983.

Fee, Gordon D. *The First Epistle to the Corinthians.* New International Commentary on the New Testament. Grand Rapids, Mich.: Eerdmans, 1987.

————. *1 & 2 Timothy, Titus.* New International Biblical Commentary. Peabody, Mass.: Hendrickson, 1988.

Field-Bibb, Jacqueline. *Women Towards Priesthood: Ministerial Politics and Feminist Praxis.* Cambridge: Cambridge University Press, 1991.

Filson, Floyd V. *The Gospel According to St. Matthew.* London: Adam and Charles Black, 1960.

Fiorenza, Elisabeth Schüssler. *In Memory of Her.* New York: Crossroad, 1983.

Fisher, Fred L. *1 & 2 Corinthians.* Waco, Tex.: Word, 1975.

Fitzmyer, Joseph A. "Another Look at *Kephalē* in 1 Corinthians 11:3." *New Testament Studies* 35, no. 4 (1989): 503-11.

Flanagan, N. M., and E. H. Snyder. "Did Paul Put Down Women in 1 Cor. 14:34-36?" *Biblical Theology Bulletin* 11 (January 1981): 10-12.

Foh, Susan T. "Woman Preachers: Why Not?" *Fundamentalist Journal,* January 1985.

————. *Women and the Word of God.* Phillipsburg, N.J.: Presbyterian & Reformed, 1979.

Foster, J. "St. Paul and Women." *Expository Times* 62 (Summer 1951): 376-78.

Foulkes, Irene W. "Bible and Tradition." *Midstream* 21, no. 3 (July 1982).

Frame, Randy. "Vote Overturns Women's Ordination." *Christianity Today* 38, no. 9 (August 15, 1994)

Frantz, Nadine Pence, and Deborah L. Silver. "Women in Leadership: A Theological Perspective." *Brethren Life and Thought* 30 (Winter 1985).

Fraser, D. B. "Women with a Past: A New Look at the History of Theological Education." *Theological Education* 8, no. 4 (Summer 1972).

Freedman, David. "Woman, a Power Equal to Man." *Biblical Archaeology Review* 9, no. 1 (January-February 1983).

Frymer-Kensky, Tikva. "Law and Philosophy: The Case of Sex in the Bible." *Semeia* 45

(1989): 89-102.

Fung, Ronald Y. K. "Ministry in the New Testament." In *The Church in the Bible and the World*, edited by D. A. Carson. Grand Rapids, Mich.: Baker Book House, 1987.

Funk and Wagnalls New Standard Dictionary of the English Language. New York: Funk and Wagnalls, 1965.

Galbraith, John Kenneth. *The Anatomy of Power*. Boston: Houghton Mifflin, 1983.

Gardner, John W. *On Leadership*. New York: Macmillan/Free Press, 1990.

Getz, Gene A. *The Measure of a Family*. Glendale, Calif.: Gospel Light/Regal Books, 1976.

Gill, David W. J. "Importance of Roman Portraiture for Head-Coverings in 1 Corinthians 11:2-16." *Tyndale Bulletin* 41, no. 2 (1990).

Gilligan, Carol. *In a Different Voice*. Cambridge, Mass.: Harvard University Press, 1982.

Goguel, M. *The Primitive Church*. Translated by H. G. Shape. London: Allen and Unwin, 1964.

Greenleaf, Robert. *Servant Leadership*. New York: Paulist, 1977.

Gregory of Nazianzus. "An Examination of Apollinarianism." In *Documents of the Christian Church*, edited by Henry Bettennson. 2nd ed. London: Oxford University Press, 1963.

Grenz, Stanley J. *Reason for Hope: The Systematic Theology of Wolfhart Pannenberg*. New York: Oxford University Press, 1990.

_____. *Sexual Ethics*. Dallas: Word, 1990.

_____. *Theology for the Community of God*. Nashville: Broadman & Holman, 1994.

Grosheide, F. W. *The First Epistle to the Corinthians*. Grand Rapids, Mich.: Eerdmans, 1953.

Grudem, Wayne. "Does Kephalē ('Head') Mean 'Source' or 'Authority Over' in Greek Literature? A Survey of 2,336 Examples." *Trinity Journal* n.s. 6 (Spring 1985): 38-59.

_____. *The Gift of Prophecy in 1 Corinthians*. Washington, D.C.: University Press of America, 1982.

_____. "The Meaning of *Kephalē* ('Head'): A Response to Recent Studies." *Trinity Journal* n.s. 11 (Spring 1990): 3-72.

Gundry, Patricia. *Neither Slave nor Free*. San Francisco: Harper & Row, 1987.

Guthrie, Donald. *The Pastoral Epistles*. Grand Rapids, Mich.: Eerdmans, 1990.

Guthrie, Donald, and J. A. Motyer, eds. *New Bible Commentary*. 3rd ed. London: Inter-Varsity Press, 1970.

Hall, Barbara. "Paul and Women." *Theology Today* 31, no. 1 (April 1974).

Hanson, A. T. *The Pastoral Epistles*. New Century Bible Commentary. Grand Rapids, Mich.: Eerdmans, 1982.

Hardesty, Nancy. "Women and the Seminaries." *Christian Century* 96, no. 5 (February 7-14, 1979).

_____. *Women Called to Witness: Evangelical Feminism in the Nineteenth Century*. Nashville: Abingdon, 1984.

Harnack, Adolf von. *Die Mission und Ausbreitung des Christentums in den ersten Jahrhunderten*. Leipzig: 1906.

Harris, Timothy J. "Why Did Paul Mention Eve's Deception? A Critique of P. W. Barnett's Interpretation of 1 Timothy 2." *Evangelical Quarterly* 62, no. 4 (1990).

Hassey, Janette. *No Time for Silence*. Grand Rapids, Mich: Zondervan/Academie Books, 1986.

Heine, Suzanne. *Goddesses and Images of God*. Translated by John Bowden. Minneapolis: Augsburg, 1989.

Héring, Jean. *The First Epistle of St. Paul to the Corinthians*. Translated by A. W. Heathcote and P. J. Allcock. London: Epworth, 1962.

Hestenes, Roberta. "An Historical Perspective of Women in Christian Leadership." Paper presented at the North American Professors of Christian Education Annual Conference, October 21-24, 1993.

Hestenes, Roberta, and Lois Curley, eds. *Women and the Ministries of Christ*. Pasadena, Calif.: Fuller Theological Seminary, 1979.

Hill, David. *New Testament Prophecy*. Atlanta: John Knox, 1979.

Hoerning, Erika M. "Upward Mobility and Family Estrangement Among Females: What Happens When the 'Same Old Girl' Becomes the 'New Professional Woman'?" *International Journal of Oral History* 6, no. 2 (June 1985).

Holmes, Urban T. "The Sexuality of God." In *Male and Female: Christian Approaches to Sexuality*, ed. Ruth Tiffany Barnhouse and Urban T. Holmes II. New York: Seabury Press, 1976.

Hommes, N. J. "Let Women Be Silent in the Church." *Calvin Theological Journal* 4, no. 1 (1969).

Hooker, Morna D. "Authority on Her Head: An Examination of 1 Corinthians 11:10." *New Testament Studies* 10 (1964): 410-16.

House, H. Wayne. "Distinctive Roles for Women in the Second and Third Centuries." *Bibliotheca Sacra* 146, no. 581 (January-March 1989).

———. "Neither . . . Male nor Female . . . in Christ Jesus." *Bibliotheca Sacra* 145, no. 577 (1988).

Howard, J. Keir. "Neither Male nor Female: An Examination of the Status of Women in the New Testament." *Evangelical Quarterly* 55, no. 1 (January 1983).

Howe, Margaret. "The Positive Case for the Ordination of Women." In *Perspectives on Evangelical Theology: Papers from the Thirtieth Annual Meeting of the Evangelical Theological Society*, edited by Kenneth S. Kantzer and Stanley N. Gundry. Grand Rapids, Mich.: Zondervan, 1979.

———. *Woman and Church Leadership*. Grand Rapids, Mich.: Zondervan, 1982.

Hughes, Philip E. *The Book of Revelation: A Commentary*. Leicester, U.K.: Inter-Varsity Press, 1990.

Hull, Gretchen Gaebelein. *Equal to Serve*. Old Tappan, N.J.: Revell, 1987.

Hulse, Erroll. "The Man-Woman Controversy." *Reformation Today* 119 (January-February 1991).

Hurley, James B. "Did Paul Require Veils or the Silence of Women?" *Westminister Theological Journal* 35 (Winter 1973): 190-220.

———. *Man and Woman in Biblical Perspective*. Grand Rapids, Mich.: Zondervan, 1981.

Hutchens, S. M. "God, Gender and the Pastoral Office." *Touchstone* 15, no. 4 (Fall 1992).

Irenaeus. *Adversus Haereses*. In *The Ante-Nicene Fathers*, edited by Alexander Roberts and James Donaldson. Grand Rapids, Mich.: Eerdmans, 1975.

Jacob, Edmund. *Theology of the Old Testament*. London: Hodder & Stoughton, 1958.

Jenson, Robert W. *The Triune Identity: God According to the Gospel*. Philadelphia: Fortress, 1982.

Jeremias, Joachim. *Jerusalem in the Time of Jesus*. Translated by F. H. Cave and C. H. Cave. 3rd ed. Philadelphia: Fortress, 1969.

Jewett, Paul King. *Man as Male and Female: A Study in Sexual Relationships from a Theological Point of View*. Grand Rapids, Mich.: Eerdmans, 1975.

———. *The Ordination of Women*. Grand Rapids, Mich.: Eerdmans, 1980.

———. "Why I Favor the Ordination of Women." *Christianity Today* 19, no. 18 (June 6,

1975).

Jewett, Robert. "Paul, Phoebe and the Spanish Mission." In *The Social World of Formative Christianity*, edited by Jacob Neusner et al. Philadelphia: Fortress, 1988.

Johnson, Ron, and Deb Brock. "Gender-Specific Therapy." *Journal of Psychology and Christianity* 7, no. 4 (Winter 1988).

Josephus. *Antiquities.*

———. *Contra Apionem.*

Joy, Donald M. *Men Under Construction.* Wheaton, Ill.: Victor Books, 1989.

Kagan, Jerome. "Psychology of Sex Differences." In *Human Sexuality in Four Perspectives*, edited by Frank A. Beach. Baltimore: Johns Hopkins University Press, 1976.

Kaiser, Walter C., Jr. *Toward an Exegetical Theology: Biblical Exegesis for Preaching and Teaching.* Grand Rapids, Mich.: Baker Book House, 1981.

Käsemann, Ernst. *Essays on New Testament Themes.* Translated by W. J. Montague. London: SCM Press, 1964.

Keener, Craig S. *Paul, Women and Wives: Marriage and Women's Ministry in the Letters of Paul.* Peabody, Mass.: Hendrickson, 1992.

Kelly, J. N. D. *Early Christian Doctrines.* 5th rev. ed. London: Adam and Charles Black, 1977.

———. *The Pastoral Epistles.* Harper's New Testament Commentaries. San Francisco: Harper & Row, 1960.

Kilmartin, E. J. "Apostolic Office: Sacrament of Christ." *Theological Studies* 36, no. 2 (1975).

Kimberley, David R. "1 Timothy 2:15: A Possible Understanding of a Difficult Text." *Journal of the Evangelical Theological Society* 35, no. 4 (December 1992).

Kittel, Gerhard, and Gerhard Friedrich, eds. *Theological Dictionary of the New Testament.* Translated by Geoffrey W. Bromiley. 10 vols. Grand Rapids, Mich.: Eerdmans, 1964-1976.

Knight, George W., III. "*Authenteō* in Reference to Women in 1 Timothy 2:12." *New Testament Studies* 30, no. 1 (January 1984).

———. "Male and Female Related He Them." *Christianity Today* 20, no. 14 (April 9, 1976).

———. "The Ordination of Women: No." *Christianity Today* 25, no. 4 (February 20, 1981).

———. *The Role Relationship of Men and Women.* Rev. ed. Chicago: Moody Press, 1985.

Kraemer, Ross S. "Ecstasy and Possession: The Attraction of Women to the Cult of Dionysus." *Harvard Theological Review* 72 (January-April 1979): 55-80.

Kroeger, Catherine Clark, and Richard C. Kroeger. *I Suffer Not a Woman: Rethinking 1 Timothy 2:11-15 in Light of Ancient Evidence.* Grand Rapids, Mich.: Baker Book House, 1992.

Kroeger, Richard, and Catherine Clark Kroeger. "Pandemonium and Silence at Corinth." In *Women and the Ministries of Christ*, edited by Roberta Hestenes and Lois Curley. Pasadena, Calif.: Fuller Theological Seminary, 1979.

———. "Subordinationism." In *Evangelical Dictionary of Theology*, edited by Walter A. Elwell. Grand Rapids, Mich.: Baker Book House, 1985.

Kurzinger, Josef. "Frau und Mann nach 1 Kor 11, 11ff." *Biblische Zeitschrift* 22, no. 2 (1978): 270-75.

Landau, Sidney I., ed. *The Doubleday Dictionary for Home, School and Office.* Garden City, N.Y.: Doubleday, 1975.

Lane, William. *The Gospel According to Mark.* New International Commentary of the New Testament. Grand Rapids, Mich.: Eerdmans, 1974.

Lasch, Christopher "Women as Alien." In *The Woman Question in American History*, edited by Barbara Welter. Hinsdale, Ill.: Dryden, 1973.

Leenhardt, Franz J. *The Epistle to the Romans.* London: Lutterworth, 1961.

Lenski, R. C. H. *The Interpretation of St. John's Revelation.* Minneapolis: Augsburg, 1963.

Lewis, C. S. "Priestesses in the Church?" In *God in the Dock.* Grand Rapids, Mich.: Eerdmans, 1970.

Liddell, H. G., and R. Scott. *A Greek-English Lexicon.* Oxford: Clarendon, 1992.

Lilburne, Geoffrey R. "Christology: In Dialogue with Feminism." *Horizons* 11, no. 1 (Spring 1984).

Linss, Wilhelm C. "St. Paul and Women." *Dialog* 24 (Winter 1985).

Lippert, Peter. *Leben als Zeugnis.* Stuttgart: Katholisches Bibelwerk, 1968.

Lock, Walter. *A Critical and Exegetical Commentary on the Pastoral Epistles.* Edinburgh: T & T Clark, 1924.

Lowe, Stephen D. "Rethinking the Female Status/Function Question: The Jew/Gentile Relationship as Paradigm." *Journal of the Evangelical Theological Society* 34, no. 1 (March 1991).

Luther, Martin. *Lectures on Genesis: Chapters 1-5,* translated by George V. Schick. In *Luther's Works,* edited by Jaroslav Pelikan and H. T. Lehmann. St. Louis, Mo.: Concordia, 1958.

MacGorman, J. W. "Glossolalic Error and Its Correction: 1 Corinthians 12-14." *Review and Expositor* 80 (Summer 1983): 389-400.

MacNair, Donald J. *The Living Church: A Guide for Revitalization.* Philadelphia: Great Commission, 1980.

Martin, Ralph P. *The Spirit and the Congregation.* Grand Rapids, Mich.: Eerdmans, 1984.

Marty, Martin E. *The Pro and Con Book of Religious America.* Waco, Tex.: Word, 1975.

Mattingly, Harold. *The Man in the Roman Street.* New York: W. W. Norton, 1966.

Maxwell, Joe. "Churches Challenge Synod Ruling." *Christianity Today* 38, no. 11 (September 12, 1994).

May, Rollo. *Power and Innocence: A Search for the Sources of Violence.* New York: W. W. Norton, 1972.

McBeth, Leon. *Women in Baptist Life.* Nashville: Broadman, 1979.

McCoubrie, Susan. "Happy Birthday: Now We Are Four! A Brief History of Christians for Biblical Equality." *Priscilla Papers* 5, no. 3 (Summer 1991).

McDonald, Margaret Y. "Early Christian Women Married to Unbelievers." *Studies in Religion* 19, no. 2, 1990.

McFadyen, Alistair I. *The Call to Personhood: A Christian Theory of the Individual in Social Relationships.* Cambridge: Cambridge University Press, 1990.

Meeks, Wayne A. *The First Urban Christians: The Social World of the Apostle Paul.* New Haven, Conn.: Yale University Press, 1983.

Mickelsen, Alvera, ed. *Women, Authority and the Bible.* Downers Grove, Ill.: InterVarsity Press, 1986.

Mickelsen, Berkeley, and Alvera Mickelsen. "The 'Head' of the Epistles." *Christianity Today* 25, no. 4 (February 20, 1981).

Micks, Marianne H. *Our Search for Identity.* Philadelphia: Fortress, 1982.

Migliore, Daniel L. *Faith Seeking Understanding: An Introduction to Christian Theology.* Grand Rapids, Mich.: Eerdmans, 1991.

Milne, Bruce. *Know the Truth.* Downers Grove, Ill.: InterVarsity Press, 1982.

Mollenkott, Virginia. *Women, Men and the Bible.* Nashville: Abingdon, 1977.

Moltmann, Jürgen. *Trinity and the Kingdom.* San Francisco: Harper & Row, 1981.

Montegiore, C. G. *The Synoptic Gospels*. London: Macmillan, 1909.

Moo, Douglas J. "The Interpretation of 1 Timothy 2:11-15: A Rejoinder." *Trinity Journal* n.s. 2 (Fall 1981): 198-222.

_____. "1 Timothy 2:11-15: Meaning and Significance." *Trinity Journal* n.s. 1, no. 1 (1980).

Morris, Joan. *The Lady Was a Bishop: The Hidden History of Women with Clerical Ordination and the Jurisdiction of Bishops*. New York: Macmillan, 1973.

Morrison, Ann M., Randall P. White and Allen van Volsor. "The Narrow Band." *Issues and Observations* (Center for Creative Leadership, Greensboro, N.C.), Spring 1987.

Moule, F. D. *Worship in the New Testament*. London: Lutterworth, 1961.

Muir, Elizabeth Gillan. *Petticoats in the Pulpit*. Toronto: United Church Publishing House, 1991.

Murphy-O'Connor, Jerome. *1 Corinthians*. Wilmington, Del.: Michael Glazier, 1979.

_____. "The Non-Pauline Character of 1 Corinthians 11:2-16." *Journal of Biblical Literature* 95 (December 1976): 615-21.

_____. "Sex and Logic in 1 Corinthians 11:2-16." *Catholic Biblical Quarterly* 42 (October 1980): 482-500.

Murray, John. *The Epistle to the Romans*. Grand Rapids, Mich.: Eerdmans, 1965.

Nafzger, Samuel H. "The Doctrinal Position of the LCMS on the Service of Women in the Church." *Concordia Journal* 18, no. 2 (April 1992).

Nelson, James B. *Intimate Connection*. Philadelphia: Westminster Press, 1988.

Nixon, Rosemary. "The Priority of Perfection." *Modern Churchman* 27, no. 1 (1984).

Novak, Michael. "Women, Ordination and Angels." *First Things* 32 (April 1993).

Odell-Scott, David W. "In Defense of an Egalitarian Interpretation of 1 Cor 14:34-36: A Reply to Murphy-O'Connor's Critique." *Biblical Theology Bulletin* 17, no. 3 (July 1987).

_____. "Let the Women Speak in Church: An Egalitarian Interpretation of 1 Cor 14:33b-36." *Biblical Theology Bulletin* 13, no. 3 (July 1983).

O'Grady, John F. "Authority and Power: Issues for the Contemporary Church." *Louvain Studies* 10, no. 2 (1984).

Okure, Teresa. "The Significance Today of Jesus' Commission to Mary Magdalene." *International Review of Mission* 81, no. 322 (April 1992).

Omanson, Roger L. "The Role of Women in the New Testament Church." *Review and Expositor* 83, no. 1 (Winter 1986).

Origen. *Epistolam ad Romanos Commentariorum*.

Osborne, Grant R. "Hermeneutics and Women in the Church." *Journal of the Evangelical Theological Society* 20, no. 4 (December 1977).

_____. "Women in Jesus' Ministry." *Westminster Theological Journal* 51 (Fall 1989): 259-91.

Packard, Vance. *The Sexual Wilderness*. New York: David McKay, 1968.

Packer, J. I. "Let's Stop Making Women Presbyters." *Christianity Today* 35, no. 2 (February 11, 1991).

_____. "Postscript: I Believe in Women's Ministry." In *Why Not? Priesthood and the Ministry of Women*, edited by Michael Bruce and G. E. Duffield, revised and augmented by R. T. Beckwith. Appleford, U.K.: Marcham Books, 1976.

Padgett, Alan. "Feminism in First Corinthians: A Dialogue with Elisabeth Schüssler Fiorenza." *Evangelical Quarterly* 58, no. 2 (April 1986).

_____. "Paul on Women in the Church: The Contradictions of Coiffure in 1 Corinthians 11:2-16." *Journal for the Study of the New Testament* 10 (1984).

————. "Wealthy Women at Ephesus: 1 Timothy 2:8-15 in Social Context." *Interpretation* 41, no. 1 (January 1987).

Padgett, Kenneth T. "Paul on Women in the Church." *Biblical Theology Bulletin* 17, no. 2 (April 1987).

Parvey, Constance F. "Where Are We Going? The Threefold Ministry and the Ordination of Women." *Word and World* 5, no. 1 (Winter 1985).

Payne, Philip B. "Libertarian Women in Ephesus: A Response to Douglas J. Moo's Article '1 Timothy 2:11-15: Meaning and Significance.'" *Trinity Journal* n.s. 2 (Fall 1981): 169-97.

Peiser, Andrew. "The Education of Women: A Historical View." *Social Studies* 67, no. 2 (March-April 1976).

Perriman, Andrew C. "What Eve Did, What Women Shouldn't Do: The Meaning of *Authenteō* in 1 Timothy 2:12." *Tyndale Bulletin* 44, no. 1 (1993).

Pfitzner, Victor C. *Paul and the Agon Motif: Traditional Athletic Imagery in the Pauline Literature.* Leiden: Brill, 1967.

Philo. *On the Special Laws.*

Pierce, Ronald W. "Evangelicals and Gender Roles in the 1990s: 1 Tim 2:8-15—a Test Case." *Journal of the Evangelical Theological Society* 36, no. 3 (September 1993).

Piper, John. "The Order of Creation." *The Standard,* April 1984.

Piper, John, and Wayne Grudem, eds. *Recovering Biblical Manhood and Womanhood: A Response to Evangelical Feminism.* Wheaton, Ill.: Crossway, 1991.

Pliny. *Letters and Panegyrics.* Translated by Betty Radice. Loeb Classical Library. Cambridge, Mass.: Harvard University Press, 1975.

Pomeroy, Sarah B. *Goddesses, Whores, Wives and Slaves: Women in Classical Antiquity.* New York: Schocken, 1975.

Porter, Stanley E. "What Does It Mean to Be 'Saved by Childbirth' (1 Timothy 2:15)?" *Journal for the Study of the New Testament* 49 (March 1993): 87-102.

Rahner, Karl. *Theological Investigations.* Translated by Kevin Smyth. New York: Crossroad, 1982.

Räisänen, Heikki. *Paul and the Law.* Philadelphia: Fortress, 1983.

Raming, Ida. "The Twelve Apostles Were Men." *Theology Digest* 40, no. 1 (Spring 1993).

Raser, Harold. "Your Daughters Shall Prophesy: Women Ministers in the American Holiness Movements." *The Seminary Tower* 49, no. 1 (Fall 1993).

Rawlinson, G. "Psalms." In *The Pulpit Commentary,* edited by H. D. M. Spence and Joseph S. Exell. New York: Funk and Wagnalls, 1985.

Redekop, Gloria Neufeld. "Let the Women Learn: 1 Timothy 2:8-15 Reconsidered." *Studies in Religion* 19, no. 2 (1990).

Richardson, Peter. *Paul's Ethic of Freedom.* Philadelphia: Westminister Press, 1979.

Ridderbos, Hermann. *Paul: An Outline of His Ministry.* Translated by John Richard DeWitt. Grand Rapids, Mich.: Eerdmans, 1975.

Roberts, Mark D. "Woman Shall Be Saved: A Closer Look at 1 Timothy 2:15." *TSF Bulletin* 5, no. 2 (November-December 1981).

"Role of Women in the Church: A Report of the Study Panel of the Free Church of Scotland." *Diakonia* 4, no. 3 (March 1991).

Rossiter, Margaret W. "Doctorates for American Women, 1868-1907." *History of Education Quarterly* 12, no. 2 (Summer 1972).

Ryrie, Charles Caldwell. *The Role of Women in the Church.* Chicago: Moody Press, 1958.

Salazar, Pamela. "Theological Education of Women for Ordination." *Religious Education* 82, no. 1 (Winter 1987).

Sampley, J. Paul. *And the Two Shall Become One Flesh.* Cambridge: Cambridge University Press, 1971.

Sanday, Peggy Reeves. *Female Power and Male Dominance.* New York: Cambridge University Press, 1981.

Sanday, William, and Arthur C. Headlam. *A Critical and Exegetical Commentary on the Epistle to the Romans.* 5th ed. International Critical Commentary. Edinburgh: T & T Clark, 1902.

Saucy, Robert L. "The Negative Case Against the Ordination of Women." In *Perspectives on Evangelical Theology: Papers from the Thirtieth Annual Meeting of the Evangelical Theological Society,* edited by Kenneth S. Kantzer and Stanley N. Gundry. Grand Rapids, Mich.: Baker Book House, 1979.

Sawtelle, H. A. "Commentary on the Epistles of John." In *An American Commentary of the New Testament,* edited by Alvah Hovey. Philadelphia: American Baptist Publication Society, 1888.

Scalise, Pamela J. "Women in Ministry: Reclaiming Our Old Testament Heritage." *Review and Expositor* 83, no. 1 (Winter 1986).

Scanzoni, Letha, and Nancy Hardesty. *All We're Meant to Be.* Waco, Tex.: Word, 1974.

Schein, Edgar H. *Organizational Psychology.* Englewood Cliffs, N.J.: Prentice-Hall, 1980.

Schmidt, Alvin John. *Veiled and Silenced: How Culture Shaped Sexist Theology.* Macon, Ga.: Mercer University Press, 1989.

Schnackenburg, Rudolf. "Apostles Before and During Paul's Time." In *Apostolic History and the Gospel,* edited by W. Ward Gasque and Ralph P. Martin. Grand Rapids, Mich.: Eerdmans, 1970.

Schneider, Sandra M. "Women in the Fourth Gospel and the Role of Women in the Contemporary Church." *Biblical Theology Bulletin* 12, no. 2 (April 1982).

Schultz, Ray R. "Romans 16:7: Junia or Junias?" *Expository Times* 98, no. 4 (January 1987).

Schweizer, Eduard. *Church Order in the New Testament.* London: SCM Press, 1961.

———. *The Good News According to Mark.* Translated by Donald H. Madvig. Atlanta: John Knox, 1970.

———. "The Service of Worship: An Exposition of 1 Cor. 14." *Interpretation* 13, no. 3 (July 1959).

Scott, Anne Firor. "The Everwidening Circle: The Diffusion of Feminist Values from the Troy Female Seminary, 1822-1872." *History of Education Quarterly,* no. 1 (Spring 1979).

Selby, Gary. "Your Daughters Shall Prophesy: Rhetorical Strategy in the Nineteenth Century Debate over Women's Right to Preach." *Restoration Quarterly* 34, no. 3 (1992).

Sennett, Richard. *Authority.* London: Secker and Warburg, 1980.

Seton, Bernard E. "Should Our Church Ordain Women? No." *Ministry* 58, no. 3 (March 1985).

Shoemaker, Thomas P. "Unveiling of Equality: 1 Corinthians 11:2-16." *Biblical Theology Bulletin* 17, no. 2 (April 1987).

Sigountos, James G., and Myron Shank. "Public Roles for Women in the Pauline Church: A Reappraisal of the Evidence." *Journal of the Evangelical Theological Society* 26, no. 3 (September 1983).

Smith, Hannah Whitall. *The God of All Comfort.* Chicago: Moody Press, 1956.

Smith, Mark S. "God Male and Female in the Old Testament: Yahweh and His 'Asherah.' "

Theological Studies 48 (June 1987): 333-40.

Snodgrass, Klyne R. "The Ordination of Women—Thirteen Years Later: Do We Really Value the Ministry of Women?" *Covenant Quarterly* 48, no. 3 (August 1990).

Spence, Janet T., and Robert L. Helmreich. *Masculinity and Femininity.* Austin: University of Texas Press, 1978.

Spencer, Aída Besançon. *Beyond the Curse: Women Called to Ministry.* Peabody, Mass.: Hendrickson, 1985.

Spring, Beth, and Kelsey Menehan. "Women in Seminary: Preparing for What?" *Christianity Today* 30, no. 12 (September 5, 1986).

Stackhouse, John G., Jr. "Women in Public Ministry in Twentieth Century Canadian and American Evangelicalism: Five Models." *Studies in Religion* 17, no. 4 (1988).

Stanton, G. N. *Jesus of Nazareth in New Testament Preaching.* London: Cambridge University Press, 1974.

Stendahl, Krister. *The Bible and the Role of Women.* Philadelphia: Fortress, 1966.

Stouffer, Austin H. "The Ordination of Women: Yes." *Christianity Today* 25, no. 4 (February 20, 1981).

Talbert, Charles. *Reading Corinthians: A Literary and Theological Commentary on 1 & 2 Corinthians.* New York: Crossroad, 1987.

Tarasar, Constance J. "Women in the Mission of the Church: Theological and Historical Reflections." *International Review of Mission* 81, no. 322 (April 1988).

Tavard, George. "Theology and Sexuality." In *Woman in Christian Tradition.* South Bend, Ind.: University of Notre Dame Press, 1973.

Terrien, Samuel L. *Till the Heart Sings.* Philadelphia: Fortress, 1985.

Thayer, Joseph Henry. *A Greek-English Lexicon of the New Testament.* Rev. ed. Wheaton, Ill.: Evangel, 1974. (Original ed. 1889.)

Theissen, Gerd. *The Social Setting of Pauline Christianity.* Philadelphia: Fortress, 1984.

Thomas, Derek. "The Place of Women in the Church at Philippi." *Expository Times* 83 (January 1972): 117-20.

Thomas Aquinas. *Summa Theologica.* Translated by Fathers of the English Dominican Province. Westminster, Md.: Christian Classics, 1981.

Thrall, E. *I and II Corinthians.* Cambridge: Cambridge University Press, 1965.

Toews, John. "Women in Church Leadership: 1 Timothy 2:11-15—a Reconsideration." In *The Bible and the Church: Essays in Honor of Dr. David Ewert,* edited by A. J. Dueck, H. J. Giesbrecht and V. G. Shillington. Hillsboro, Kans.: Kindred, 1983.

Trible, Phyllis. "Depatriarchalizing in Biblical Interpretation." *Journal of the American Academy of Religion* 41 (March 1973): 30-48.

———. *God and the Rhetoric of Sexuality.* Philadelphia: Fortress, 1978.

Trompf, G. W. "On Attitudes Toward Women in Paul and Paulinist Literature: 1 Corinthians 11:2-16 and Its Context." *Catholic Biblical Quarterly* 42, no. 2 (1980).

Tucker, Ruth A., and Walter Liefeld. *Daughters of the Church.* Grand Rapids, Mich.: Zondervan, 1987.

Untener, Kenneth. "Forum: The Ordination of Women—Can the Horizons Widen?" *Worship* 65, no. 1 (January 1991).

Van Leeuwen, Mary Stewart, et al. *After Eden: Facing the Challenge of Gender Reconciliation.* Grand Rapids, Mich.: Eerdmans, 1993.

Vennum, Eileen. "Do Male Old Covenant Priests Exclude Female New Covenant Pastors?" *Priscilla Papers* 7, no. 2 (Spring 1993).

Verner, David C. *The Household of God: The Social World of the Pastoral Epistles*. Chico, Calif.: Scholars Press, 1983.

Vetterling-Braggin, Mary, ed. *Femininity, Masculinity and Androgyny*. Totowa, N.J.: Rowman and Allanheld, 1982.

Walker, David. "Are Opponents of Women Priests Sexists?" *Churchman* 105, no. 4 (1991).

Walker, William O., Jr. "1 Corinthians 11:2-16 and Paul's Views Regarding Women." *Journal of Biblical Literature* 94, no. 1 (1975).

Warkentin, Marjorie. *Ordination: A Biblical-Historical View*. Grand Rapids, Mich.: Eerdmans, 1982.

Weber, Max. *Max Weber on Law in Economy and Society*. Edited by Max Rheinstein. Translated by Edward Shils and Max Rheinstein. New York: Simon & Schuster, 1967.

_____. *The Theory of Social and Economic Organization*. Glencoe, Ill.: Free Press, 1947.

Westermann, Claus. *Creation*. Translated by John J. Scullion. Philadelphia: Fortress, 1974.

Wetmore, Gordon. "God-Called Women." *The Seminary Tower* 49, no. 1 (Fall 1993).

Whelan, Caroline F. "Amica Pauli: The Role of Phoebe in the Early Church." *Journal of the Study of the New Testament* 49 (March 1993): 67-85.

Whybray, R. N. *The Book of Isaiah*. New Century Bible. London: Marshall, Morgan and Scott, 1975.

Williams, J. Rodman. *Renewal Theology: Systematic Theology from a Charismatic Perspective*. 3 vols. Grand Rapids, Mich.: Zondervan, 1992.

Willmore, Eva. "Should Our Church Ordain Women? Yes." *Ministry* 58, no. 3 (March 1985).

Wilshire, Leland E. "1 Timothy 2:12 Revisited: A Reply to Paul W. Barnett and Timothy J. Harris." *Evangelical Quarterly* 65, no. 1 (1993).

_____. "The TLG Computer and Further Reference to *Authenteō* in 1 Timothy 2:12." *New Testament Studies* 34, no. 1 (1988): 120-34.

Wilson, Kenneth T. "Should Women Wear Head Coverings?" *Bibliotheca Sacra* 148, no. 592 (October-December 1981).

Wingfield, Mark. "Women Gaining Ground in Baptist Ministry Roles." *Religious Herald* 71, no. 1 (February 11, 1993).

Witherington, Ben III. "Rite and Rights for Women: Galatians 3:28." *New Testament Studies* 27, no. 5 (1981).

_____. *Women in the Earliest Churches*. Cambridge: Cambridge University Press, 1988.

_____. *Women in the Ministry of Jesus*. Cambridge: Cambridge University Press, 1984.

Wright, Susan Lockwood. "SBC Women Ministers Break Their Silence." *Christian Century* 103, no. 34 (November 12, 1986).

Young, Edward J. *The Book of Isaiah*. Grand Rapids, Mich.: Eerdmans, 1972.

Yukl, Gary A. *Leadership in Organizations*. 2nd ed. Englewood Cliffs, N.J.: Prentice-Hall, 1989.

Zerbst, Fritz. *The Office of Woman in the Church*. Translated by Albert G. Merkens. St. Louis, Mo.: Concordia, 1955.

Zikmund, Barbara Brown. "Women in Theological Education." *Ministerial Formation* 38 (June 1987).

Zuck, Roy B. "Greek Words for Teach." *Bibliotheca Sacra* 122 (April-June 1965).

Name & Subject Index

Scripture Index